THE DAVID & CHARLES ENCYCLOPEDIA OF EVERYDAY ANTIQUES

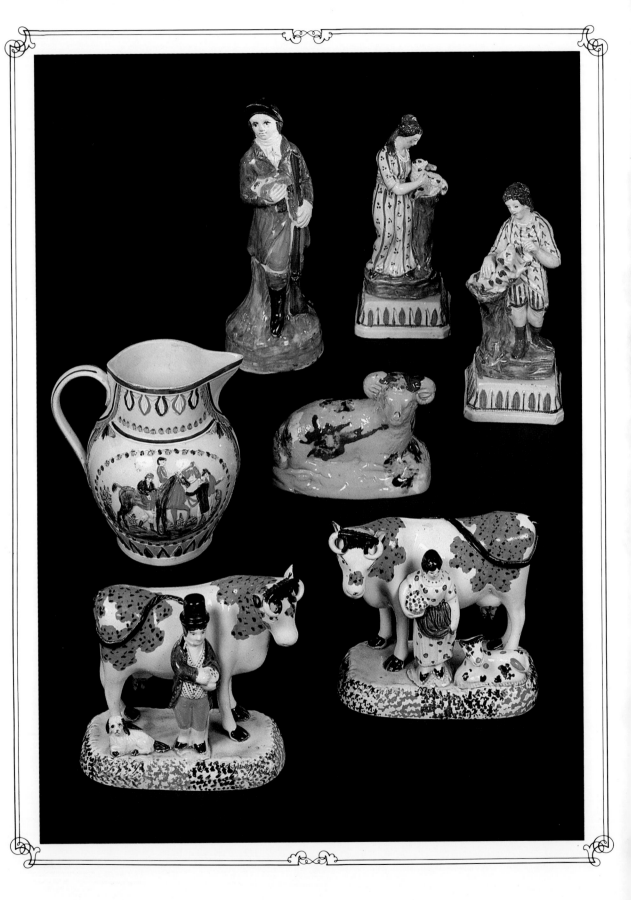

THE DAVID & CHARLES ENCYCLOPEDIA OF
EVERYDAY ANTIQUES

Ronald Pearsall

David & Charles

Page 2: Prattware figure of a sportsman c1790; Prattware figures with a dog and a lamb c1795; Prattware horse-racing jug c1800; Yorkshire figure of a recumbent ram c1790; Prattware figures of cows with farmer and milkmaid c1810.

British Library Cataloguing in Publication Data
Pearsall, Ronald
  The David & Charles encyclopedia of everyday antiques.
  I. Title
  745.103

ISBN 0–7153–9868–7

Typeset by ABM Typographics Ltd., Hull.
and printed in Hong Kong
by Imago Publishing Ltd
for David & Charles plc
Brunel House Newton Abbot Devon

Contents

Foreword

by
Richard Hamm

Fortunately the world of antiques is not just confined to valuable and stately works of art, but encompasses everyday objects of curiosity and delight. These everyday antiques often reflect fashions of a past era and give us an insight into a previous way of life, whether it's collecting thimbles, grape scissors, or jelly moulds. Most everyday objects have such a diversity of styles, quality and values it is understandable why the novice collector soon becomes 'hooked' on his or her hobby. One advantage of collecting such items is their ready availability at car boot sales, junk shops and auctions. The joy is the hunt, the reward the find. As a youngster I would spend my Saturday afternoons queuing for jumble sales where my limited pocket money would be spent on every 'treasure' available in the hope that it would be worth more than I paid for it. The best lessons came to be (and still are) that of learning by your mistakes. Gradually my knowledge grew and with it the pleasure of collecting. I am fortunate that my hobby eventually became my career and I find that even after twenty-three years I'm still learning.

This encyclopedia offers a worthy introduction into the wealth of curios and artefacts available. For those who want to discover more about any of the subjects there is a bibliography at the back. Your local library or specialist bookshop should be able to help obtain these books.

Richard Hamm A.S.V.A. of Lambrays is one of the South West's leading auctioneers of fine art and antiques welcoming novice and specialist collector alike.

Early nineteenth-century Staffordshire pottery figure of The Flight into Egypt, with the Virgin Mary and Child seated on the back of a donkey with Joseph at their side.

Introduction

Some encyclopedias and dictionaries of antiques stop at the year 1870, as if there was too much to cope with in the tumultuous years to come, when craze often succeeded craze. There are some in which the writer or writers dip and dive amongst the wealth of material available and bring up those things that appeal to them personally. And there are some, hopefully this is one, which survey the past and not only try to convey pleasure in looking at and handling the objects but also try to observe a connecting link, a common bond, between different artifacts made at the same time.

They may be quite ordinary things, and at first a resemblance may be difficult to gauge. But it is helpful to remember that what we term antiques, or bygones, or whatever, were new when they were made, perhaps so new that they were puzzling and exciting. In the nineteenth century techniques were advancing year by year, and objects which we may consider odd if not downright eccentric were symbols of progress and of the ability of modern man (and woman) to make anything from any material. An interesting parallel can be seen by comparing, for example, a papier-mâché piano, with something else made about the same time – an intricate cut-out Valentine card that opens out and displays a different picture. Both demonstate the pleasure in making something – or designing something – that could much more easily be made in another way. A piano of wood is far more sensible than one of compressed pulp; a Valentine that was merely a folded-over piece of card with an appropriate message and picture would have probably been as acceptable as a fragile concoction that began to shed bits before the day was out.

The Encyclopedia of Everyday Antiques is not merely a list. It contains sections on repairing antiques, refurbishing and cleaning antiques and is so arranged that readers can dip into it and read it for pleasure as well as use it for reference. Certain articles have been grouped together, and it is hoped that an entry such as *Dining-room Silver* will not only provide information but will show how people in the past lived. The illustrations have been very carefully selected so that they are an integral part of the book and not added extras. Using old pictures and engravings, antiques will be shown in their settings as everyday objects.

Items from the past carry all kinds of overtones, not all of them pleasant. The so-called lobster helmets from the English Civil War, still available on a modest budget, have something sinister about them. The incredibly uncomfortable hall chairs of the nineteenth century remind us that this is where the common person sat as he or she waited to be seen by someone higher in the social scale. The silver vinaigrettes, containing a perfumed sponge held in place by a perforated grille, were not pretty ornaments, but a necessary accessory when everything smelled awful and personal hygiene was not regarded as very important. But other articles to smell have different connotations. The delightful Victorian double-ended glass scent-bottles had one end for scent, one end for sal volatile (smelling salts). It was considered

good form for a young lady of delicate sensibilities to have what was known as an occasional and picturesque attack of the vapours. In other words, she felt faint, but immediately recovered when the smelling salts were exposed beneath her nose.

No-one who has had anything to do with fine

(Above) Interior of an Edwardian home. Notice the handsome fireplace of about 1910, and amongst the clutter can be seen a Jack Russell terrier; (below) A sitting room from 1921, very little different from a Victorian sitting room. The date can be deduced by the photograph of the World War I soldier, the art nouveau hood over the fire, and the curious padded fireguard.

late eighteenth-century furniture in all its elegance and sense of fragility will forget that this was the age of Doctor Johnson, of London coffee-houses, and of the ceremonial taking of tea, so expensive that it was often kept in a locked tea-caddy. No-nonsense old oak reminds us of the age of Queen Elizabeth, perhaps of Shakespeare.

Antiques, of whatever kind, from a humble postcard from Clacton to a wardrobe eight feet wide with compartments for every known accessory, are a window into the past. They make history come alive. They can be bought for use or to look at. They may have been surveyed with pleasure and affection for eight generations or more, and in some way they transmit an aura, even when they are seen hidden away on a shelf in an antique shop or nudging a Cindy Doll on a table at a boot fair. In other words, they have a presence, irrespective of the monetary value that has been allotted often by fashion or chance.

This is an encyclopedia of everyday antiques, so there is an approximate limit of £500 on an item. Most of the entries are a lot less than that; sometimes a hundred times less. Entries marked with * are likely to cost more than £500. But they are such essential antiques that no encyclopedia would be complete without them. It is possible to buy an Edwardian bureau for well under £200 if it is oak and plain, but the 'typical' bureau will cost more than £500. 1930's so-called court cupboards are worth no more than the cost of the wood, but by a court cupboard most people immediately think of a seventeenth century piece. And it is still possible to obtain an inferior long-case clock for under £500, but most reasonable examples are over. You can also obtain a musical box of a sort for £5, but that is not what one would reckon to be a real musical box. The story of English furniture would be ridiculous without mentioning the supreme achievement of eighteenth-century cabinet-makers, the bureau-bookcase. The fluctuations of fashion do mean that certain categories at present outside the £500 limit may fall below it later. Some years ago there was immense excitement when a fairing, a fairground ornament produced in Germany in the late nineteenth

A Victorian mahogany wardrobe in private collection.

century for the British market and sold for about sixpence (2½p) achieved £1,000 at auction. Fairings had become the latest fad. Eventually common sense reasserted itself, especially when the forgeries of 'rare' fairings came onto the market.

The changes in fortune that occur in the world of antiques are fascinating in themselves. Or the world of near-antiques, because there are still those who define antiques as objects at least a hundred and fifty years old. But there is really no adequate substitute for the word. So this book includes entries covering items made only a few years ago. Some were meant to be thrown away, but pop enthusiasts who went to a Beatles concert and managed to get the Beatles' autographs are no doubt delighted that they held onto their programmes.

The author has been writing on antiques for thirty years. His first article was on papier mâché for the magazine *Ideal Home*. The first antique he bought was a Parian head for fifteen shillings in Bermondsey Market in 1964 (now worth approximately £200). The first piece of antique furniture he bought was a massive ornate 1890s vitrine (display cabinet) for £6 (now worth £600 plus). He opened his first shop in Burwash, Sussex, in 1969. He has probably handled hundreds of thousands of objects. And each one was different (and a few were fakes or imitations!) Antiques mirror the life of the past, the distant past, the recent past, and always there is something new, some category of items that have emerged from anonymity. There is always something around the corner, and no-one even remotely interested in antiques or objects of the past can know too much.

As the author was thinking about this introduction a young antique-dealer friend visited him with the latest news from the front. Pine furniture was not selling at all except the very highest quality; lace was not to be found even for ready money; everyone was looking for silver. And what had he turned down lately? A massive heavily carved Indian wardrobe (with lots of ornate elaborate elephants). The cost £120. So here was something with a potential value of at least £500, a projected value of probably £1,000. And available at modest cost simply because it is unfashionable.

The author hopes that the reader will share his enthusiasm for the great game – antiques.

Major Periods

Although the following styles are English, there is often a parallel with those in Continental Europe. However, until the seventeenth century Britain, satisfied with its own often clumsy creations, lagged behind, and only with the arrival of Charles II did foreign influences, especially Dutch and French, become truly important and oak lost its predominance as the main wood to use for furniture. In the eighteenth century the position was reversed, and English designs were shamelessly copied, with regional variations and different woods, especially in Denmark, Sweden, and other countries with trading links with Britain. It is always important to realise that these periods overlap – stylistic features do not automatically change when a new monarch takes over. So historical periods are useful as a guide-line. There was also a gap between London styles and country styles; it sometimes took decades for new ideas to achieve acceptance. In the nineteenth century, and after, styles became international. Britain had the Regency; the French had the Directoire and the Empire. Different names, but sharing common features, even common aspirations. Throughout Europe during the middle years of the nineteenth century there was a nostalgia for the past. In Britain it was the Gothic Revival, in France the Troubadour style, in Italy the Dantesque style, and America had its version of High Victorianism. The Americans, because of the different nationalities represented, had a medley of styles which they managed to blend together, often with amazing skill, but amongst

Table and chair leg shapes are often important to determine an exact date.

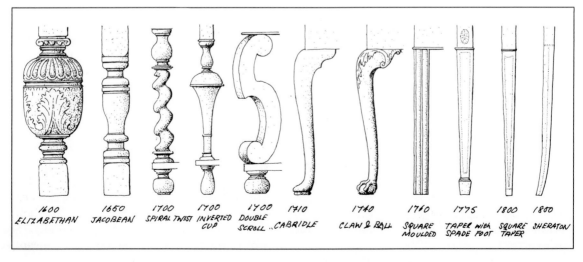

the leaders of the classless society their models of the eighteenth century were predominantly English, just as their architecture was determinedly classical.

MEDIEVAL (– 1485)

Little furniture dated before about 1500 survives, and what we know of it depends on written and pictorial evidence. In illuminated manuscripts, Books of Hours, and similar material the most important piece of furniture – sometimes the only piece of furniture – is a throne, understandable when most pictorial matter related to religion.

There is very little evidence that furniture was regarded highly; some writers have maintained that furniture was relatively scarce. This is ridiculous, as Britain was covered with forests and woods, and carpentry was certainly not one of the more arcane skills. What does seem certain was that furniture was portable, carried from castle to castle as the well-to-do carried on their noble pursuits, mostly fighting. As for the ordinary people, no doubt there were men in the towns and villages who could create simple furniture.

An interesting example of how a historical painter, Sir David Wilkie (1785–1841) imagined a room of a 9th-century cottage would look. It is even more interesting to realise that no-one has the faintest idea of whether he was right, though the powder-horns hanging from the wall would have to wait a few centuries until the introduction of gunpowder. The forlorn gentleman with a crossbow is King Alfred, and the circular objects by the fire (which would have been in the middle of the room and not at the side) are the burnt cakes.

TUDOR (1485 – 1603)

The ruggedness and austerity of the furniture is often at odds with what we know of the period, but it would seem that furniture was still not very important and was used as a background to the colourful cushions, embroideries and hangings. Decoration was predominantly carved, with linenfold panelling the most sophisticated form, though some of the chip carving has elegance and feeling, far more so than the work of Victorian improvers let loose on plain chests. New types of craftsmen such as the joiner came into being, responsible for joined (or 'joint') work (chairs, chests, doors, and tables). This was often furniture called 'dormant', meant to stay where it was and not moved from place to place.

The main pieces of furniture were the chest, which was both a container and a seat, the various cupboards such as aumbries and dole cupboards, tables and stools. The draw-leaf table came into being about 1550. The court cupboard, a three-tiered side-table, became increasingly popular in households to set off their silver and gold. The panel-backed chair was the standard model for two centuries. It was only used by the superior folk; the common man (and woman) used stools. The use of a framework to raise the bedding above the ground was not commonly practised until the early seventeenth century, so the 'traditional' four-poster bed was not universal. Existing furniture is mostly of oak, but this does not mean that other native woods were not used, and massive elm tables survive. Furniture of some woods has merely not lasted, eaten by insects or long disintegrated. Continental furniture was far more sophisticated and was often imported. Towards the end of the Tudor period, with Elizabeth on the throne, furniture became increasingly self-assertive and imposing, and upholstered furniture became fashionable.

JACOBEAN (1603 – 25)

Oak was still the most important wood during the reign of James I, but there was a change of emphasis and a new expertise in dealing with it, best exemplified in the use of elaborate turning. Small hanging cupboards were popular, often made of deal or fruitwood, as were low wide chairs and settees in the form of two chairs side by side. An interesting feature of Jacobean chairs is that they were made in response to a fashion fad, the farthingale or hooped petticoat, which made women's skirts enormous, thus demanding a very wide chair seat. Much of the furniture was undistinguished, but colour was provided by the vogue for 'Turkey' carpets (not necessarily from Turkey but rich and exotic), which were used as bed covers and hangings, as well as to walk over.

CAROLEAN (1625 – 49)

Charles I was a widely cultivated man, who strove to bring Britain's taste in line with that prevailing in Continental Europe, and had his reign not been rudely interrupted by the Civil War he might have done so. Furniture, still predominantly oak, became more refined, and gateleg tables became increasingly popular as the practice of dining at small tables became common. Chests 'with drawers' were becoming chests of drawers, though in the early stages these drawers were concealed behind doors. There was more adventure, with the use of inlay of bone and mother-of-pearl and the introduction of exotic woods, such as zebra wood.

COMMONWEALTH (1649 – 60)

Under Oliver Cromwell life was austere, and furniture reflected this. Much of the furniture that served what was considered the pampered class of the previous era was destroyed. Carving was frowned upon as being out of tune with the new age, but modest turning, especially bobbin turning, was permitted. An interesting feature was the use of leather in chairs.

RESTORATION (1660 – 89)

When he came to the throne in 1660, Charles II brought with him new ideas of furniture and fittings from the Continent, lighter, more elegant, and with walnut the key wood and not oak. Walnut was presented in veneers, not possible with oak even if wanted. Perhaps walnut would have been a court fashion only had the Great Fire of London not happened in 1666, destroying not only the houses but the contents, and encouraging those replacing their furniture to opt for other than old-fashioned oak. The main stylistic influence came from Holland, with floral marquetry, ornate chests of drawers, chests and cabinets on legs, and caned chairs. The bookcase was first mentioned in 1666. Boxes intended for a multitude of purposes, sometimes on stands, were made, and a wide variety of inlays were employed including ebony and tortoiseshell. Gilt furniture became fashionable, and fittings of iron were replaced by those of brass. Dutch influence was also seen in the great importance of tin-glazed pottery inspired by Delft. There was also a vogue for Chinoiserie, lacquer work, and brightly coloured Indian chintzes, encouraged by the imports of the East India Company. Of major importance, especially in the world of silver, was the introduction into polite society of beverages we now take for granted – tea, coffee, and chocolate – the taking of which was a ceremony necessitating a variety of wares. New methods of making clearer and brighter glass made silver goblets and other vessels partially obsolete. A desire for comfort resulted in increased use of upholstery and the evolution of furniture such as the day-bed and the couch. However, the Restoration style did not triumph overnight, and away from the urban centres oak and modest country woods continued to hold sway, with function more important than looks and keeping up to date.

WILLIAM AND MARY (1689 – 1702)

Mainly transitional, with an emphasis on comfort and lightness, heavy Dutch slowly being replaced by more elegant French styles, partly due to the arrival in Britain of Huguenot refugees from France. Walnut was still in favour for furniture, as was lacquer, and several new forms of furniture were introduced, such as the swing toilet mirror and the bureau. Looking-glasses were very popular, and there was a great variety

Queen Anne silver dish of 1704, but the rim was added in 1727.

of chairs, some of them with small shaped aprons on the seat rails, and including upholstered winged armchairs. Caned furniture was popular because it was cheap. A new type of chair foreshadowed things to come – a narrow back of curved outline, a vase- or fiddle-shaped central splat, and cabriole front legs, after Italian and French models. Ornate side-tables influenced by France were very popular. The first tables specifically made for card playing appeared, with folded tops, and dressing-tables, either of the knee-hole type or with drawers on short legs, were popular.

QUEEN ANNE (1702–14)

Typified by the cult of the cabriole leg, simplification, the decline of lacquer and carving, and the first inklings of the classicism that was to mark the later part of the eighteenth century. The claw-and-ball foot was introduced about 1720, partly replacing hoofed and scrolled feet. Chairs were more comfortable, shaped to support the user's body. Stretchers were often discontinued. 'Love-seats', settees with cabriole legs, low backs, and padded seats were introduced. The vogue for panelled rooms meant that cupboards, often called buffets, could be built in the wall. During the walnut period (1690–1730) oak was still used by those who preferred the old order or were out of touch with city fashion. Burr-walnut veneer was particularly popular during the Queen Anne period, and some chests of drawers were mounted on stands. The construction of cased furniture was also more elegant, with finer dovetailing. Bracket feet replaced ball or bun feet. Both the William and Mary and Queen Anne periods saw marvellous furniture, rich and ornate, produced by craftsmen the equal of those on the Continent.

GEORGIAN (1714–1811)

There was little change in taste when the Hanoverian dynasty took over, and the most significant event occurred in 1720 when there was a walnut famine. Walnut was an indigenous French wood, and the authorities placed an embargo on its export. There were supplies in the English American colonies, but they were insufficient, so attention was turned to mahogany,

George III mahogany reading stand with adjustable pillar and slope.

observed while in the West Indies by a carpenter on board Sir Walter Raleigh's ship in 1595, but not greatly used. Walnut continued to be used until about 1760 but the eighteenth century is dominated by mahogany. There are four great stylists in the Georgian period, and one maverick, William Kent.

THE WILLIAM KENT OR PALLADIAN STYLE: William Kent (1685–1748) was an architect, born in Yorkshire, who went to Rome in 1710 and returned to promote classical styles and values in relation to houses and furniture in the grandest of manners. His market was the rich and only the rich. His hallmarks are the broken pediment, the supporting eagle, festoons of fruit, carved masks, lion heads, shells and acanthus motifs, all on a massive and often brooding scale. His most typical piece of furniture was the French-derived console table. He favoured gilding and part ('parcel') gilding. His clients did not mind being surrounded by ponderous furniture if it helped to establish their superiority.

THE ADAM STYLE: one of the most important styles in European furniture, initiated after 1758 when Robert Adam returned from four years' architectural study in Rome with ideas for a new kind of architecture and furniture, not naturalistic and frivolous like the fashionable rococo, not solemn and ponderous, but based on motifs and designs he had seen in ancient baths, villas, and tombs. These included corn husks, bell-flowers, shells, honeysuckle and foliage scrolls, which formed a rich repertoire of ornament for him to select from, both for architectural work and for furniture. The Adam style involves sophistication and refinement; typical of his furniture detail is the square-section straight tapering chair leg, sometimes with inlaid oval medallions, and shaped stretchers incorporating urns. It is reckoned that Adam was at his peak in the 1770s and that by the end of the decade his decorations had become trivial and spineless. He established the dining-room sideboard as a major article of furniture with its flanking urns or pedestals, and his designs for mirrors, side-tables and pier-tables were numerous. Adam greatly influenced Chippendale in his neo-Classical period, and Hepplewhite's taste and discretion owes much to Adam's example.

THE CHIPPENDALE STYLE: extremely eclectic and open to influences from all over the world and from any century. Chippendale himself (1718–79) is a shadowy figure. Among the features which Chippendale announced in his pattern book were fretwork (sometimes blind fret where the piercing does not go all the way through), lacquer-work, pagoda-shaped tops, Gothic cusps, arches, and tracery, and he also applied rococo forms and motifs in a wholly new and adventurous way, twisting French designs so that they conformed perfectly to English furniture. When he became acquainted with Adam's neo-Classical work, Chippendale immediately set to work on his own versions, as valid as his earlier furniture if perhaps not so immediately eye-catching. Had he lived longer and experienced the subtle changes in customer demand that marked the 1780s and 1790s maybe he would have moulded a different taste to that

catered for by Hepplewhite and Sheraton. Furniture described as in the Chippendale style can sometimes be misleading, the triumph of optimism over observation.

THE HEPPLEWHITE STYLE: the merit of Hepplewhite, who died in 1786 and whose book *The Cabinet-Maker and Upholsterer's Guide* was published two years later by his widow, was that his designs were of domestic furniture, such as bedroom and dressing-room furniture, and he was not so concerned with furniture for the grand houses. A byword for elegance and grace, the Hepplewhite style includes beautiful chairs with oval, heart and shield backs; he is especially associated with the Prince of Wales's feathers, and the influence of the neo-Classical movement is seen in the urns, vases, husks and similar motifs that adorn his furniture, as well as straight tapering round and square legs. Although he took over the Adam concept of the sideboard group he also evolved a one-piece ensemble for the smaller home. His painted and inlaid furniture is always in keeping, and he is particularly associated with the secretaire-cabinet, and four-poster beds with very slender, often fluted, posts, few of which have survived probably because of their fragility. He was not averse to taking over curved rococo forms for legs, arms, seats and back rails of chairs and sofas.

THE SHERATON STYLE: Sheraton's furniture was strongly influenced by Adam and neo-Classicism, especially in his chair designs. However, his square-backed chairs were utterly distinctive, and there is a perceptive change in direction between the furniture of the 1780s and that of the 1790s. He also evolved new decorative motifs, such as the lattice and lozenge, deriving from France, and it was the richness and delicacy of French furniture that so appealed to Sheraton, as well as a fondness for strong perpendicular lines, as in chair backs. With less formality in the home, there was a demand for less ceremonial tables, and Sheraton was at his best in casual tables that could be set up anywhere such as Pembroke tables, sofa tables, Carlton House tables, card tables and 'quartetto' tables, designed in sets of four. A Sheraton innovation was the domed top given to ladies' furniture, such as the upper stages of writing tables and dressing tables. Sheraton also showed great interest in multi-purpose furniture typified by tables and chairs which doubled as beds, some of his designs being bizarre and perhaps anticipating his later derangement.

REGENCY (1811–20)

Strictly speaking 1811–20, but generally understood to cover the years from 1793, when the French wars began, to 1830 and beyond, sometimes nudging the Victorian period and disregarding William IV. There was a reaction against spindly shapes, and an emphasis on straight clean lines exemplified in such classic pieces as the chiffonier. Horace Walpole probably summed it up best in his phrase 'an august simplicity'. The main show wood was rosewood, although mahogany and satinwood continued to be used in quantity. Marquetry was unfashionable, brass inlay was welcomed, reeding was a popular decorative finish, and there was often an underlying desire for economy as the war with France was hurting the economy. As in France, much of the furniture was powerful, with the use of novel motifs. There was a taste for contrast, not only in furniture but in draperies, wallpapers (the Regency stripe) and upholstering materials. One of the most influential designers was Thomas Hope who in 1807 published his *Household Furniture and Decoration*. George Smith's *A Collection of Designs for Household Furniture and Interior Decoration* followed a year later. He promoted Egyptian, Greek and Roman styles, and there was also an engaging interest in Chinese-type designs, without any attempt at imitation. Silver was made in a severe style, but from 1804 there was a frivolous phase, almost rococo in flavour.

WILLIAM IV (1830–7)

The most important thing to happen during William IV's brief reign was the publication of the widely influential *Encyclopaedia of Cottage, Farm and Villa Architecture and Furniture*, by J. C. Loudon in 1833, which set out the guide lines for the future. Loudon named the four prevailing styles as Grecian, Gothic, Elizabethan and Louis Quatorze. He gave respectability to the revival of old styles of furniture, with a deferential nod towards French elegance.

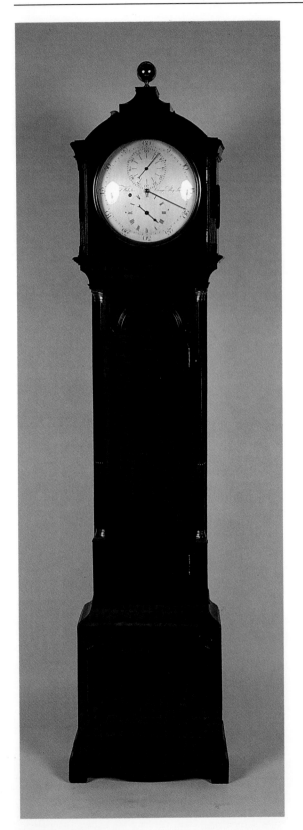

Regency mahogany long-case clock by Richard Webster.

VICTORIAN (1837–1902)

There was not a dramatic break in tradition when Queen Victoria ascended the throne, and Regency designs remained popular, albeit with some coarsening and elaboration, but a fondness for show, experiment, and glitter marked subsequent years, together with a nostalgic look back at older styles, such as the Gothic, which was rejigged for a new prosperous and machine-orientated age. Objects that were once made in limited quantities were mass produced, and new technology made it possible to produce fussy and over-decorated articles at little cost, fantasy pieces on a reckless scale, demonstrated to the world in the Great Exhibition of 1851. Decoration and surface flourish was all, or so it seemed, but exhibition pieces did not necessarily represent furniture and other pieces in the average home, and modest items continued to be made, some of which were classics of their kind, such as the balloon-back chair, made in various forms for decades. The techniques were available for anything to be made, and they were. Manufacturers were constantly striving after novelty, plundering the past for ideas, and on the look

Pair of gilt Regency open armchairs of about 1826.

out for new stimulants, such as the Japanese furniture and decorative pieces in the exhibition of 1862. Throughout the period there were constant movements against ugliness and the law of the jungle, such as the Arts and Crafts Movement from 1861, the Art Furniture phase, and the Aesthetic Movement, with small firms fighting a battle against the big battalions, though many of the large factories, such as Minton, had their studio-pottery wing. It is easy to be dogmatic, and even furniture and decorative objects that seemed unbearably ugly are now much admired.

EDWARDIAN (1901–10)

The end of the Victorian period saw the emergence of art nouveau, signalling a total rejection of what is now known as Victoriana, and also at the opposite extreme a return to eighteenth-century-type furniture in mahogany and satinwood, superbly made by indentured cabinet-makers. The Edwardian period was a

THE CONNOISSEURS.

smooth continuation of the last glowing years of the nineteenth century, given a momentary jolt by the Boer War, but there were tensions between those who were not going to give up their clutter and dark shiny woods, their pampas grass in bright-coloured vases and their overburdened mantels crammed with knick-knacks, and those who wanted to project what has been termed 'a special kind of poverty'. These were the 'arty', with a fondness for light-coloured natural woods, waxed not varnished, fabrics of wool and cotton and not silk, the handmade or imitation handmade. Their provider was Ambrose Heal, who had set up in business in 1893, and whose country-cottage furniture was simple and inexpensive. What is often overlooked is that from the last part of the nineteenth century many more people lived in substantial houses which needed furnishing, and furniture was used from all periods, often placed in bizarre juxtaposition. The antique trade as we know it today dates from the Edwardian period. Very few people lived in 'the styles' of the period except the very particular and the very rich.

GEORGE V (1910–36)

There was no general style during the reign of George V. After World War I the accent was on comfort, novelty, and the pursuit of the chintzy. Lack of domestic servants led to the desire for clean surfaces needing a minimum of dusting. Some of this furniture is the dullest ever made, even more boring than the chain-store furniture that offered a bright cheap glitter for the £5-a-week artisan. In 1925 the Salon des Arts Décoratifs was held in France and, shortened to art deco, the name given to a style that existed until the outbreak of World War II in 1939, or coexisted, for many ordinary people remained

A cartoon of 1922 when antique shops were the province of the rich.

oblivious to it and if observed at all it was in the foyers of cinemas (an alternative name for art deco was the Odeon Style). The accent of art deco products was on movement, streamlining, zigzags, geometry in action and startling colour schemes. There was also a passing nod at the fitness-for-function lobby represented by the German Bauhaus, the most influential design school of the twentieth century. The seeds of art deco were sown in the rectilinear aspect of art nouveau, and even earlier in the 1880s in the pitchers, candlesticks, and tea services designed by Christopher Dresser (1834–1904). The influences that went to shape art deco were many and various – Aztec architecture, Egyptian motifs, and African tribal art. The Aztec influence can be seen in the fashionable stepped shapes on such articles as wireless sets. In a perverse way the pioneers of art deco were doing what the Victorian furniture designers had done nearly a century earlier – plundered the past in a bright and breezy manner looking for elements which they could exploit and thereby make a good deal of money, for art deco was nothing if not commercial. Art deco furniture could be exotic using expensive and little-known woods contrasted with metal and plastic, or it could be chain-store, using laminated plywood with a veneer of loudly figured walnut, given the requisite razzle-dazzle by the addition of chrome.

POST-WAR YEARS (1945–).

It is rather a question of paying your money and taking your choice. The consumer-orientated society gets what it wants. Plastic furniture often in red? Cheap foam-rubber-type (fireproof of course) upholstery? Reproduction Georgian-style furniture which looks as though it is made from candle grease? Office-style smoked-glass-topped tables and chairs which have somehow escaped into the living room? G-plan? Habitat? The American 'womb-chair'? It is no wonder that the market for antique furniture is so buoyant.

Cleaning and Refurbishing Antiques

No damage can result to any object if common sense is used. Soap and water are invaluable aids for materials such as horn, tortoiseshell, white marble, and amber. Coloured marble and alabaster should be cleaned with petroleum. Ivory can be sponged with water but not soaked. A mild ammonia solution is a good brass cleaner, followed up with vinegar with a dash of salt, but for copper there is a trade recipe that works remarkably well – brown sauce, applied liberally, left overnight and then thoroughly washed off with water. Bronze can be washed and dried, but bronze often acquires an attractive patina which is part of its appeal. This is not bronze disease, indicated by greenish spots. All soft substances such as silver and pewter should be cleaned with care, and patent substances should be shunned except for prosaic everyday ware. A chamois leather is ideal for silver, and whiting and silver sand is used to clean pewter, though some people prefer soap and water, followed by a coating of petroleum jelly. Iron is not often met with in antiques, except perhaps in fire grates and similar fireside objects. If corrosion has set in, there is no way to reverse the process, but it has to be stopped. Rust-remover as sold by garages and car accessory retailers may have to be used, or even wire-wool.

The question of cleaning furniture is a personal matter; there can be no set rules. But the older the piece the more thought has to go into the task, with advice being to underclean rather than overclean. Grime on furniture can be removed with vinegar and water, applied in small areas at a time and wiped dry. There is nothing to better a wax finish, and there are finishes to suit all tastes, from beeswax to proprietary furniture polishes, but the key to success is periodical polishing with a soft rag. Sometimes a piece of furniture needs 'reviving', given a bit of sparkle. Vinegar and water may be sufficient, although other recipes include raw linseed oil and white spirit in equal proportions, with a dash of vinegar; or raw linseed oil, methylated spirits and vinegar in equal parts. Perhaps more of a shine is wanted, and the answer may be French polishing. Items destined for French polishing should be carefully evaluated before the task is carried out. Mahogany furniture of the eighteenth century was not intended for French polishing, though it is likely that during the Victorian period, with a horde of servants who liked nothing better than to spend hour after hour painstakingly engaged in cleaning activities encompassing everything from grates to the furniture, the temptation to put a gloss on anything that stood still was impossible to resist. Previous French polishing can be lifted by using a lint-free rag impregnated with methylated spirits, passed in even strokes over the surface. If there is some doubt whether a piece of furniture has been French polished, a drop of methylated

Walnut stool of indeterminate date in the manner of George I.

spirits on an unimportant section will provide an answer. If the surface blisters and dissolves French polish has been used. If there is dirt and grime, fine steel wool with methylated spirits can be used, not rubbing too hard, though it is likely that filler used to fill in the grain of the wood will be disturbed. This will probably be plaster of Paris, and may need to be replaced, using plaster of Paris again tinted with powder colour to match the surrounding wood.

With so many excellent products on the market, much of the legend has departed from French polishing, but it still demands a degree of patience though not enough to be pathological. French polish involves blending shellac with methylated spirits, and there are various kinds. Some have strange names. Button polish is so called because it comes in solid button shapes. White French polish is used for light wood, button is yellowish, orange a golden brown, garnet is dark brown, and ebony or ebonised woods should be treated with black. There is also a transparent French polish. The surface to be polished should be prepared, sanded if necessary, with all cracks and fissures filled and stained. If filling in has been necessary, the surface should be given a thin coat of linseed oil then rubbed down with very fine glass paper. French polish is not applied with a brush but with a rubber, which is a square of wadding approximately 10in x 10in (25cm x 25cm) folded and wrapped in a square of material of about the same size. This should be something that does not shed unwanted particles, and a piece of good-quality sheet or a large handkerchief are ideal. The polish should be poured on the wadding a little at a time, squeezed so that it permeates through the covering and recharged at intervals. There are several ways to fold the rubber, but the main object is to keep the wadding in place and a mushroom shape, with the covering twisted at the top, is perhaps favourite. The rubber should be applied with the grain in gentle even strokes, making certain that at no time does the rubber stick to the surface otherwise a pitting texture will result. Several coats need to be applied. This can be a fairly lengthy process as the coats have to dry between each application. Towards the end, a smear of linseed oil should be applied as a lubricant, preventing the polish already laid down from lifting. Between coats there is a danger of the rubber drying out, so it needs to be kept in an air-tight container. Finally a new rubber is prepared, like the first one. A figure-of-eight action is now used, followed by up-and-down as first practised. A touch of linseed oil is applied to the rubber, and later (six hours or so) removed with methylated spirits (though this is optional). For carvings French polish is applied with a brush, thinned down with 25 per cent methylated spirits. An important thing about French polishing is that the process is reversible.

Rather more adventurous is colouring or staining woods, and there is a wide variety of agents available which can be water-based, spirit-based, oil-based, or chemical. Manufacturers' instructions should be followed, and what is a suitable procedure for one type of stain may not be so for another. Most woods can be simulated. Varnishing is a simple process, and is of two basic kinds – spirit and oil. One slight disadvantage with oil varnish is that the drying time is fairly lengthy, and, unless the atmosphere is dust-free, particles may adhere to the sticky surface during the drying process. As with French polishing, application with the grain rather than figure-of-eight is advisable, and a soft brush is preferable so that the hairs leave no texture. A standard varnishing consists of three coats, with the first diluted with turpentine or white spirit. Spirit varnish dries quickly, and the surface should be sealed with two brush strokes of French polish before beginning. Between the coats of spirit varnish the surface can be rubbed down with very fine steel wool. Polyurethane should be used with discretion. Its advantage is that it is heat-resistant as French polishing is not. Its disadvantage is that it can impart an unacceptable level of gloss. It is very useful for pine as it hardens it and takes away pine's natural woolliness.

One of the many ebonised little pieces that were very popular towards the end of the 19th century. This one is slightly unusual in that there are painted panels.

The two most drastic processes are bleaching and stripping. There is no question that these remove old unwanted finishes of whatever kind, but they can destroy the value of a piece of furniture and there is always the risk that stripping will actually cause a piece of furniture to disintegrate. Heavy stripping involves the use of caustic soda; a stripping tank is standard equipment for a dealer in pine, but for the occasional item a bucketful may be sufficient, with soda added to the water and never the other way about. Protective clothing should be worn, a mop is the preferred applicator, and the process should be carried out speedily, with the caustic soda solution applied, sluiced down, dried off, and swabbed down with a vinegar solution. Stubborn paint or other finishes may need to be tackled with a stiff brush, a knife, or a scraper. Bleaching takes out stains as if by magic; household bleach can be used, though there is a more potent two-part pack available. Furniture which is in any degree valuable should never be subjected to it, though bleaching can be stopped by the application of vinegar.

Repairing Antiques

POTTERY AND PORCELAIN

Repairs can be basic or cosmetic. It is often a temptation to try to smarten up old repairs, but this can result in reducing the value of a piece. If a plate is riveted, and has been riveted for a long time, it may be advisable to leave it as it is rather than take the pieces apart and glue. On the other hand, old amateur gluing by someone not very good at it may be improved upon, so there is no hard or fast rule. Nor is there a hard and fast rule about the kind of adhesive to use. It is tempting to declare unequivocally that it is better to use adhesives that can be easily removed, perhaps by dissolving in hot water, but the advantages of instant glue can never be overlooked, and a crisp break in a piece of pottery or porcelain can be remedied immediately so that there is absolutely no sign that damage has been sustained. The repair of china has always had its pros and cons. A piece of valuable china that has been invisibly mended may convince by touch and by sight, but subject to ultra-violet light a repair, no matter how immaculately carried out, will show up. Perhaps of no consequence if it is, for example, a Victorian figurine worth maybe a hundred pounds; but if it is an eighteenth-century piece nudging four figures? Figures and decorative ceramics are more difficult to repair than vases, cups and saucers. Chips can be filled with a mixture of epoxy resin and whiting (powdered chalk). Missing parts such as an arm can be replaced by making a mould with dental impression mould from a dental supplies manufacturer or Plas-

ticine, using the undamaged arm as pattern – if it matches. The material used in lieu of pottery or porcelain can be a filler of one's choice, with Araldite a good standard replacement. Unfortunately, if a piece is broken off it is debatable whether a match can be found on that particular figure, so such repairs are only possible with symmetrical pieces or where there is a repeating pattern. There are experienced restorers who can fashion replacement parts so that superficially they look right – but to whom? Certainly not the expert. Most fillers being an off-white or a grey, when a replacement section has been glued back it needs painting. Oil or acrylic colours can both be used, using a gloss or matt medium depending on the surface texture required. Dark colours are the easiest to match, whites the hardest, because they usually have a tinge of some other colour that is often difficult to specify. Where an item of no great value has been messily repaired some time in the past, it is better to take apart and reassemble than attempt to improve. Often ugly cracks are ugly simply because of accumulated grime and dirt. If there are segments missing from such pieces as cups or plates the problem of supplying a replacement piece is considerable, often unsurmountable. On the other hand, a chip is often easier to repair than a crack as the replacement piece is small enough to work in and where a chip occurs it is often on a decorated section, and it is simpler to work on a coloured or decorative surface than a plain surface. Where a plate or a cup has been shattered and all the pieces have been retained, it is a good idea to back the largest piece with brown paper

William Moorcroft pomegranate pattern vase signed and dated 1913. Ceramics of this type are so distinctive that they are extremely difficult to repair.

gummed strip and work from there, assembling in the manner of a jigsaw puzzle, adding extra pieces of gummed strip as the work proceeds. Gummed strip is far better than brown parcel tape, which has more grip, simply because it can all be soaked off in hot water after the repair has been carried out, while parcel tape can pull the pieces apart.

FURNITURE

To repair or not to repair is the first question. A repair does not necessarily add value to a piece of furniture, and may reduce it. Wear and tear is expected in old furniture of whatever status. Some kinds of damage are superficial, needing just common sense and a small range of basic tools and materials.

SURFACE REPAIRS

Burn marks can be taken out with fine steel wool, a scalpel or good-quality craft knife, or a razor-blade, but what might appear initially to be a minor job may turn out to be more exacting if there is a degree of charring not seen at first and only coming to light after the work has started. In any case, there will be a shallow hole that needs filling. There are a number of ways to do this – oil paint worked in with the fingertip, coloured beeswax, epoxy resin, or shellac mixed with powder pigment. A traditional filler is beaumontage, made by mixing equal quantities of beeswax and rosin, plus a few flakes of shellac, melted in a tin with powdered colour added. Stick stopping is a ready-made substance, used like sealing wax. New easy-repair products are constantly coming on the market. White circular patches are heat marks, the indication of a carelessly placed cup, removable by the use of turpentine and linseed oil in equal parts rubbed well in, allowed to penetrate, then finished off with a wipe with a vinegar-impregnated rag. Methylated spirits can do the job, and so can cigar ash mixed in water (cigar ash is a mild abrasive). Black spots and rings are due to contact with water over a period. Oxalic acid (3 heaped tbsp – 405ml – in a cup of hot water), brushed on and wiped off, can be used. Oxalic acid will not hurt the furniture but it is poisonous. It is a useful substance, and can cope with ink stains, which are also susceptible to household bleach, washed off with water. For stubborn stains, diluted nitric acid can be tried; this can leave stains of its own, removable with linseed oil. Superficial scratches on furniture can be taken out using fine glass-paper dipped into linseed oil. Deeper scratches may need filling with one of the fillers mentioned earlier. A deep scratch may indicate the beginning of a split, especially if it is 'eccentric', ie following the line of the grain.

VENEER REPAIRS:

Superficial repairs to solid furniture are far easier than repairs to veneer. Veneer can be straight-forward, relying on the figure of the wood, or it can be picture or pattern (marquetry or parquetry). Strips of veneer as used in banding or other decorative finishes will not present too much of a problem, as it is most likely that any damage will be in the form of missing segments, which merely need to be matched up and replaced. Small pieces of veneer can be obtained from marquetry sets as sold in toy and craft shops, although these will probably be thinner than old veneer and may need to be glued in two or more layers. Old-fashioned Scotch glue (treacly brown and boiled up in a saucepan or tin) is best. If a section of veneer is to be replaced it is better to remove any existing polish and grime either by using white spirit, or a proprietary stripper, or by sanding down. It does not matter that the old veneer will be discarded. However, the removal of a surface finish helps the next process, which is to apply heat over a damp cloth using a fairly hot iron. This melts the underlying glue and the veneer will strip off. For small sections, an electric soldering iron can be used. There are still many suppliers of veneer to the trade and the public, located by means of the Yellow Pages or in craft and woodworking magazines. As most veneers are made of the 'standard' woods there should be few problems, though if zebra wood or amboyna or other exotic woods have been used as inlay it may be necessary to doctor available veneers (staining, painting, etc). The new veneer should be dampened and flattened between weighted wood for twenty-four hours and relaid while slightly damp. It should be slightly 'proud', rather above the existing surface, so that it can be sand-papered down rather than built up. Blisters in veneer can either be treated by making two tiny holes, preferably with a hypodermic syringe, and squirting glue in one of them then pressing flat (the second hole is to let air escape), slicing neatly across and inserting glue, or by removing and replacing with a new shape. Marquetry and parquetry repairs need patience and some skill, for it is necessary to match new areas of veneer with the old, copying existing sections of patterns using tracing paper. Acetate, from drawing-office suppliers, can also be used. Templates can then be made.

STRUCTURAL REPAIRS
Chairs

The cardinal rule is to repair as soon as possible, for if there is a fault it will throw a strain on other parts of the furniture and a minor problem may turn into a major project. All pieces that chip off or break off should be put in a container and labelled. Chairs are especially vulnerable to breakage, especially the back and back legs where sitters have been balancing on them. If there are slats and rungs that have worked loose, regluing may be sufficient, applying glue to one end only. A loose rung can also have a sliver of wood inserted before gluing. Some rungs are straightforward, and broken ones can be replaced by dowelling, shaped with a plane and finished off with a spokeshave. Intricate turned and shaped members can be bought from suppliers, and these pieces only need to be inserted. This may necessitate dismantling the chair, which is a simple structure, though a check must be made to see that no-one has done any repairs using screws or even nails. If a chair, or, indeed, any article of furniture needs to be knocked apart a mallet is better than a hammer, and a batten of wood should be interposed to spread the force of the blow. Major repairs, such as inserting a new section of wood in a chair leg, need preparation and forethought. It is often better to put in new legs than try to mend the originals, but all depends on the quality of the chair. A chair leg that has been cut down because the foot has rotted away is easier to repair than one which has been subject to woodworm, where the damage is unseen, and a promising section may be painstakingly taken out only to find that the woodworm has spread to superficially healthy sections. The professional way is to cut our the damaged section with a chisel and straight edge and insert replacement wood. But this does mean a certain amount of woodworking skills and confidence. All repair jobs should be looked at practically. It may be tempting to remove metal braces on long-damaged furniture and renew or repair any damage to the wood; but some furniture was fitted with metal reinforcing braces when it was made. Shaky furniture may merely mean that a mortise and tenon joint has lost its peg, and if it is a simple piece of furniture, such as a chair, it is often better to replace the peg rather than use glue. The construction of most articles of furniture can easily be disco-

Before repairing an article ascertain that it is worth repairing. This 'George III' armchair of about 1900 is, despite its inappropriate legs and high ugly arms.

vered as it was done with the simplest of tools, most of which are in the average handyman's workshop. Replacing broken carving demands certain skills; photographs should be taken of the damage before anything major is carried out. Corner blocks are used to strengthen the seat framework of many upright chairs, as well as settees and furniture such as chests of drawers. This is one of the few processes where screws are used as a matter of course. A missing or loose corner block can easily be fixed. In all furniture repairs Scotch glue should be used. Although there is a slow drying time, meaning that repaired or replaced pieces need to be clamped together or held together in some way (sometimes using sandbags), the process is always reversible by the application of heat.

Carcase furniture

In carcase furniture, such as chests of drawers, sometimes what might seem a major problem is resolved by common sense. If a drawer sticks it

may be a missing or worn guide underneath, cured by the application of plastic wood or a small fillet of wood – or rubbing a candle on the runners and sides may be sufficient; if it goes too far in, it is almost certainly because the drawer stops at the back have broken off, and are easily replaced. If a drawer will not open it may be that there is something quite small inside jamming it, perhaps removed by using a knife blade. If not, and there are other drawers, it may be possible to remove them to get at the culprit. A locked drawer may pose problems. Perhaps the only way is by dismantling the furniture, or removing the back. If the bottom of a drawer is split, it is often easier to replace than repair. A split that is just starting is harder to repair than one that has 'matured' and it is sometimes better to finish the split before setting to work with glue. The linings or sides of a drawer should be treated with respect. The essence of drawer construction is the dovetail joint; this may be of high quality, may be a clue to the age of the piece of furniture, and should not be meddled with unduly. Loose wooden knobs on drawers or doors are easily dealt with by taking out, removing the old glue, and wrapping a glue-saturated cloth round the dowel of the knob. Sometimes a knob needs to be replaced. A knob is of little intrinsic value, but it may be on a veneered drawer or door, in which case it is advisable to chisel off the knob so that there is no possible damage to the veneer. If mouldings are broken, and if they are integrated with the furniture rather than glued on, they can be replaced by dowelling and then carved and trimmed to match the surrounding or adjoining section. Complicated mouldings, no matter how they were made originally, can be made in more than one piece and then assembled on the spot. For high-quality furniture, broken mouldings or pieces can be left as they are as indications that the piece is what it purports to be, warts and all, or they can be given a cosmetic treatment with coloured wax. The construction of not only carcase furniture but tables and chairs often involves dowels, and these may need to be removed or replaced, in which case the best way is to drill them out or poke them out with a sharpened screwdriver. When replacing dowels it is important that they are the right length; this can be found out by inserting a pencil in the hole and marking how far it goes in.

Tables

Framed tables with a leg at each corner are strong; tables with an X-shaped underframe are weaker because of stresses to the grain direction; tripod tables are inherently suspect; tripods with a platform less so as the stress is dispersed. Even more than chairs, the structure of a table can be ascertained in a minute or two by turning it upside down and looking at it. The legs of tripod tables are often slot-dovetailed in, and many tables were fitted with metal plates when they were made. If regluing is necessary, the tripod table needs to be held together using a form of tourniquet, while the glue is drying. It is vital to prevent bruising, and sheets of foam rubber are useful. Table tops sometimes split, often due to warping or a hidden stress difficult to work out. The table top may need to be taken off and worked on. If the split is narrow it may be advisable to expand with a saw, preferably a flexible one so that it follows the line of the crack, which in turn will follow the line of the grain, so that a sliver of wood can be inserted, slightly proud so that it can be sandpapered down. It will need to be glued and the two pieces held together under pressure; the tapes used by furniture removers are ideal as they will not harm the wood. If simple gluing is not sufficient, it may be necessary to insert a butterfly-shaped piece of wood to hold the two sections together, but this is a fairly major woodworking job and it will not add to the value of a good table, a crack being preferred. Round tables are often reinforced by a substantial length of wood screwed to the underside. This will need to be removed if repairs are carried out to the top. When replaced, the existing screw holes should not be used, but fresh ones drilled, the batten, placed at a slightly different angle, covering the old screw holes. A warped table top may be cured by screwing on battens, even if it had no battens previously. The leaf of a drop-leaf or gateleg table can be battened, but at an angle so that it does not interfere with the raising and lowering of the leaf. Damage to table legs is not uncommon. If they are sturdy, a cosmetic repair using wax or plastic wood may be sufficient. If they are mahogany, eighteenth-century, perhaps with inlay, lining, or banding, more discretion is needed. The extent of the repairs depends on ability and on the value of a piece. Eighteenth-century furniture does not have to be perfect to be valuable. A

Customer. "IS IT REALLY TUDOR? SHOULDN'T HAVE THOUGHT SO; DON'T SEE ANY WORM-HOLES."
Dealer. "AII, SIR, EVEN THE INSECTS DIDN'T HAVE THE HEART TO DEFACE ITS BEAUTY."

The world may have changed in seventy years, but not the antique-dealer's sale talk.

worn-down leg of a seventeenth-century table is acceptable, whereas an added-on section is not. Quality marquetry with bits missing is preferable to a botched job. In all repairs, discretion is of the essence.

Furniture accessories

Furniture is made of materials other than wood, and the decorative extras and accessories can be of almost anything, with brass predominant, especially with handles which replaced wooden knobs or iron pulls with the introduction of walnut, inlay and marquetry. The loop, with sockets at the heads of bolts, came in about 1710. In about 1780 handles were stamped out in sheet metal, and these are often found with splits and dents, especially the backplates. Brass is malleable and, by persistent hammering with a round-

from 1807 in a variety of styles. One of the most common was the Ogee clock, a weight-driven striking clock in an oblong case. On the lower part of the glass was a picture, either hand-painted or a print, and pasted to the inside back of the case was advertising material with instructional details. There were forty parts in what was called the shelf-clock, and assembly took, it was claimed, a few minutes. The cases were usually of softwood, with crude joining of the glue-and-nail order. Amongst the designs were Beehive, where the movement was reached from the back (unusual for American clocks), the Cottage (a squat Ogee), and the Sharp Gothic, with a pointed top, a favourite design for alarm clocks and made well into the 1940s.

AMERICAN FURNITURE

In early years America was a land of regions and different nationalities who brought their own languages, traditions, and ideas of what constituted acceptable furniture with them. The Dutch colonised the Hudson Valley, the Germans settled in Pennsylvania, and the English occupied New England and the far south. Little American furniture survives from the seventeenth century. It was rugged, functional and without adornment except for decorative turning, but very soon American furniture-makers were copying European and especially English furniture. The American Colonial style is characterised by simplicity, the use of native woods such as hickory and maple, and versatility – combination-furniture, the chair which served as a table and vice versa. With the rise of an urban elite, furniture became as sophisticated and elegant as in Europe, and the return to classical models in the late eighteenth century by European furniture-makers was followed in America. The cabinet-maker Duncan Phyfe was as famous in the United States as Chippendale was in Britain (and in more recent years in Australia as well). Because of the size of the country, communities could live self-contained existences, persisting in using furniture which logically belonged to a previous age. Typical of such communities were the Shakers. Individual and expressive names were given to certain pieces of furniture, especially chairs. The Hitchcock chair, popular in Connecticut 1820–50, was painted black, stencilled with fruit and

flower designs; the Brewster chair was a Dutch-style armchair made of turned posts and spindles with a rushed seat, named after the leader of the *Mayflower* colonists; it was also called the Carver chair, named after the first governor of the Plymouth colony. The New England armchair was a hoop-back Windsor; the Martha Washington was a mid-eighteenth-century armchair with arms tapering down and a high back. The Boston rocker was based on a curved-arm Windsor, often with an ornamental top rail. Chests were important pieces of furniture in the American household; the Hadley chest was made in Connecticut 1675–1740, with flat carving of leaves and flowers covering the entire front of the chest. The Connecticut chest had tulip and sunflower carving, often with split baluster mouldings. The hope chest was the American name for a dower chest. The period 1785–1830 is known as the Federal style, with strong European influences, for when an enthusiasm for a particular style struck Europe, Americans followed suit with even more zest. Thus American Gothic can be more outrageous than anything in Britain, and nineteenth-century extravagances could be produced more cheaply and on a massive scale because of the American superiority in mass-production techniques. Sometimes they produced pieces of furniture unknown in Europe such as the Wells Fargo desk, more properly the Wootton Patent Office desk, which opened at the front and the sides to reveal scores of drawers and pigeon holes – the roll-top desk driven to its limits. In the 1890s and 1900s adventurous furniture was made by Frank Lloyd Wright, and America continued to be in the fore during the art deco period. The formative geometric furniture of the 1920s and 1930s was largely a European phenomenon, but the furniture and decorative art produced in America had a wider influence on the man and woman in the street simply because of the cinema. Audiences not only in America but throughout the world saw this fresh, uninhibited, streamlined furniture in the Hollywood films, and without realising it wanted the same kind of environment, happily supplied by the chain stores. In 1940 the Museum of Modern Art in New York inaugurated a competition for 'Organic Designs in Home Furnishings', and the one-piece seat shell form made its appearance.

Tiffany glass was well ahead of its time in its use of bold colours, anticipating by many decades types of abstract painting. Only over the last twenty years has its merit been recognised and its unique qualities valued, so much so that genuine Tiffany glass is out of reach of the average lover of antiques. This is a modern lamp in the Tiffany style. In another twenty years no one will know the difference.

AMERICAN GLASS

The first glass (making) house was established by English settlers in Virginia in 1608, and this and others made fairly crude domestic glass and window glass, together with beads for trading with the Indians. Most glasshouses were short-lived, and glass was mainly imported until 1739 when a progressive company opened in New Jersey, bringing workers from Germany and Holland, which made the standard wares, such as drinking glasses and decorative ware, but also experimented with new techniques resulting in the 'lily pad' design, pulling the material into the form of a water-lily stem and pad. As the

frontiers of the United States stretched further west new glass factories opened; the New Geneva Glassworks in western Pennsylvania, started in 1797, was the first glasshouse west of the Allegheny Mountains. The first commercial cut glass was produced in America by Bakewell and Company in 1808. The New England Glass Company (1818–1888) was one of the largest glass factories in the world, prominent in its use of pressed glass. By 1840 there were more than eighty-one glasshouses in the USA. In 1864 soda-lime glass was produced, not known in Europe, cheaper than lead glass. Influences came from Bohemia, as well as Britain, and although the Civil War reduced the demand for luxury items the glass-makers survived and what is known as the 'Brilliant Period' began in 1880, with deep and lavish cut glass. The demand for novelty resulted in exotic and elaborate art glass, such as Amberina, Amber, Agata, Satin Glass, Crown Milano, Burmese and Peachblow, leading to art nouveau glass and inevitably Tiffany, a producer of genius, whose stained-glass lamps were unique.

AMERICAN POTTERY AND PORCELAIN

American ceramics have been overshadowed by American furniture and glass. Early pieces were functional, derived from European models, but in the eighteenth century a distinctive style began to emerge. A pottery was established at Bennington, Vermont, in 1793, producing stoneware by 1815 and a type of Parian ware in the 1840s. One of the most important nineteenth-century porcelain factories was the Union Porcelain Works established in 1848. Wedgwood-style pieces of the highest quality were made in the 1870s. The American Pottery Company, founded in 1833, was the first to succeed in producing printed wares to compete with those imported from England. Later American ceramics, though little-known, are often superb.

AMERICAN SILVER

The chief centres of production of silver in the seventeenth century were Boston and New York. By 1680 Boston had twenty-four silversmiths, most of whom had received their train-

ing in London. Design was derived from English models, but in New York there were strong Dutch and French influences as well. Many Huguenots came to New York in the late seventeenth century, bringing with them characteristic French techniques and motifs. In the eighteenth century the practice of engraving coats of arms on silver was taken over from England. British silver models dominated, though after the French Revolution there was a new influx of French silversmiths. American silver of the nineteenth century, as in Britain, was lavish and spectacular, relatively restrained in Boston, exuberant in New York and the more recent silver centres of Baltimore and Philadelphia. Art nouveau was not so strong in America as in Europe, but splendid art nouveau pieces were made, alongside sober functional silver in the Arts and Crafts style.

ANCHOR ESCAPEMENT

Invented about 1670, the anchor represented a revolution in timekeeping, as the pallets are in the same plane as the escape wheel instead of being at right angles to it as in the escapement it replaced, the verge. It enabled long pendulums to swing more slowly, cutting down on cumulative error. It is also known as the recoil escapement, this recoil being observed on the second hands of long-case clocks, which shudder at each beat. Many escapements have been refinements on those that have preceded them, often invented for use in smaller watches, but the anchor escapement represents a completely new attitude, a technological breakthrough of its time.

ANDIRONS

Mostly ornamental, these are the pair of outsize firedogs in front of the 'working' pair holding the logs. The early examples were of wrought iron, but later brass, silver, bronze and silver-gilt were used. The wide use of coal in the eighteenth century and the introduction of the grate rendered andirons superfluous, but with the reintroduction of the open fire as a fashionable institution, andirons have once again become necessary. Fireplace furniture has often been ornate and imposing, as the fireplace was usually the focal point of a room.

ANIMALIERS, LES

A school of French sculptors specialising in bronze animals, amongst the best known being Barye, Cain, Frémiet and Mène, much imitated by present-day practitioners in the art of cold-cast bronzes (bronze powder), easily distinguished if not deliberate fakes by the presence of bright green baize beneath the base.

ANNEALING

A process used in glass-making and metal-working involving the heating and slow cooling of an object, reducing brittleness and internal stresses. Silver sheet becomes brittle when repeatedly hammered, but raising the temperature solves the problem.

APOSTLE SPOONS

The only examples of pre-Restoration silver now found outside museums are spoons, large numbers of which are available because they were treasured as heirlooms, because they were sometimes the only piece of silver in the household, and because their scrap value was too small to melt down. Early spoons have decorative finials in immense variety – diamond point, acorn, fruit, and, the most sought after, the apostle spoon. There are twelve apostles and the master or Christ spoon, and most apostle spoons available today were made in the nineteenth century and after, because they became very popular as christening presents. The apostles are identified by the symbols they hold, though these are sometimes missing, as are their haloes.

APPLIQUÉ

The sewing of patches or pieces onto a material, often outlined by embroidery, a process used in the Middle Ages as a cheap substitute for tapestry. During the sixteenth and seventeenth centuries motifs of animals, insects, and foliage were worked in tent stitch on canvas, cut out and applied to cushion-covers or hangings. Appliqué or applied work could also involve lace, silk and metal thread, and in the nineteenth century was much used on workboxes and in home embroidery. A very popular medium amongst twentieth-century artists.

ARABESQUE

A pattern used from ancient times, usually symmetrical, in which interlaced branches, scrollwork, leaves, stylised fruit and animal forms are employed. Found in carpets, tapestries, on types of pottery, on silver, and on furniture.

ARBOUR GROUP

An arbour is a leafy alcove, and the group usually consists of two lovers, popular in porcelain in Germany and in pottery (Staffordshire and Whieldon) in the eighteenth century, revived in the late nineteenth century for sentimental pieces.

ARMILLARY SPHERE

A simple demonstration device, made from the second century to the nineteenth depicting the moon, sun, and planets in relation to the earth, usually made of bronze or brass, and periodically revised as theories of cosmology changed. The most attractive examples were made in the eighteenth century. The orrery is a sophisticated version, usually worked by clockwork.

ARMOIRE

French term for a wardrobe; today it is a name for a large upright cupboard, often in pine, with two long doors and with one or more shelves in a plain interior. The French examples could be lavish, sometimes in Boulle work.

ARMORIAL CHINA

These are miniatures bearing an armorial crest, and the principal maker is Goss, although other factories such as Arcadian, Crescent, Carlton, Grafton, and Shelley produced much the same kind of small porcelain pieces. William Henry Goss founded the Falcon Pottery at Stoke-on-Trent in the late 1850s, and in 1887 his son obtained permission from the boroughs and cities of Britain to reproduce their coats of arms on miniature china. Goss insisted that these novelties should be sold only in the town whose crest was depicted, and consequently there was a ready sale to tourists who wanted a memento.

Goss used a wide variety of shapes and subjects and was always ready to capitalise on local places of interest. He made a speciality of archeological finds, such as urns. During World War I miniature tanks, aircraft, ships and other wartime objects were made in large quantities. In 1936 the firm was taken over by Cauldon Potteries, and, although the original moulds were used, the standard of finish was inferior. A variant of the armorial Goss china was the Goss commemorative ware, especially for royal occasions. The early Goss pieces are characterised by the presence of a serial number related to the patent number, and those who have sufficient interest can date them.

ARMORIAL ENGRAVING

Carried out especially on silver, and most pieces of large silver prior to about 1830 bore engraved armorials, since removed to the detriment of the piece and to its value. The 'crossed plumes' cartouche (the decorative surround to the coat of arms) was used 1650–85, with coarse vigorous cutting, refined gradually, with baroque carving 1705–40, incorporating shells and masks. In the 1730s asymetric designs were prominent, leading to neo-Classical styling about 1770. In about 1785 came bright cut engraving, cuts made at an angle to reflect the light, popular until about 1805, when the 'leafy' cartouche was introduced. All styles were used in the nineteenth century, often lavishly and pretentiously by the new rich with doubtful armorials.

ART DECO CERAMICS

Art deco pottery and porcelain could be frivolous and humorous, or it could be serious and elegant, as in some Royal Doulton products in a Chinese style with flambé glaze, and in the work of many French potters, many of whom carried on the traditions of art nouveau as though World War I had never happened. French art deco pottery is often subdued and subtle, though the potters' names (René Buthaud, Jean Mayodon, Jean Besnard, Emile Decoeur, and Emile Lenoble) are little known in Britain and America. In Britain, interwar ceramics can seem an uncharted area, with a few chosen potters and manufacturers standing

Italian art deco figure of a lady.

as beacons, such as Clarice Cliff, Susie Cooper, and Charlotte Rhead. Clarice Cliff is the most important, introducing her 'Bizarre' range in 1928, with its strong, simple, designs and bright colours including an individual orange she called tango. Her ceramic cut-outs featuring dancing couples were entirely new to Britain. Susie Cooper's work was quieter, more leisurely, Charlotte Rhead's pottery more subtle and redolent of art nouveau. Much of the British pottery was anonymous – rectangular vases with Z-shaped handles, geometric candlesticks with a sharp cutting edge, cubist teapots with inset handles and spouts, angular animal forms, and pretty-pretty wall plaques in the shape of a woman's head. Some of the most dramatic and uncompromising ceramics were produced in Russia, often designed by abstract

Three Art Deco figures made in Austria.

painters such as Malevich. Even more than in art nouveau, art deco was a universal language, and it is difficult to ascertain countries of origin without examining potters' marks. American art deco ceramics were exceptionally original and vigorous, well attuned to the times, and the potters excelled in figurative work, often using skyscraper, lightning-bolt, and neon-sign motifs. In the geometric work most typical of the period, glazes were of less importance, though sometimes in figurative work potters used ingenious glazes to get the appearance of a bronze patina.

ART FURNITURE

A term first used by Charles Eastlake in *Hints on Household Taste* (1868). The Art Furniture Company manufactured pieces designed by E. W. Godwin, and the aim was to combat florid flashy furniture by the use of plain pieces with simple lines, made of homely wood especially oak and walnut, and waxed rather than French polished. Decoration was often in the medieval style, though later there were fashionable Japanese influences.

ART NOUVEAU

A deliberate attempt to create a new end-of-the-century style. The results were seemingly contradictory, either sinuous, free flowing, curved and undulating (as in much French furniture and art glass) or stark and geometric (as in the furniture of J. R. Mackintosh). There was a strong Japanese influence in the earlier manifestations of art nouveau and in the fashionable furniture of about 1890 advertised as 'Fanciful' and 'Quaint', which was spindly and marked by a multiplicity of legs, totally unlike the later furniture, a characteristic of which was that legs, normally ending under the tops of tables and other furniture, continued on and above, sometimes ending up beneath a cornice or moulding or free standing, when they were topped by rectangular caps. Stretchers were almost at floor level instead of the usual six or eight inches (15–17cm) above. Carving was replaced by inlay of wood, pewter, mother-of-pearl, enamel, and stained glass, sometimes with stunning effect, sometimes in a random way, as in the ubiquitous pewter panels on wardrobes. Mottoes were also incorporated into furniture to match those on house beams and on walls. Amongst the best designers, such as C. F. A. Voysey, there was a conscious effort to think vertically. Voysey used unstained unpolished wood, and made a feature of his hinges, which could be the most important design element. Ambrose Heal advocated 'admirable proportion, harmonious design and rigid economy of ornament', and he and his firm had a great influence on future furniture development up to and after the Utility furniture of World War II. Important as art nouveau furniture was and is, the movement is seen at its most extreme in glass, architecture, jewellery, and graphics, in which the designers seem determined to explore how much manipulation the various materials will take.

French art nouveau cameo glass vase made by Daum.

ART POTTERY

The seeds of art pottery were sown in the 1830s, when there was a clamour against the lack of style of mass-produced products. In the 1850s John Ruskin railed against the ugliness of factory-produced objects. Large potteries such as Minton and Doulton took note, and amidst their commercial ware produced specialised pieces, not always profitably. Art pottery is the name given not to the products of the major potteries but to small adventurous and innovative firms. The most original of the small potteries was Martin Brothers (1873–1914), famous for its stoneware grotesque birds and animals, which sometimes look as though they have been made on the spur of the moment and in drink. One of the least known but most important is Linthorpe, founded in 1879 and existing for about ten years, known for original streaky glazes on browns, blues, and greens. When Linthorpe closed, exiles moved elsewhere, some of them to Bretby, founded in 1883. Two Linthorpe designers left to join the new firm of Burmantoft, which specialised in heavy glazed majolica. William Ault began his firm in 1887. Moorcroft was a good deal later, starting in 1913, specialising in fruit and flowers in lustrous colours against a dark background. There are three other major art potteries that are a world apart from these. Ruskin pottery, founded in 1898, was subtle and refined, famous for an eggshell-like ceramic with pitted granular glazes. Pilkington's Royal Lancastrian pottery was founded in 1892, first of all making tiles and then decorative wares, particularly vases adorned with Greek-style boats, fish, animals, and sinuous plant forms. William de Morgan began in 1872 by decorating ware bought 'in the white' from Staffordshire. He has been described as the ultimate Pre-Raphaelite potter, experimenting with lustre painting on very large dishes and enamelled work suggesting Islamic sources. Other important names are Howell & James, Craven Dunnill & Co, Della Robbia Pottery, Brannam, and Elton. Some potters such as Bernard Moore and the Upchurch Pottery preferred simple adorned forms, which remained the stock-in-trade of the hobbyist and back-garden potter. There are potteries that are commercial but have roots in the art pottery past, such as the three Devon factories of Watcombe, Aller Vale, and Longpark, which specialised in red earthenware coated with a creamy slip and adorned with a motto, souvenir work that transcended the genre. Occasionally a small pottery receives flattering attention, as has been accorded to Wemyss. a Scottish firm operating from the 1880s until 1930, which produced 'ox-blood' vases and their speciality, animals adorned with flowers and other motifs – especially the famous Wemyss pig.

ARTS AND CRAFTS MOVEMENT

Social, moral, intent on 'art made by the people, and for the people' (William Morris 1879). A number of guilds and societies such as the Century Guild (1882) and the Guild of Handicraft (1888) were formed to revive craftsmanship and encourage a greater co-operation between the various crafts. The co-operative was the ideal structure for these dedicated men. Although the influence of the Arts and Crafts Movement was great, especially on the present century, its products were minimal because they were handmade and therefore even the simplest chair – preferably made by one man throughout – was expensive. The ordinary man- and woman-in-the-street, the target customer, could not afford to buy. Arts and Crafts furniture does, however, have a curious identity, and

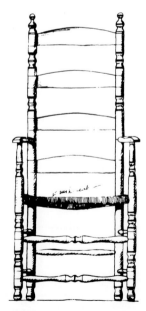

An Arts and Crafts Movement chair by Ernest Gimson.

can often be recognised amongst superficially similar furniture by an unaccountable 'something', as though the care bestowed by the craftsman in its making has permeated through.

ASSAY

The testing of metals to ensure that they are of a standard fineness. The Goldsmiths' Company at the Goldsmiths' Hall in London received its Charter in 1327, which gave it the authority to assay and mark articles of gold and silver. In 1363 it was decreed that each master goldsmith in London was to have his or her own mark registered at Goldsmiths' Hall. In 1681 a fire destroyed all these records. The main mark on sterling silver (silver containing the legally required proportions of silver and copper) is the lion. In 1697 a higher standard of purity was required, denoted by a seated Britannia, but the lion was restored in 1720. Provincial silver was stamped by regional assay offices, the most important being Birmingham, Chester, Dublin, Edinburgh, Exeter, Glasgow, Newcastle, and Sheffield. Many articles not of silver were given assay marks that look, at first glance, like the real thing and are intended to confuse.

AUBUSSON

High-quality knotted-pile carpets were made from 1742, designed by the Court painters, with gradually some deterioration of quality during an export boom in the early nineteenth century. Carpets in the Aubusson style are often described as Aubusson. Tapestries were made from early times and by 1637 there were about two thousand weavers, but little survives earlier than the eighteenth century. Lavish and visually spectacular, favourite subjects were landscapes, bucolic scenes, Chinoiserie, rococo taste. In the eighteenth and nineteenth centuries much tapestry for upholstery was made and exported.

AUTOGRAPHS

Autographs are often more interesting than valuable, and even an autograph book bulging with personalities' names may be worth very little. An autographed letter is more valuable than just a signature, which may have been cut off and

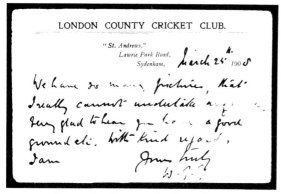

A postcard, signed and written by the cricketer W. G. Grace, of great interest to collectors of sporting memorabilia.

stuck in a book, and the content and nature of the letter may increase the value tenfold, even a hundredfold. A signature of Mozart is acceptable; a signature and part of a music manuscript, or the manuscript without a signature, are invaluable – the difference between something done and a mere token of identity. An autographed letter signed is known as an A.L.s; of less consequence is a letter with the signature only in the handwriting of the important personage – but if the content of the letter is important this may not be so inconsequential after all. A document signed is a Doc.s., a typed letter signed is a T.L.s. Autographed photographs and picture postcards may not be what they appear; sometimes the facsimile signature on actors' and actresses' postcards are very good. Autograph manuscripts of course vary enormously in value; a trunkful of manuscripts by a nonentity can be worth less than a couple of lines scribbled on the back of an envelope by someone who is passably well known. However, American universities are taking on board tons of autographed and typed material by little-known writers just in case posterity re-evaluates them. Forgery is rampant in this area, as famous peoples' signatures are easy to find out; it was an incredibly popular subject for articles in Victorian and Edwardian magazines such as *Strand* and *Macmillan's Magazine*.

AUTOMATA*

Mechanically operated figures, mostly of the eighteenth and nineteenth centuries, some simple and hardly more than toys, some elaborate and involving complex gearing, often with a musical accompaniment furnished by a music-box movement. Amongst the popular subjects were piano players, women dancing, men smoking, life-size moving, fluttering and singing birds, and comic monkeys. A favourite form of display was in a picture frame with a multitude of participants. The most common picture automaton was a ship on a sea. The figures in automaton tableaux were often superbly dressed and presented. Tiny automata were fitted in snuff-boxes and watches, such as a singing-bird, the voice produced by minute bellows.

AXMINSTER CARPETS

A type of carpet not necessarily from Axminster. From 1735 machinery was used by British carpet manufacturers, and until 1906 machinery could not make knots, so the British carpet is totally unlike the classical Middle Eastern type, fluffier, thicker, and more luxuriant with wide sweeping designs. A charter was granted to weavers in Axminster in Devon as early as 1710. The Axminster Carpet Manufactury had a fire in 1828, could not recover and closed in 1835, with looms and orders taken over by Wilton, which kept the name Axminster.

BABY WALKER

Known from the sixteenth century, the baby walker is an open frame consisting of two horizontal wooden rings connected by struts. The lower ring has castors at intervals around it. The upper wooden ring is smaller than the lower, and the baby stands with his or her head and upper body through this. It was also known as a baby cage.

BACHELOR CHEST

Auctioneer's name for small eighteenth-century chest of drawers with folding table flap.

BALANCE

The oscillating wheel in the escapements of certain clocks and watches, erratic until the balance spring, usually a flat spiral, was developed about 1675. The word balance can also refer to the weighted bar of a chronometer.

BARBER'S BOWL

Bowl or dish with segment missing, used probably from the fifteenth century and placed against neck. The best known were delftware blue-and-white. The design often bore references to the barbers' trade, which was not merely cutting hair but drawing teeth and carrying out modest operations (thus the red and white barber's pole representing blood and bandages). Barbers' bowls were made later in silver and pewter.

BAROMETERS

There are two types of barometer, the mercury and the aneroid, the latter being worth little and depending for value on the quality of the case (usually circular and of oak). The theory of measuring atmospheric pressure using mercury was described in 1643, and stick barometers were made in Britain from about 1670, first of all in walnut mounts, later in other woods but especially mahogany, and between about 1710 and 1740 lacquered barometers were made, commanding a premium. The stick barometer is a column of mercury in a very thin wooden case, with a graduated card behind the column. It could be plain or ornate, especially from about 1750. Thermometers and other useful gauges were often included on the case. The wheel barometer, in which there is still a column of mercury but the measurements are shown on a dial, was introduced about 1770, and is known as a banjo barometer because of its shape. The aneroid works on a spring mechanism enclosed in a drum, and was patented in 1844. An unusual type of barometer is the diagonal, used from about 1720, rare and not very elegant. One of the most collectable barometers is the Admiral Fitzroy, a stick thermometer often looking older than it is, which has a specific and quaint tabulation of winds and climatic conditions. This is usually housed in a very handsome case and is being made today. A bubble on the top of the mercury column of a barometer means that the barometer is faulty.

BAROQUE STYLE

Originating in Italy in the late sixteenth century, baroque is ebullient, richly decorative, heavily symmetrical, with dynamism replacing the order and rest of classicism. Essentially a forward-looking style, interpreted in a hundred different ways. Some sought harmony, some sought grandiloquence, some merely wanted something new, and it eventually drifted into the prettiness of rococo, which did not pretend to be harmonious.

BARREL

In clocks and watches, the metal drum that contains the driving spring. As the spring unwinds the power is reduced, but this can be 'equalised' by the use of the device known as the verge. In long-case clocks and other weight-driven clocks, the barrel is nothing more than the drum around which the cord or chain is wound.

BATH CHAIR

A chair on three wheels for invalids in spa towns, invented about 1750, with a steering handle attached to small front wheel.

BAT PRINTING

Bat is a sheet of glue or gelatine and used instead of transfer tissue in transfer-printing on ceramics or enamels, used from about 1780, employed by prestige potters such as Minton and Copeland in the nineteenth century and also by cheap potters making fairing-type novelties at the end of the century.

BEAD-WORK

Popular from at least the seventeenth century, bead-work included shallow baskets with flat bottoms decorated with beads sewn onto canvas, pictures made out of beads, looking-glass frames, and caskets, some of which have miniature gardens inside made out of beads on wire. The most common articles are bead-purses and bags, often with a draw-string, made from the seventeenth to the nineteenth centuries, and much collected.

BEAKER

A drinking vessel usually of tapering cylindrical form, made in glass, wood, silver, gold, and ceramics. Known in Britain since at least the

eleventh century, losing popularity in the eighteenth century when it was replaced by table glasses. Beakers have continued to be made, especially for children and the tourist market, with and without mottoes, probably because they are suitable for cold drinks.

BEAR JUG

An atavistic curiosity relating to bear-baiting and depicting a bear crushing (genteel writers prefer hugging) a dog, made in salt-glazed and brown stoneware, with the detachable bear-head acting as a cup for some noxious liquid.

Made during the eighteenth and early nineteenth centuries in the Midlands and in Yorkshire, some in enamel.

BED

Beds have a high survival rate as they are customarily handed down through the family. This has worked against them, for there was a time

Edwardian satinwood bed with caned front and back, painted oval panels, and banding and stringing of rosewood, boxwood and ebony.

Iron and brass bedsteads were introduced in the mid-19th century as an alternative to unhygienic wood, and many were very elaborate affairs.

not so many years ago when there were so many seventeenth-century four-poster beds about that they were cannibalised, the uprights becoming plant stands and any carved section incorporated into more saleable items. Where they remain, the headboard is usually panelled, carved, arcaded, and often inlaid, with decorative friezes and turned or carved pillars supporting the canopy, often incorporating the melon shapes used in the court cupboard. Eighteenth-century four-posters often had slender posts, often fluted, with the vase-shaped lower section usually adorned with classical ornament. French beds were either genuine imports or English, made in what was known as the Louis style (the particular Louis not specified). Some were in the form of a gondola, others were derived from daybeds. There were beds in which a fixed canopy was replaced by a tentlike structure on a pole. In the nineteenth century there was a tendency during a period of hygiene consciousness to regard wooden bedsteads as dirty and insanitary. This led to the iron and brass bedstead, which

became very popular, and still is, whether or not the brass is superficial, on a core of iron. The bedroom suite of bed, washstand, and wardrobe did much to stabilise bed design until the arrival of the divan bed.

BELCHER CHAIN

Chain worn in the nineteenth century with big equal-size links. The belcher ring is a neckerchief or scarf ring worn by men (named after the English pugilist, J. Belcher, died 1811).

BELLARMINE

Made in astonishing numbers, this is a stoneware big-bellied long-necked ale-house jug produced originally in Cologne in the sixteenth century, modelled on a cardinal of that name, and made in England, especially at Fulham, in the seventeenth century. Frequently mentioned in the literature of the time, it has been associated with witchcraft and magic.

BELLOWS

Dating from at least 1500, many were very ornamental, with carved and inlaid wood, needlework ornament, and sometimes silver decoration. The hand bellows has not changed over the centuries, consisting of two shaped boards, a spring to keep them apart, and the leather bellows section. One of the wooden boards is pierced and fitted with a flap of leather inside, which acts as a valve, letting air enter but not allowing it to escape except via the nozzle. The leather is vulnerable, and in old bellows is usually creased, thin, cracked, and often repaired or replaced. Most bellows seen today are for the tourist industry. Heavyweight bellows on a stand, operated by a lever or a wheel-and-cord mechanism, were for servants with a lot of fires to light before breakfast.

BELL-PULL

An ornamental handle usually of brass attached to cord or strap and connected to a system of wires, which rang bells in servants' quarters. Sometimes the bell-pull was fixed to the wall, usually by the side of the fireplace, with the cords and connections hidden from view.

BELLS

The familiar flared shape of church bells was adopted throughout Europe about 1500, and bells in glass, silver, bronze and other materials follow this shape, some more elongated than others. Household bells for summoning servants are usually fairly plain, as are those used for handbell ringing (which bear numbers). Glass bells, produced mainly as novelties in the nineteenth century, have a good deal of variety in colour and design, among the most attractive being handbells of 'Bristol' blue with diamond moulding. Ships' bells are the most collectable, often discovered by underwater divers. Large bells are made from a special type of bronze called bell metal.

BENCH

Used from the earliest times, a basic backless long seat used against a wall or at the long trestle or refectory tables of the old oak period.

BENIN BRONZES*

Among the most important items of African sculpture are the Benin bronzes of Nigeria, which have a history going back to the thirteenth century, though how the skills reached Nigeria is not known. They varied in constitution from almost pure copper to brass, and production reached a peak between 1550 and 1700 when copper became available in large quantities due to the *manilla*, a horseshoe-shaped bar of copper or brass used by European traders as currency in exchange for slaves, ivory, palm oil and other useful commodities. In 1897 a British expedition sacked Benin, and as was the custom raped and looted, resulting in more than 3,000 art objects in bronze, ivory, wood and stone being brought to Britain, where some remained whilst others were put up for sale, many bought by Continental museums. These astonishing objects caused a great stir, and along with other ethnographica influenced such artists as Picasso. The principal Benin bronzes are heads and plaques depicting battles and historical events, but other articles included ritual bronzes such as staves, cocks, bells, and a large number of objects depicting the leopard, a symbol of power, and other animals and birds. Less localised are the minature bronze and brass weights of the Ivory Coast and Ghana, geometric and figurative, decorative and anecdotal, used for weighing gold.

BENTWOOD FURNITURE

In about 1830 Michael Thonet of Vienna discovered that moist beechwood could be steamed and bent into a circular shape, eliminating joints completely. By 1850 bentwood furniture was immensely popular in England especially for use in clubs, restaurants and hotels. It was copied in metal for rocking chairs, and in the 1920s and 1930s the shape was revived in chrome and other metals, often by key designers in the modern movement, which has made humdrum office furniture of the time ludicrously expensive.

BERLIN IRON JEWELLERY

Cast-iron jewellery made from about 1804 was given a fillip during the Napoleonic Wars when

German women were asked to give up their gold and silver jewellery in return for iron jewellery, suitably inscribed with the nation's thanks. Early work is neo-Classical, particularly medallions with classical portraits or subjects linked together to form bracelets, etc. This was followed by naturalistic and Gothic subjects.

BERLIN WOOLWORK

Embroidery in coloured wools on canvas, with designs provided. The craft, brought to England about 1810, became extraordinarily popular from 1830 and woolwork was used to adorn footstools, chairs, slippers, and almost anything that could be upholstered, and also to make pictures, often in association with beads. The usual stitches were tent-stitch and cross-stitch. Many of the designs were taken from well-known paintings, though floral subjects were perhaps the most popular. Berlin woolwork is often confused with tapestry.

BIJOUTERIE

A small display or show-case on tapered legs with a hinged glass lid, usually rectangular but sometimes oval or kidney shaped, often lined with velvet. Made in many woods including rosewood, mahogany, and satinwood, perhaps with inlay including Buhl and marquetry. French examples had ormolu mounts.

BILLIES AND CHARLIES

A name given to fake medallions, pilgrim badges, amulets, and similar nonsense made usually in pewter and lead by two London japers in the nineteenth century, unutterably crude and transparent – naturally they deceived all the experts. Billy Smith and Charlie Eaton of Tower Hill, London, are but two of thousands of nineteenth-century fakers whose work has yet to be uncovered (if it can be prised from museums).

BIN LABEL

Pottery label dating from the seventeenth century pierced with a hole for suspension from a hook or nail beside a wine bin, not to be confused with the label suspended round a bottle's neck.

BIRDCAGE

Hinged mechanism on tables of the eighteenth century, allowing the top to revolve or tip vertically when not used. Two squares of wood are joined by pegs, the upper square hinged beneath the table top, while a shaft on the pedestal head goes through a central hole in the lower square, permitting the top to rotate.

BIRDCAGES

The first birdcages were of wicker, from the eighth century of iron, and there are countless references to cage-birds from the fourteenth century onwards. Cages of silver and silver-gilt were features of the court of Queen Elizabeth I (but the birds were often stuffed), and the interests of Charles II are reflected in the name of Birdcage Walk, St. James's Park. By his time cages were of wood with bars of iron, but there was also a type resembling a lantern in metal, and during the eighteenth century birdcages were made to match the walnut or mahogany furniture. There was often a semi-circular bow at one end of the cage, so that the cage could be placed on a table by an open window and the bow would extend outside as it was considered healthy for the birds to bathe in the rain. The most fashionable birdcages were those in the form of a mansion. Others were rectangular or were in two compartments, and the cabinet-makers of the time often used fretwork and lattice-work and based their designs on Indian and Chinese models. Towards the end of the eighteenth century the wood was sometimes inlaid with shells or banded with boxwood, and the lantern cages had bars of cane instead of metal. During the nineteenth century cages were made of ebony and ivory, Sheffield plate, and glass and wood with ormolu fittings, and often tortoiseshell and other materials were incorporated, though the everyday cage in the traditional style was made of brass, which could be gilded or lacquered. Wicker and basketwork cages, often referred to in the literature of time, do not appear to have survived intact.

BLACK FOREST CLOCKS

Clocks with wooden parts had been made in the Black Forest area of Germany since the late seventeenth century, initially a cottage industry with the simplest of movements and a weight in the form of a stone from the nearest stream. The first clocks ran for twelve hours and were not very accurate, gaining or losing about twenty minutes a day. The first of the striking clocks was evolved about 1730, less important than the introduction of the cuckoo mechanism about the same time. Ten years later the makers used pendulums, placed in front of the dial rather than behind it. Early dials were of wood, followed by painted designs on paper and stuck on the dial. The circular part of the dial was raised from its background. Wooden parts were replaced by metal as clocks began to be made in quantity. In the 1840s the picture clock appeared, with the movement set in the centre of a painting set in an ornate frame, but the production of cheaper mass-produced American clocks began to have an effect on the export trade and the Germans copied them almost exactly. These copies are known as Amerikaners. The Germans also copied other nations' clocks, superior ones known as Massivs and the ornate hanging clock known as the Vienna Regulator (still being reproduced, not necessarily in Germany).

BLACKJACK

A jug made from leather from the seventeenth century, sometimes with silver rim. Quite common in the early years of the twentieth century, but increasingly rare. Leather was also used for making buckets and other objects.

BLOWING-TUBE

A cylinder of brass or copper, which when blown down would start or revive a fire, used in the eighteenth and nineteenth centuries and probably good for lazy servants who, left to themselves, would use bellows.

BLUE-AND-WHITE CHINESE PORCELAIN

Perhaps the most important and influential of all porcelain, well-known in the fourteenth century and reaching its peak in the fifteenth century, with fine forms, rich colour, splendid glazes, lively dragon and floral motifs. Imported into Europe from about 1600, first of all thin

porcelain plates and bowls with indented edges, later vases, bottles, and other decorative items. In the eighteenth century much Chinese porcelain was made to European order. Chinese export ware is known by a large number of names, often those of the trading centres and exporting ports such as Nankin and Canton.

BLUE-AND-WHITE TRANSFER-PRINTED WARE

Ceramics were transfer-printed in blue dating from the end of the eighteenth century, the first designs being based on Chinese models but later ones derived from engravings and books. Among the various patterns of the early years of transfer printing are 'fisherman', 'plantation', 'pine cone', 'Chantilly sprig', 'zig-zag fence', 'peony', 'bat' or 'vase', 'boy on a buffalo', 'the dromedary on a raft', and, of course, 'willow' which varied with the factory and proved to be the most popular of all.

BLUE-DASH CHARGERS

These were large delftware dishes made in the seventeenth and eighteenth centuries painted with figures or floral subjects, with strokes or dashes on the rims, with the foot-rim perforated so that the dish could be hung. The archaic name 'charger' was given by a collector. Among the best-known designs were portraits of various English kings, armoured horsemen, and Adam and Eve. Blue was the predominant colour, but these dishes were also made in grey, orange, yellow, green, purple and turquoise.

BLUE JOHN

A fluorspar, a natural substance, mined in Derbyshire, first of all by the Romans, often violet-blue but also in other colours, used for vases, urns, and candlesticks from the late eighteenth century. The name is said to be a corruption of bleu-jaune (French for blue yellow).

BOCAGE

A name given to the greenery surrounding the main subjects in ceramic figures and groups. This could sometimes be botanically correct but was usually ambiguous.

BONBONNIÈRES

Small gold, silver, enamel or porcelain boxes for sweetmeats.

BONE CHINA

The most popular type of English porcelain since about 1800, though bone ash as an ingredient was proposed in 1649 and first used in soft-paste porcelain in 1749. As much as 40 per cent of the mix can be bone ash.

BOOKCASE

First mentioned by Samuel Pepys in his diary, bookcases fall into two types, the first, from the eighteenth to the early nineteenth century, are from floor to ceiling, sometimes with a break-front (the centre section jutting out beyond the side sections) and an intricate pattern of glazing bars; the second are of low height, sometimes known as dwarf bookcases, a popular Regency and Victorian piece and often difficult to segregate from cabinets and credenzas. Large plain bookcases with panelled doors beneath were made without change for more than half a century, being library and study furniture and not needing much decoration, although there was a fad for Gothic and 'old oak' bookcases from the early Victorian period onwards among the self-conscious literati. In the early years of the twentieth century low bookcases tended to acquire an angular air, sometimes with art nouveau cut-outs in the space above the top shelf. Many small bookcases were made to accommodate the volumes of the Everyman library and the Collins classics, then published for the first time. The 1920s and 1930s saw banks of shelves with the minimum of support, as well as bookcases combined with a bureau facility, usually squat and neither one thing nor the other. Revolving bookcases, used since the eighteenth century and usually in mahogany, have always been in demand, but for a book-lover they always seem to hold far too few books.

BOOK-REST

A stand used in eighteenth-century libraries to support large books, consisting of a square or rectangular frame with cross bars, the upper one of which was supported by an upright, adjustable on a base. Sometimes a desk adjunct.

BOOT AND SHOE TREES

Dating from the Middle Ages, sometimes segmented for easy use, these wooden objects have a certain unpretentious charm. Some of them have a screw fitment. There is an abbreviated form, with a wooden toe piece connected to a spiral spring or flexible piece of metal, in turn connected with a sphere that fits inside the heel. Mostly of beechwood, waxed and polished, or sometimes varnished. A cobbler's or specific customer's name engraved or printed on the boot or shoe tree adds considerably to the modest value. As with cobblers' lasts, boot and shoe trees are very common indeed.

BOTTLES

The British bottle industry began in the early seventeenth century and from 1623 to 1860 it was illegal to sell wine by the bottle. Bottles were expensive because of a high tax on glass. The rich ordered wine by the barrel, and had a stock of personalised bottles by having a glass disc or seal applied to them. The merchant filled these bottles from the barrel. These bottles are known as seal bottles. Crafty inn keepers did sell wine in bottles which had no seal, and this was unlawful. Early bottles were shaft and globe (bulbous body, long neck); about 1680 necks became shorter and bodies broader, but in the early eighteenth century a mallet-shaped body was favoured. From about 1730 bottles were moulded, tending towards the cylindrical, and by about 1760 the diameter of the bottle was down to about five inches (12.5cm), and there was a pronounced kick in the base. By the early nineteenth century the diameter had shrunk to about three and a half inches (8.75cm), and by 1840 the height was approximately ten inches (25cm). In 1840 machine-moulded bottles were first produced, and there were endless variations. Schweppe introduced soda water in 1790, and bottles were kept on their side as otherwise gas would have escaped through the dry cork. As these bottles had rounded bases they were called torpedo bottles, and were made in several colours, the rarest being dark blue. The Codd lemonade or ginger-beer bottle (1875–1930) (still made in India) had a marble imprisoned in it to act as an internal stopper when filled with gas, and these were also made in various colours (blue the most valuable). Beer bottles were often embossed with makers' names and trade marks, and were usually of green, brown, or black glass (to disguise the contents). Spirits and ginger-beer were housed in brown or brown and buff stoneware bottles and flasks, often bearing the names and trade marks of the maker, or, in the case of spirit flasks, caricature figures in relief. There were numerous varieties of poison and medicine bottles; the poison bottles were often ribbed or quaintly shaped so that they could be identified in the dark, and sometimes had trick openings to dissuade young fingers. Throughout the nineteenth century millions of bottles were produced, some of the most interesting bearing advertising embossing or labelling. Ink bottles were made in a multitude of shapes including cottages, kettles, tops and birds, and colours, and are widely collected.

BOTTLE TICKET

Contemporary name for a decanter label, hung by a chain around the neck and made in enamels or silver, often including designs of chubby boys (putti) engaged in wine making.

BOUGIE

Sometimes called a taper box, this is a drum for feeding out taper (or wick) with a winding handle and a nozzle through which taper protrudes. Usually made in silver or Sheffield plate, it sometimes had a pierced body with a glass liner. An extinguisher was usually attached by a chain. Used from the late eighteenth century.

BOULLE OR BUHL

Inlay invented by the person of that name in the late seventeenth century and consisting of tortoiseshell on brass, sometimes combined with materials such as copper, pewter, and mother-of-pearl. Boulle furniture was often equipped with ormolu mounts. Less used in Britain than France, boulle can be found in the credenzas and show furniture of Victorian England. Modern reproduction furniture uses imitation boulle.

BOURDALOUE

Although strictly speaking out of fashion by about 1790, this delicately named object was made at least until the 1830s, when Davenport produced a blue-and-white version. During the eighteenth century there was a preacher named Bourdaloue, whose fame was so great that queues formed long before the service was to begin. Ladies often needed to relieve themselves or lose their place in the queue. The bourdaloue was thus a portable sauce-boat-shaped chamber-pot. A variant was also used in early corridor-less trains.

BOW PORCELAIN

The famous factory dates from the 1740s, and a patent was taken out in 1749 for 'phosphatic porcelain', ie including bone ash or 'Virgin Earth'. Many figures were produced, especially of women and children with round doll-like heads and receding chins, and some figures were inspired by or copied from Meissen originals. An immense amount of domestic ware including blue-and-white china was made, often with a mauve tint, and Oriental designs and shapes were much used. It was a short-lived concern. After 1760 standards went down, and although the later figures retained their charm they had a grey tinge and the decoration became excessive. The factory closed in 1776, and the moulds were taken over and used at Derby. Bow china bore numerous and confusing factory and workmen's marks, and prior to 1760 can be identified only by other qualities.

BOX BEDSTEAD

Bed with high top, bottom, and one side, the open side with curtain on rails. Although a medieval design, made well into the nineteenth century.

BRASS

Versatile alloy from copper and zinc, varying enormously in proportions and colour and known from ancient times. It can be hammered, rolled, drawn into wire, and cast, and takes a high polish. In the Middle Ages centres of production were Flanders and Germany, and commercial brassmaking began in Britain in the late sixteenth century, with a wide range of products such as candlesticks, lamps, and domestic ware. Brass could be tinned to emulate silver. In the eighteenth century Birmingham became the main producer, a position strengthened in the nineteenth century, with products such as bedsteads, imitation Indian brass trays, inkstands, and novelties of all kinds. Brass was often lacquered to prevent tarnishing.

BRETON WORK

A form of embroidery derived from French peasant costume, worked in coloured silks and gold thread, mainly employing satin and chain stitch and used for the borders of garments and novelties such as bookmarks. A popular Victorian hobby in England after art needlework became a laudable pursuit.

BRISTOL DELFTWARE

A pottery was founded near Bristol by Southwark potters about 1650, and several factories grew up, Temple Pottery (1683–1770), Limekiln Lane (1700–54) and St Mary Redcliffes (1700–77). Bristol delft is distinguished by a lavender-blue glaze, and characteristic products include puzzle-jugs, flower bricks, chargers, and porringers with a circular handle and a hole in the centre. Colours often include a rich red, and in the early eighteenth century there were strong Chinese influences.

BRISTOL GLASS

An important glass-making centre, with fifteen factories recorded in the early 1700s, most of them making window or bottle glass. Noted for opaque white glass similar to porcelain, enamel-

Early 18th-century Bristol delft charger with oak leaf motifs.

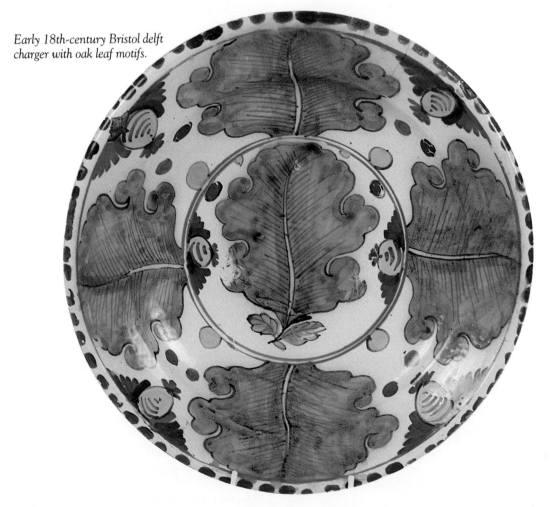

led with birds, flowers, and Chinese subjects. Items of white glass include small boxes and 'toys', as well as vases, candlesticks and other decorative work. Bristol is best known for its blue glass, often gilded, used for decanters, dishes and other suitable pieces.

BRISTOL PORCELAIN

Soft-paste porcelain was made from Cornish soapstone from 1749 to 1752 when the factory amalgamated with Worcester. Existing pieces include Chinese-type figures and sauce-boats. Hard-paste porcelain was made 1770–81, and the products included ordinary china as well as elaborate figures and groups in the French style, spectacular table services, and large hexagonal vases. A distinctive teapot in the shape of an inverted pear with double curve handles was made. An assortment of marks was used during this limited period, some of them copies of those used at Meissen.

BRITANNIA METAL

An amalgam of tin, antimony and copper, also known as white metal, first produced in 1769 as a cheap substitute alloy. It is often mistaken for pewter although it is much harder. The process used was usually spinning, cheaper than casting, and Britannia metal was initially used mainly for teapots, with wooden and other handles, and much Britannia metal is hollow-ware. With the coming of electroplate in the middle of the nineteenth century, Britannia metal was chosen as one of the candidates, and some thoroughly nasty pieces were made, for when the plating wears off it leaves an ugly grey under-surface. Products are marked EPBM (electro-plated Britannia metal).

BRONZE

Alloy of copper and tin, often with lead and zinc added, usually cast, and lending itself to chiselling, chasing, and engraving; much used for statuary and decorative objects and for household utensils demanding strength, such as buckets and basins. Over the years bronze acquires an attractive sheen known as patina, distinct from bronze disease which is bright green spotting.

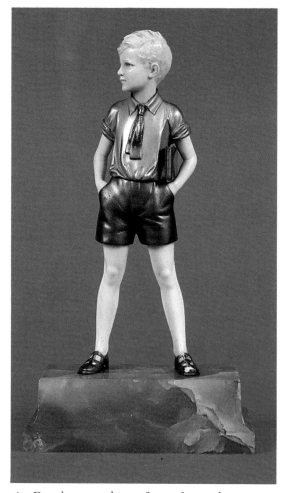

Art Deco bronze and ivory figure of young boy.

BUCKLES

Metal fasteners especially for belts and shoes, used for many centuries. Belt buckles were made in most metals, including silver, which, as it is soft, is often over a steel core or used where there is no tension. Military belt buckles, both for the waist belt and for the belt across the chest, are desirable, especially if they have regimental marks. The Highland belt buckle was fashionable from about 1820 with the coming of Scots self-awareness fuelled by the novels of Sir Walter Scott. Belt buckles were used by many organisations in the nineteenth century, including the police and fire brigades, and buckles were also made as dress accessories, in which semiprecious stones or gold were inlaid. There is a continuous demand for silver nurses' buckles, not by collectors but by nurses themselves; nurses' buckles of the art nouveau period can be very decorative. Shoe buckles were a fashion phenomenon of the 1660s, and it was not until about 1880 that straps and laces returned, except on some ladies' shoes and Highland footwear and, as with belt buckles, semiprecious stones could be incorporated in the design. Besides metal, buckles were made of ivory, tortoiseshell and when plastics first began to be widely used in the 1930s they proved to be ideal for ladies' wear. Some buckles had fancy devices to make locking them easier or safer, and some were fitted with a spring mechanism.

BUFFET

Synonymous with court cupboard, the buffet was also used in the eighteenth century for a set of shelves, a cabinet with doors, and a butler's pantry. As a receptacle for glass, china, plate, etc, it was replaced by the sideboard towards the end of the eighteenth century. Its use as a railway eating place is fairly recent.

BUREAU*

The bureau evolved from the portable boxes with sloping lids used from earliest times, but towards the end of the seventeenth century the box was placed on a stand, and soon progressed into a desk with pigeon-holes and drawers. A characteristic of the bureau is that the front flap, hinged at the bottom, comes forward, and resting on pull-out slides or lopers, forms a writing surface. It was common practice to develop pieces of furniture in rather a slow leisurely way, and the next step was to replace the stand by a set of drawers. All bureaux were high-quality pieces, and are amongst the gems of English furniture. No expense was spared, and the drawers, pigeon-holes and hidden compartments were masterpieces of compression. Towards the end of the eighteenth century as new forms of writing furniture were produced the bureau tended to fade into respectability. Because of the lack of knee room it was never comfortable to sit at.

BUREAU BOOKCASE*

Perhaps the ultimate test for a cabinet-maker, and to acquire one is certainly the dream of the provincial antique dealer. The upper section is a set of usually adjustable book shelves enclosed by doors or glass, the bottom a bureau with customary drawers and pigeon-holes and fall-front writing surface. Sometimes the upper section is a cabinet with a multitude of sections. Often the bookcase was surmounted by a pediment, often of the broken type (shaped like a swan's neck). The upper part could be in the shape of a double dome. All woods were used, especially walnut and mahogany, with lacquer particularly desirable today. A superior bureau bookcase can easily top £100,000.

BUTLER'S TRAY

A rectangular, oval, or kidney-shaped tray mounted on legs or on a X-shaped trestle, used from the mid-eighteenth century, and having a gallery pierced with hand-holes.

BUTTONS

Glass, gold and pottery buttons were used by the ancient Greeks, Egyptians, and Persians. Button-making was established as an industry in France in the thirteenth century, but buttons, although increasingly widespread, were mainly for decorative purposes until the opening of the nineteenth century, when changes in fashions and the rise of the Birmingham button industry coincided and brought the utilitarian button into use. During the first half of the eighteenth century buttons were made in enamel, pearl shell, silver, gold, gems of many kinds, brass, pewter, copper, bone, and tortoiseshell, the better ones made in France and all now rare. Throughout the subsequent years dozens of materials were used, including porcelain, often painted with French pastoral scenes, and cut steel, and amongst the most exquisite were buttons with minute scenes under glass. In 1802 the so-called Florentine button came along, a fabric-covered button which competed with the brass button. With the introduction of button-making machinery in the mid-nineteenth century even more substances were used, and the long period of Queen Victoria's mourning made jet fashionable as well as French jet (black glass imitating natural jet). Her fascination with Scotland likewise created a vogue for Scottish-style buttons (tartans, Celtic symbols, etc).

Machine-made shell or 'pearl' buttons were very much used from about 1850 onwards. Nineteenth-century buttons are generally half the size of the eighteenth-century examples. Throughout the centuries the sizes, materials, and designs of buttons have been dependent on the demands of fashion, and each passing phase has been mirrored. Some very adventurous buttons were produced in the art nouveau period, and even more in the 1920s and 1930s when plastics and every conceivable natural and synthetic material were used, often in an outrageous and aggressive way. Buttons no longer needed to be round or even symmetrical. Buttons are marvellous for a starter collection, as every open market has at least one stall with a tin of buttons. There is also an inexpensive opening for theme collectors, for distinctive metal buttons were worn by schools and colleges, railway companies, police forces and most formal organisations, especially the armed forces, the buttons of which are perhaps the most in demand except for the sporting buttons made between 1820 and 1850 in sets depicting creatures of the hunt and chase (these are being reproduced). Military buttons can often be dated almost exactly. In 1767 regimental numbers were shown, discontinued in 1871 (for other ranks) and 1881 (for officers, when the numbers were replaced by regimental names); in 1880 manufacturers' names were stamped on the back, and in 1850 addresses and trade marks were added. In 1830 regular regiments began to wear gold instead of silver buttons (except the militia which kept to silver). The practice of other ranks of most regiments wearing a general service button without regimental number was reversed in 1920.

CABARET SET

Porcelain tea-set for one or two people consisting of a tea or coffee-pot, sugar-bowl, jug, cups and saucers, on a porcelain tray. Sometimes, especially in the more modern casual sets, saucers are dispensed with and there is a shallow depression in the tray for the cups.

CABRIOLE LEG

In the late nineteenth century the term was used to describe the double curved table and chair legs of the eighteenth century. The leg curved outward at the knee and inwards towards the foot in the shape of an elongated 'S'. Sometimes the knee bears an ornament, often a shell. It was introduced to Britain during the William and Mary period after being revived by French and Dutch furniture makers from Greek models. Because of the way the grain of the wood runs, the cabriole leg is vulnerable to damage. A great favourite of manufacturers of reproduction furniture.

CADOGAN TEAPOT

An unmistakeable object as it is filled from a hole in the base, lidless, and first made about 1795 in a purply-brown. It was later made by several potters including Davenport and Copeland.

CAMEO

A shell or substance cut to leave a design in relief, a process carried out from at least 350BC, and used for medallions and jewellery, often in ornate frames. Revived in the Italian Renaissance, and again in the eighteenth century. The most famous cameos are those by Wedgwood in pottery, the most common are the shell cameos, using the layers of different coloured shells, harder than mother-of-pearl but still able to be hand-carved. Cameos today are produced on a production line, and often the cutting is crude and perfunctory. Moulded cameos in plastic can often be confused with shell cameos at first glance.

Cameo portrait set in gold, seed pearls, and agate.

CAMERAS

The principles of photography were discovered by Niepce in 1816, although projecting an image had been known for hundreds of years in the form of the camera obscura, a kind of magic lantern. The problem was fixing the image and there were many ways of doing this. The Daguerreotype process was patented in 1839; each picture was a one-off, and there was no way further prints could be obtained, unlike the wet-plate process (1840–1880), which was cumbersome and needed an awesome amount of equipment. Early wet-plate cameras consist of two wooden boxes, sliding into each other, and the later ones have bellows. The dry-plate camera was patented by George Eastman in 1879, and brought the camera within the reach of almost everyone. In 1888 the Kodak camera appeared, taking roll film, and in 1896 modern snapshot photography was born with the first folding pocket camera. Since then it has been consolidation – better lenses, more accurate shutters, and the modern emphasis on making complex

Daguerreotype camera.

cameras easy to operate using modern technology. A dry-plate camera can be confused with a wet-plate; at the back of the camera is the plate carrier. Wet-plate cameras contain a length of silver wire for the wet plate to rest on. Dry-plate cameras do not need this feature. Some dry-plate cameras may not be as old as they look as they are still used by some photographers. The lenses of cameras 1918-39 made by such makers as Rollei, Leica, and Zeiss are very much sought after. It is always worth while examining the bellows on older cameras – they may be replacements as the leather is vulnerable on the folds.

CAMPAIGN FURNITURE

Military furniture for the use of officers characterised by portability (so that chests, etc, are in easily divided sections), strong wood (so teak is often used), and resistance to damage (so that handles are recessed and edges are brass-bound). Common in the Napoleonic and Crimean wars.

CANDELABRUM

A standing branched candlestick, usually used in the plural form of candelabra, with designs

Copper tea urn of about 1840, brass commemorative plaque relating to the actor David Garrick, and a pair of 17th-century brass pricket candlesticks.

conforming to those used in candlesticks. Victorian candelabra can be very elaborate and many-branched, and can sometimes form part of an epergne (centre-piece). Most of those on the market are silver and silverplate, and because they often have interchangeable sconces it is wise to check that all the individual parts match, often best checked by taking out the sconces and replacing them to ensure that the fit is snug.

CANDLE BOX

A rectangular or cylindrical box, usually lidded, and made from wood or metal. They are attached to walls and used to store candles and were used up to the nineteenth century. Eighteenth-century candle boxes are sometimes japanned.

CANDLESTICKS

Made in brass since the Middle Ages, there has been one major development – the replacement of a spike on which the candle was stuck by a socket. Early candlesticks have a wide grease-pan halfway up the stem, but this disappeared with improvements in candle technology, being replaced in the 1720s by the detachable sconce at the top of the stem, used for catching the drips. The baluster stem dating from the sixteenth century became the most popular shape. Brass casting improved in the 1690s to give a finer texture. The bases of candlesticks conformed with fashion; square and octagonal bases began to have their corners rounded off, and were succeeded by scalloped and petalled forms,

A candlestick of 1885–6 made by Toft and Cope, Stoke.

and column and urns, best in silver and Sheffield plate. The Victorians made their candlesticks into confections, and were served by the invention of electroplate, which brought silver-appearing objects into the middle-class home. The Arts and Crafts movement produced candlesticks with a plain stem, a broad drip-pan and a high circular case which were fondly believed to be medieval in style. Glass candlesticks first appeared in the seventeenth century, and later followed metal counterparts or wineglass design; cut-glass candlesticks were first advertised in 1742, and later there were candlesticks with fluted column steps and terraced feet. Some opaque-glass candlesticks were produced, either enamelled or painted. Pewter was used instead of brass in the seventeenth century, but fell out of favour, was revived in the early nineteenth century and again during the art nouveau period. It was never an ideal metal, as pewter is inclined to melt. Silver candlesticks can often be unexpectedly heavy, leading the uninitiated to believe that they are solid when in fact the core is resin. 'Old' brass candlesticks are relentlessly faked, are often too crude, and an examination of the base reveals that the pattern of concentric circles resulting from the cleaning-up process in genuine old candlesticks is lacking. The chamber candlestick in all materials from tin to silver has a saucer-like dish and a prominent handle.

CANTEEN

Originally a small leather or shagreen case containing knife, fork, spoon, condiment box and beaker for travellers; later a container which could contain three hundred of everything.

CANTERBURY*

In the late eighteenth century a kind of tea-trolley with three divisions to hold cutlery with a curved end for plates, but by about 1800 the name was given to a small piece of furniture to hold music, of rectangular form with sides and partitions of open fret with turned or carved posts extending below the base to form legs, usually terminating in castors. There was often a shallow drawer for sheet music. Regency Canterburies often have diagonal latticework between square-cut rails, claw feet, and featured

often very ornate and sometimes incorporating grotesque masks, which worked well in silver. About 1770 candlesticks became taller, and this coincided with the evolution of die-core casting in Birmingham so that brass candlesticks could be made in one piece, without tell-tale seams. Taller candlesticks demanded elegance, with fluted and gadrooned tapering stems, though the Corinthian-column style remained popular. Some candlesticks were made from sheet metal, and these often had a sliding rod in the stem to regulate the height of the candle and eject the stub. The neo-Classical movement introduced new patterns and motifs such as the square base

The canteen of cutlery reached its apotheosis in the Victorian period, as evident from this 1894 advertisement.

lyre motifs. Victorian Canterburies were more ornate, and the show woods were often used, such as rosewood and walnut, as well as papier mâché. During the Aesthetic period, bamboo with lacquer panels made a brief appearance. Sometimes a writing slope was added to the top, and a brass gallery was an optional extra.

CANTON ENAMELS

Enamel on copper often in famille rose style made in China for export to Europe and consisting of teapots, tea caddies, bowls and trays painted with views, fruit, or flowers.

CAPODIMONTE

Italian porcelain from factory founded in 1743 with a wide range of products especially fancy snuff-boxes, cane handles, and lively tableware and ornamental vases. Perhaps best known for its figures, still being made in quantity.

CARD CASES

Flat rectangular cases for visiting cards, often surprisingly large because early visiting cards were the same size as playing cards. Up to about 1780 visitors desirous of being thought elegant used playing cards, writing on them their names and addresses, and one day men and women realised they could use plain card. Later, playing-card-sized cards were reduced in size. Early card cases were made of silver or silver-gilt, but by the middle of the nineteenth century anything could be used including ivory, bone, wood, leather, papier mâché, tortoiseshell, sometimes inlaid with gold and silver, and mother-of-pearl. Pictures of buildings were very popular especially on silver cases, as were cases bearing a diamond pattern. Novelty card cases could be in the form of a small purse (sometimes taken to be a child's toy purse), a book, or could incorporate a stamp holder. Card cases are ideal for a starter collection.

CHAIRS

A seat for one person with a back and/or arms, derived from the throne and until the seventeenth century a prestigious piece of furniture reserved for the highly placed (the chairman). Ordinary folk used stools. From the seventeenth century, increasing attention was given to the design and comfort.

Back stool: stool with back attached evolved in the late sixteenth century, a transitional piece heralding the end of the stool as the predominant kind of seat for the ordinary person.

Balloon-back chair: classic Victorian chair with the back in the form of an upright oval, often bowed for comfort.

Banister back chair: American chair of the early eighteenth century with turned uprights of split balusters.

Barber's chair: one of the specialised chairs, with an adjustable head-rest, sometimes with swivel seat, designed, like dentists' chairs and silhouette chairs, to keep the sitter still.

Bergère chair: originally an upholstered armchair with a rounded back and wide seat, upholstered between arms and seat, and dating from about 1725. Today it is a general name for a caned chair, often in a suite.

Box chair: high-backed panelled chair with arms with a hinged seat forming the top of a box and dating from the sixteenth century.

Cabriole chair: eighteenth-century name for a chair with a padded back.

Cameo chair: chair with a horizontal open oval shape inset in the back.

Cane chair: chair with a seat and often back of tightly woven cane.

Caquetoire: sixteenth-century French small low chair. The title is French for chatter, and it was a favourite chair with women.

Caxton chair: cane-seated chair with turned front legs and stretchers, made at High Wycombe from the mid-nineteenth century.

Children's chairs: these follow the same styles as those for adults, except for high chairs, produced from the seventeenth century, and specialised chairs such as the Astley Cooper chair, designed to make children sit upright. Some children's chairs have a rocking

mechanism beneath the seat.

Close chair: chair with concealed compartment for the chamber-pot.

Corner chair: three-legged chair, with the yoke or back rail usually curved. Sometimes called a Dutch chair.

Crapaud: nineteenth-century French heavily upholstered armchair.

Cromwellian chair: auction-room jargon for oak armchair with square leather seat and back studded with brass large-headed nails; much reproduced in the Victorian period.

Curricle chair: early nineteenth-century chair

Brazilian carved padoukwood dining chair from about 1900.

Prior to the Victorian period most children's furniture was a smaller version of that for adults. These three children's chairs were depicted in J. C. Loudon's Encyclopedia of Cottage Farm and Villa Architecture and Furniture (1833).

❧

with rounded or tub-shaped back.

Derbyshire chair: seventeenth-century chair with the back in the style of an arcade or with hooped designs.

Dining chairs: made in sets and heavier than casual or fancy chairs.

Easy chair: a general-purpose name for a comfortable upholstered chair.

Elbow chair: the chair with arms in a dining-room set, usually known as a carver.

Farthingale chair: the farthingale was a crinoline of whalebone for distending women's dresses, fashionable in the late sixteenth and seventeenth centuries. So a farthingale chair has an unusually wide seat. In the 1850s the crinoline reappeared, necessitating similar types of chair.

Fauteuil: elegant French armchair with deep rounded back, often in gilt, much copied in England.

French chair: used in the seventeenth century to specify a high-backed upholstered armchair, and later a meaningless term for a chair that did not look particularly English.

Glastonbury chair: flat-backed uncomfortable chair with a vaguely ecclesiastical look and much faked in the nineteenth century.

Hall chair: hard uncompromising wooden chair of the eighteenth and nineteenth centuries, often with a carved or pierced back depicting coats of arms or other designs.

Hogarth chair: splat-backed cabriole-legged chair appearing in the prints and paintings of William Hogarth and thus named.

Hunting chair: upholstered nineteenth-century chair with section that extends to form a foot rest.

Library chair: eighteenth-century armchair with padded leather-covered saddle-shaped seat with an adjustable platform at the back for holding a book, so that the user can sit facing the back. Sometimes called a cock-fighting chair.

Monastic chair: mock-medieval nonsense chair of the mid-nineteenth century often made up from genuine panels and pieces of wood. Sometimes encountered today under the guise of 'bishops' thrones'.

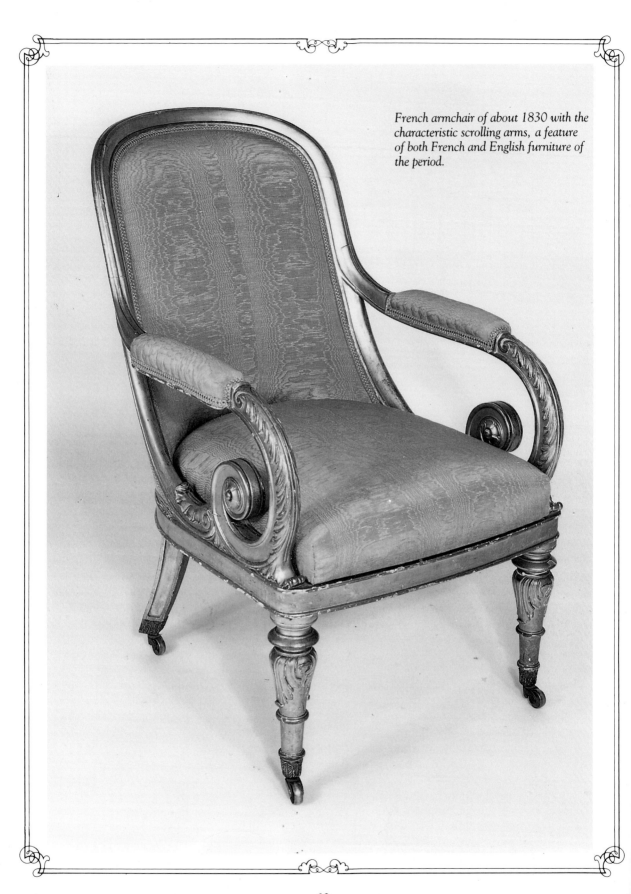

French armchair of about 1830 with the characteristic scrolling arms, a feature of both French and English furniture of the period.

Morris chair: mid-nineteenth-century armchair with adjustable hinged back.

Nelson chair: chair commemorating Battle of Trafalgar, with relevant motifs such as ropes, dolphins, and anchors.

Nursing chair: Victorian upholstered chair, low with square seat and no arms.

Oxford chair: meaningless term for a cane-seated chair with splayed legs or for an armchair with high back and open padded arms.

Parlour chair: originally a single chair with a pierced back, but in the Victorian period used to describe a heavy type of chair with an upholstered seat, as well as any odd chair that did not have a name to itself.

Porter chair: wing chair upholstered in leather, with the wings extending upwards and over to form an arch.

Prie-Dieu: Victorian chair for praying on with a very low seat and a tall straight back often adorned with needlework such as Berlin woolwork.

Quaker chair: country chair of mid-nineteenth-century with balloon back, upholstered round seat and turned front legs.

Rocking chair: mounted on curved pieces of wood, not greatly seen before the eighteenth century though used on cradles for centuries. Bentwood and metal streamlined rocking-chair design, and a platform model on a solid base using spiral springs was introduced in the late nineteenth century.

Rout chair: a rout was an eighteenth-century party, and as these often tended to get out of control the rout chair was a simple, painted, caned chair hired out to party-givers and essentially valueless and disposable.

Sedan chair: enclosed structure containing a seat and carried by two men using horizontal poles, popular from the seventeenth century until about 1800.

These chairs with leather backs and leather seats of 1926 could pose a puzzle, apparently modelled on South African farmhouse chairs, whatever they may be.

Set of six 19th-century Windsor chairs with hooped stretchers.

Sewing chair: low armless upholstered chair of the 1850s with a very wide sometimes serpentine-fronted seat and a sloping back. Legs were squat, often in cabriole form with carved knees, and the chairs were often made in rosewood or walnut.

Sleeping chair: upholstered armchair with a winged back adjusted by a ratchet mechanism to any angle. This was a very popular form in the 1920s and 1930s.

Slipper back chair: Victorian upholstered chair with scooped out back often richly carved and buttoned. These were often made in walnut or rosewood.

Spoon back chair: Victorian upholstered chair with shaped back. Not dissimilar to the slipper back chair.

Thrown chair: armchair with the triangular seat and turned uprights of the sixteenth and seventeenth centuries.

Tub chair: compact easy chair, partly winged to keep out draughts, introduced in the late eighteenth century.

Voyeuse: low-seated chair with padded top to the back so that the occupant could rest his arms whilst sitting astride. A variation was provided for women to kneel on. Known also as a conversation chair.

Windsor chair: traditional country chair with a shaped solid seat into which the legs, the bow and spindles of the back are dowelled.

Wing chair: introduced towards the end of the seventeenth century, with the wings or side pieces extending upwards from the arms to the top of the back. Often made in leather.

X-frame chair: any chair on a structure shaped like an X in rigid or folding form. This was a long-established chair in Europe, particularly Spain and Italy where there were types sometimes known as Saranarola and Dante.

CARNET DE BAL

Dance card, usually in ivory, sometimes in a batch and pinned in the corner, often expensively cased, occasionally with inset miniature. The dancing partner's name was written in pencil and later erased with a damp cloth.

CARPET BALLS

Large marbles or taws used in the Victorian game of carpet bowls, made in brown stoneware, agate ware, or pottery striped, ringed, or painted with flowers or stars. A set of carpet balls comprised one plain and six patterned balls.

CARRIAGE CLOCKS

Portable clocks have been made from the sixteenth century, similar to outsize watches, but the true carriage clock, the *pendule de voyage*, was evolved about 1770 for the use of army officers. It was small, square, and in brass or gilt metal with a shockproof mechanism. It has a rectangular face, usually three glass sides and a prominent carrying handle on top. Made from 1820 in Austria, Britain and America, the carriage clock could be unadorned or decorated with enamelling, engraving, or filigree work. It was produced almost unchanged until about 1910 when it suffered a decline, but has been revived in recent years, often in replica form.

CARTOUCHE

Ornamental surround for coats of arms, heraldic symbols and miscellaneous decorative devices often used on silver and on furniture.

CARYATID

Figure of woman, naked or semi-naked, used as a support in lieu of a column, mostly in architecture but occasionally in grandiose furniture. The male version is Atlas.

CASKET

A box usually with a lock for keeping money or jewellery. Among the materials used in manufacture were ebony, mother-of-pearl, enamel, and especially iron for the large examples, often with elaborate decoration such as filigree work or engraved with scenes. Iron caskets fell out of fashion in the sixteenth century, but they were made in the nineteenth century to cater for the interest in the Gothic revival.

CASTLE HEDINGHAM POTTERY

A curious type of ware made by a potter named Bingham (born 1829) in a quaint ramshackle old style, often mistaken by even experts for genuine fifteenth, sixteenth and seventeenth-century pottery.

CASTOR

The small wheels on furniture intended for moving it about, made from a number of materials including brass, leather, wood, china, and composition. The castor is either fixed with a socket or a long screw into the leg.

CAT

A spindly wooden stand used in the eighteenth century to warm plates in front of the fire with three arms and three feet.

CAUDLE CUP

Caudle was a spiced drink for invalids and especially pregnant women, and the cups were made in the seventeenth and eighteenth centuries from silver, pewter, and ceramics. There were various shapes, and they were fitted with a domed lid topped by a finial. Posset, warm milk curdled with liquor, was also drunk from similar vessels.

CAUGHLEY

An important Shropshire pottery founded in 1754, and from 1772 was making porcelain similar to that made by Worcester, mostly in blue-and-white, and often confused with it. A high proportion of the output was transfer-printed from 1770. Besides staple wares such as mugs, sauce-boats, cream boats, spittoons, and a characteristic cabbage-leaf jug, Caughley produced many smaller items, such as egg drainers, spoon trays, eye-baths, asparagus servers (not tongs), and miniature tea-services. It was not a major producer, closing in 1814, but from the late 1960s it became very popular for collectors frightened off the big and expensive areas such as Bow and Worcester.

CAULDRON

Associated naturally with witches, these were the earliest known type of cooking utensils, first made of hammered sheet bronze, and from the sixteenth century of cast iron. Small cauldrons were known as crocks. Cauldrons are still being made for decorative purposes and, as iron rusts rapidly, modern examples may be taken for old ones.

CAULIFLOWER WARE

Throughout the eighteenth century cauliflowers and other vegetables and fruit were taken as models for ceramic teapots and similar objects. These were not strictly novelties, being made by major potteries such as Chelsea, Worcester and Longton Hall, and it is a trend that has persisted throughout the nineteenth and twentieth centuries.

CELLARET

An eighteenth-century box on legs or a stand; a wine cooler where the wine was stored or chilled before use at the table. Mostly made from mahogany, although there are Sheraton types in satinwood inlaid with tulipwood. It was made in many shapes including oval, round, and octagonal and was often bound with brass. The most handsome are the sarcophagus-shaped examples from the Regency period.

CHANDELIER

A branched, hanging candle-holder, made in wood and brass for churches, and later brass and silver for domestic use as well as the church. Wrought iron was also widely used, not only for the chandelier itself but for the suspension rods that sometimes replaced chains for hanging from ceilings. They became immensely popular and increasingly ornate with the widespread use of cut glass, and the overall design followed fashions. Even though gas lighting was introduced during the nineteenth century, and the chan-

delier was technically obsolete and replaced by the gasolier, the rich continued to use candles in their chandeliers until the coming of the electric light bulb meant that the candles could be replaced by something more convenient that would make the glass drops glitter even more brightly.

CHARGER

A very large dish primarily intended for display, but a name given to any outsize ceramic (especially delft) or pewter plate or plate-type object.

CHASING

Decorating gold and silver by hammering so that a design appears in relief, either quite prominent or shallow, when the process is known as flat chasing. It was usually used alongside engraving to give contrasting textures. It is used in a subsidiary sense in connection with filing or cutting away the roughness of cast metalwork, and a form of chasing is used with leather.

CHATELAINE

Fastened at the waist, the chatelaine was a clasp from which numerous articles were suspended by a wife or housekeeper, the most prominent of which were keys but which could also include watches and other useful accoutrements. In itself it was not decorative but it could be adorned with ornaments such as cameos.

CHELSEA

The factory responsible for the first known English soft-paste porcelain, founded about 1745, closed in 1784, with some moulds being moved to Derby. There are four Chelsea periods, denoted by the marks on the china; Triangle (1745–9), Raised Anchor (1750–3), Red Anchor (1753–8), and Gold Anchor (1758–70). Chelsea produced a higher percentage of non-useful wares than any other factory, and the figures in the Red Anchor period have been said to equal any produced on the Continent. The best known products of the rare Triangle period are the 'goat-and-bee' jugs, cream jugs with the lower part shaped as two reclining goats. Beneath the lip was a bee in relief. Chelsea was always a wealthy man's firm; its products were collectors' pieces from the start, including salts in the form of crayfish and the immensely valuable 'tea plant' coffee-pots (bearing a tea plant design in relief). Early Chelsea ware was greatly influenced, of course, by Chinese designs, but contemporary silver and Meissen also provided impetus. Teawares, bowls, and cream boats were often octagonal, and finely painted botanical china was characteristic of the two middle periods. The Gold Anchor period was rococo, with rich gilding, flamboyant, with Sèvres a major influence. It must not be supposed that all Chelsea is marked. It is not.

CHENILLE AXMINSTER

Chenille is a thick velvety cord of silk or wool resembling a woolly caterpillar (chenille is French for caterpillar), and following its use as curtain material it was pressed into service for carpets in 1839, revolutionising the industry and providing an unending number of colours and designs.

CHESS PIECES

Although known for thousands of years, it is rare to find chess pieces earlier than the eighteenth century, though medieval chessmen made from ivory or wood are reproduced in abundance, especially the so-called Lewis chessmen discovered in 1831. Chessmen for play were usually made of wood, but Wedgwood, Minton, and the Staffordshire potteries also made them in ceramics. A very interesting set was made by Doulton in which the pieces are represented by mice. No silver chessmen have been discovered earlier than the nineteenth century, though a set was made in 1815, half of them being gold plated. There was little standardisation in shape or size before the nineteenth century, and as the number of chess tournaments increased there was a desperate need for a model, provided in 1835 (the Staunton, still the main design). French chess sets are highly regarded. German turners produced splendid wooden chess sets mounted on silver bases, and the Italians made sets of glass. Hong Kong still exports twenty different types of ivory chessmen. Most materials are used, including onyx from Mexico and bronze from Africa, but these are mainly tourist

items. Painted alabaster, marble and synthetic marble may be impressive but in terms of value they do not rate much higher than plastic.

CHESTNUT URN

Sometimes called a chestnut server, this originated from Holland in the eighteenth century, and was made in silver and other metals including copper. It was supported on a spreading round or square foot and a short stem. There were often lion masks and ring handles with a domed lid topped by a finial, sometimes acorn-shaped. The hot chestnuts were lifted from the urn with a fork and, salted and de-husked, were eaten accompanied by the taking of coffee, a custom that died out in the nineteenth century.

CHESTS

The most important piece of furniture in the medieval house. The earliest were hollowed-out tree trunks (made until the seventeenth century), but by the thirteenth century chests had simple carved decoration and hinged lockable lids. Chests with rounded arches are known as Romanesque; the French favoured elaborate carving and scrollwork in iron; the Spanish used geometrical designs influenced by Islam, while the British preferred the carving of roundels. The simplest chests were plank coffers; boards nailed onto slab ends. The sides could extend past the body of the chest to form legs. In the fifteenth century thin wood panels were set loosely in the chests (to reduce warping); these were carved to imitate linen, thus the name linenfold. Church chests had more than one lock, with individual keys held by various church officials. In the seventeenth century chests were made with drawers, and although single-compartment chests continued to be made, a sequence of drawers (the chest of drawers) proved to be more useful than the simple chest.

CHEST OF DRAWERS

A piece of storage furniture in which the interior is entirely made up of drawers, deriving from a development of the chest about 1650 where sets of drawers were concealed behind doors. The fronts of the drawers were subjected to all kinds

Victorian mahogany specimen chest.

of embellishment, sometimes excessively with veneer gone mad, especially when oyster and sycamore veneer were used. There is more restraint and decorum when mahogany replaced walnut, and the most refined, and among the least expensive, are the bow-fronted chests of drawers made towards the end of the eighteenth century. The chest of drawers has either bracket feet or bun feet, sometimes swapped around in the interests of fashion. Later varieties can be set on a plinth. From the beginning of the nineteenth century heavier and more ponderous pieces came into being, some of them with pillars at the side. The chest of drawers ceased to be a show-piece and became a utilitarian object for the bedroom (and sometimes the bigger the better) although throughout the Victorian

period earlier designs were copied. Between 1900 and 1910 there was a fashion for simple well-designed chests of drawers, often of unvarnished oak, anticipating the functional designs of the 1930s and the Utility furniture of World War II.

CHEST ON CHEST*

A double chest of drawers, with the top one usually less wide. Looked at philosophically a rather curious and ungainly object, because the people who could afford such furniture would have had plenty of room to dispose two chests of drawers, with far more ease of access to the contents.

CHEST ON STAND*

A piece of furniture with few marks for fitness for function, as the stand supporting the chest of drawers commonly collapsed, even when extra legs were provided (four on the front, two on the back). Replacement stands were known as Hackney Road stands from the area where they were made. With the vogue for cabriole legs, less strong under a dead weight, instead of turned legs, this possibility was enhanced, so all stands are suspect. Design features approximated to those of the chest of drawers, though in some examples a writing facility is provided between chest and stand. The chest on stand did not survive as a viable piece of furniture as the chest on chest did, which in turn faded in the early nineteenth century.

CHIFFONIER

A side cabinet with shelf or shelves above developed from the eighteenth century, and used for books, music, knick-knacks, or as a sideboard. A characteristic of Regency chiffoniers was a brass latticed door, square or arched, backed with silk. The superstructure could be plain or ornate, with an ornate scroll topping the back, and drawers on the upper stage could be an optional extra. It avoided the extravagances of much nineteenth-century furniture with the possible exception of some over-exuberant scroll-work. It has proved an irresistible temptation to turn ordinary Victorian cabinets and sideboards into chiffoniers by taking out the panels in the base and putting in a

Late-18th-century satinwood and tulipwood commode.

brass latticed door. In France the name has been given to a tall many-drawered commode or chest of drawers.

CHIMNEY CRANE

A bracket of wrought iron attached to the back wall of an open fireplace from which a kettle or other container was suspended. Depending on what the container was, the crane could be small or large, simple or complicated, with pulleys, swivels, and ratchets so that the pot or kettle could be easily swung to any position around or over the fire. Because of its widespread use it had a large number of names including the cobrell, cottrell, jib-crook, trammel, or sway (sometimes swey). Used until quite recently in rustic parts, it may prove difficult to identify if its purpose is not divined.

CHIMNEY ORNAMENTS

Knick-knacks designed to stand on mantelpieces and made throughout the nineteenth century in a variety of materials such as Britannia metal, pewter, lead, brass, and bronze. Classical figures were popular as well as animals, birds, and romanticised rustics.

CHINA CLAY

A white clay, called by the Chinese 'kaolin', mined in Cornwall and an essential ingredient of hard-paste porcelain. It is also used in the manufacture of certain kinds of paper.

CHINA STAND

An ornamental stand for displaying china or flowers introduced towards the end of the seventeenth century, taking many forms, the early ones being low pedestals on carved feet. In the eighteenth century they resembled stools with cabriole legs, and in the 1750s fanciful rococo stands were produced, mentioned by Chippendale. Later ones were akin to candle stands, with three uprights. Small four-legged stands with shelves were made for flowerpots. A china stand is one of the general-purpose terms used for a nondescript item of indeterminate usage.

CHINESE CARPETS

Old Chinese carpets are subdued in colour, mostly in browns, whites, blues and yellows and, despite the size of the country, there was a national style, a central figurative device on a plain or lightly decorated background. The thick-piled luxuriant carpets were made for the European market, and a carpet industry was built up in the Peking district to cater for the demand. These carpets carry the title 'Continental'.

CHINESE FURNITURE

Chinoiserie, the European conception of Chinese products, was not like the real thing, least of all in furniture, which was often characterised by quiet restraint and superb workmanship. Furniture was well developed by the Han dynasty (206BC–AD221) in the form of low platforms, occasional tables, and stools, and towards the end of this period the chair was evolved. As well as such woods as rosewood and chestnut the Chinese used native woods not known in the west and, in the warmer south, bamboo was extensively used, as well as lacquered furniture which, unlike bamboo, was insect-resistant. Nails and dowels were never used in Chinese furniture but only the mortise and tenon joint and the meagre use of dovetailing. Rounded members were cut by hand, and not turned, and veneer was not common until a late date. Metal mounts were employed, often countersunk, and sometimes several different woods were used in one piece of furniture. The way of life dictated the form of furniture, so that the quintessential European chest of drawers was not used as clothes were placed in a chest. What is known as 'Chinese brownwood' furniture is very expensive, even modern pieces.

CHINESE GLASS

Probably first used as a cheap substitute for jade and carved in the same way, glass was not regarded highly and much was imported. Glass blowing possibly was introduced by Jesuit missionaries in the seventeenth century, but moulding was preferred. The glass often had an oily texture. High-quality opaque white vases were produced, and glass was used to simulate gemstones. The Chinese also produced cameo glass in several layers, but the high point was the snuff bottle, the creation of which became an art form.

CHINOISERIE

With the spread of Chinese taste from the seventeenth century to the early nineteenth century as a result of the expansion of trade, there were deliberate attempts to reproduce certain Chinese goods such as their blue-and-white china. Chinoiserie is not concerned with these, but with imaginative ventures into what Europeans thought China was all about, often based on books of engravings and travellers' tales. The result was that basic western objects such as furniture had pseudo-Chinese details grafted onto them, often with taste and refinement, often with ludicrous inappropriateness. At its best, as with Chinese Chippendale furniture, the merger between east and west was marvellous, for the furniture-makers integrated real or imaginary Chinese detail fully into their products, just as the neo-Classical makers, such as Robert Adam, had incorporated classical devices with no hint of strain or self-consciousness. The outstanding monuments to Chinoiserie are the Brighton Pavilion and the pagoda at Kew, plus the Willow Pattern design.

CHISELLED AND CUT STEEL

Steel chiselling was a by-product of gun and lock making. In the seventeenth and eighteenth centuries pierced and ornate snuff-boxes, etuis, scissors, tweezers and thimbles were produced in Italy and France, with coarser work made in Germany. Larger items including fireplaces were produced at Tula in Russia. The centre of English production was Woodstock in Oxfordshire, and later the Soho works in Birmingham, which drove Woodstock out of business. The Soho works concentrated on cut steel, producing sword furniture, buttons, buckles and cheap jewellery, often emulating marcasite.

CHRISTMAS CARDS

The first Christmas card dates from 1843, and was slow in being accepted, but from about 1850 cards became very lacy and lavish, with heavy embossing, rich colour, and complicated folding – so that scenes could change by manipulating the paper – and even include mechanical devices. Some cards incorporated sachets of scent. Many of the most charming cards are hand-painted. The most interesting are probably the artist-designed cards of the Aesthetic and art nouveau periods.

CHRONOMETER

The chronometer is a plain-dialled clock fitted face upwards in a wooden box and invented in 1735 by John Harrison to be absolutely accurate for use at sea in association with navigational instruments. Because of the movement of the ship ordinary clocks were inefficient; the success of the chronometer was due to the grid-iron pendulum and 'compensation' using the unequal contraction of two metals. Later chronometers incorporated two balance wheels oscillating in opposite directions. By 1850 most well-equipped ships carried them.

CIGARETTE CARDS

Cigarettes were first of all sold in packs protected with a card stiffener bearing the maker's name, but about 1885 it was realised that sets of picture cards would build up a loyalty to the brand, important when there were dozens of small com-

panies anxious to establish themselves. The cards issued by these small and transient companies are naturally the most sought after. Between 1885 and 1902 more than 10,000 sets were published in Britain. In 1902 the Imperial Tobacco Company was formed to fight off American big business, and the large combines were engaged in a trade war, using the cigarette card as the medium of battle. Cards became sophisticated art products, employing the latest technology; perhaps the most immediately appealing, though of modest value, are the silk cards. During this period the reverse of the card was given over to information on the picture, instead of advertising matter. From about 1930 the reverse of the card was coated with adhesive so that it could be stuck in a specially provided album. Some collectors prefer their cards to be unmounted. Cards from 1918 to 1939 are available in vast quantities at negligible cost, simply because so many millions were produced. During World War II cigarette cards were discontinued and there has not been sufficient interest shown to revive them seriously, though a tepid attempt was made in the 1950s. Makers of tea and other products have continued the tradition, and these cards now have their collectors.

CLASSICAL STYLE

A style based upon the principles of proportion and order as in ancient Greece and Rome, re-evaluated during the Renaissance, but descriptive mainly of the efforts of Robert Adam and others in the second half of the eighteenth century to introduce styles, motifs, decorations and what might be termed classical ambience into sophisticated furniture, architecture, and silver. Many of the cabinet-makers and architects of the time did not know much about the classical style, and cared even less, and their attempts to graft on motifs in the manner of icing a cake were less than happy.

CLOBBERING

A term used for adding overglaze enamels to early porcelain, either in a naive attempt to make it more interesting or to make it more expensive, an early form of faking in a mostly innocent world. This form of improvement is often difficult to spot.

CLOCK DIALS

In the early days of the long-case clock, dials were of brass, with a silvered brass ring about 2in (5cm) wide with Roman numerals for the hours. The minutes were marked with Arabic numerals around the rim of this ring, known as the chapter ring. Dials increased in size, and were square until about 1710 when they became arched, leaving a semi-circular space for a calender (first introduced about 1690), phases of the moon, and whatever else the maker cared for in the way of extras. From about 1690 the centres of the dials were frosted and engraved, either with scroll-type decoration or with quaint flowers, birds, and other devices. Until about 1800 the hands of the dial were handmade, but then they were stamped from thin steel. Early clocks sometimes had one hand only, which was no great loss as accuracy was poor or non-existent. In 1770 the painted dial appeared, plain, in black and white, with discreet hand-painting in the corners. In the early nineteenth century Roman figures were often replaced by Arabic numbers for the hours and there was an increase in decoration, and little pictures made their appearance. Although clock design changed continuously, there was little that could be done about the dials, as their main purpose was to be instantly legible. The 1920s and 1930s brought in the figure-less clock, with the hours marked out in small squares, circles, or triangles to conform with a more geometric type of case.

CLOCKS

There are two types of traditional clock. One relies on the fall of a weight, the other on the recoil of a spring. The action of the driving force needs to be interrupted at regular intervals, and this is the function of the escapement, which periodically checks and releases the driving train. Mechanical clocks first appeared in the thirteenth century and began to replace water-clocks, though the sundial remained popular for many centuries. The domestic clock first appeared in the fifteenth century, the pendulum clock in the seventeenth. The reign of the spring and the weight lasted until the arrival of first the electric clock and then the battery clock, perhaps the antiques of the future. Electric clocks of the 1930s enjoy a modest vogue.

Mantel clock of about 1890.

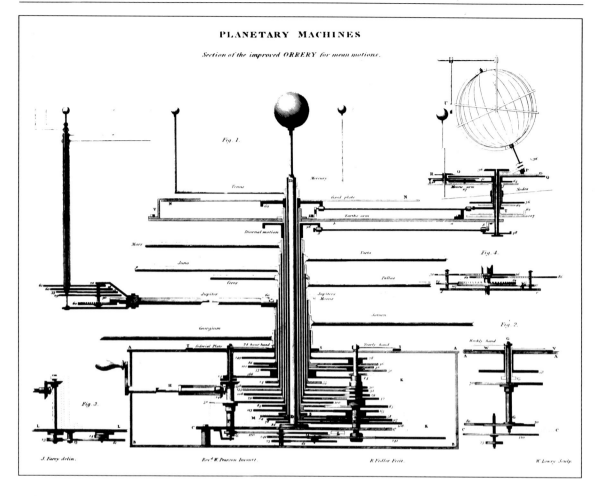

PLANETARY MACHINES

Section of the improved ORRERY for mean motions.

A diagram of an orrery, in which clockwork mechanisms reached a peak.

CLOSE-PLATING

A method used for primitive silverplating, in which an iron or steel object is dipped in flux, then molten tin, whereupon silver foil is applied to the surface to be plated. The application of a hot iron causes the tin to react as a solder. The process was briefly revived in the early nineteenth century, but was no contender to Sheffield plate.

CLOTHES PRESS

Many people have opened the upper doors of what they think is a wardrobe and have come across large plain open drawers instead of hanging space. The clothes press, akin to the cabinet on chest, was introduced in the seventeenth cen-

tury, and very popular in the eighteenth, where it began to acquire the name of wardrobe. Previously clothes were folded, but new fashions dictated that they should be hung. Until about 1975 they were disregarded, and were bought, if at all, for the sake of the wonderful sheets of veneer, especially flame mahogany, which covered the upper doors. The bottom of the clothes press could consist of drawers or, less common, cupboards. Extra value is added by mouldings, especially top mouldings, cornices, and original brass fittings.

COACH- AND POST-HORNS

Made in a single straight tube, usually of copper with a short section near the mouthpiece of another metal (coach-horns) or brass (post-horns). The length can be anything from 30 to 45 inches (75 to 135cm). The vast majority seen today are reproduction, some of them being of high quality for coaching enthusiasts.

COADE'S STONE

A peculiar process in which carved stone was imitated in moulded stoneware by the Misses Coade of 'Coade's Lithodipyra, Terra Cotta or Artificial Stone Manufactory' which existed in one form or another from 1769 to about 1840. Although much of the work was architectural, statues and busts were made, usually impressed with the maker's name.

COAL

Perhaps the least promising material for making anything in. Nevertheless the Victorians made a chair out of coal, illustrating their ability to make the best use of anything. They also made furniture from gutta percha (India rubber).

COALBROOKDALE COMPANY

Iron works established in 1709, the most permanent monument being the Iron Bridge, much illustrated especially on Sunderland lustre ware. Among the many objects, mostly in cast iron, the company made were gates, railings, furniture for indoors and outdoors, door furniture, and hall-stands.

COALPORT

Porcelain factory founded by John Rose (died 1841), who had trained at the Caughley porcelain factory. Rose set up at Jackfield in 1780, then later moved to Coalport. He bought Caughley as well as the Nantgarw factory in 1819, the owner of which was the brilliant porcelain-painter W. Billingsley, who had started Nantgarw in 1813. Billingsley then worked for Coalport. Coalport produced translucent porcelain with bright flower painting, particularly roses, often over pink or purple guide-lines which were transfer printed. Coalport was thus able to keep pace with demand, still retaining some of the qualities of hand-decorating. Continental porcelain was also copied. Amongst the more unusual items were plaques with fruit and flower paintings. From the middle of the nineteenth century less elaborate domestic ware was made. Coalport is still a major porcelain factory, its flower groups very much in the nineteenth-century style.

A Worcester Barr, Flight and Barr plate, a Coalport vase, and a Coalport plate.

Collectables hover uneasily on the borderland of antiques, dismissed by many with scorn. Some of them may have been rubbish, rediscovered and promoted, and when the fashion has passed may easily return to the dust heap of history. Many collectables have a nostalgia content, reminding collectors of days gone by, and are often associated with pleasurable activities, such as smoking, drinking and motoring. Looked at logically, there is a yawning chasm between an eighteenth-century silver tankard and a beer mat, between a Meerschaum pipe and a cigarette card, between a Rolls-Royce Silver Ghost and an oil can, but all have their devotees. A beer mat collector (a tegestologist) may not have the money for an eighteenth-century tankard, but he may not want one, content to pursue his/her own particular and specific interest. Some collectables, such as picture postcards and pot lids, now have auctions devoted to them. Perhaps cigarette packets and gramophone needle tins will soon join them as fully paid-up members of the antique fraternity. A complete list of things people collect would fill a dozen volumes. Milk-bottle tops? Yes. Jars of rusty nails? Not likely, but everything is possible in this shifting and fascinating world. Here are a few of the recognised collectables:

Beer bottle labels: printed paper labels were first stuck on beer bottles to identify the brewers in the 1850s, and were oval shaped. In 1876 the Trade Marks Registration Act came into force, and Bass was the first brewer to register, its logo being a triangle. One German collector has over 300,000 labels.
Beer mats: patented in Germany in 1882 as a wood pulp drip mat, and introduced to Britain in the 1920s to advertise brewers, individual public houses, cigarette brands and large companies.
Billheads: these came into their own after the introduction of the penny post in 1840, and nineteenth-century billheads were mostly engraved, using a mixture of types and incorporating a view of the factory, shop, or product. New printing technology brought in full colour, but many of the nineteenth-century bill heads were used unchanged into the 1950s.
Biscuit tins: production of biscuit tins with designs printed directly onto the metal began in the 1860s, and adventurous manufacturers realised that the tins did not have to be rectangular but could be any shape. These included lorries, baskets, vases, urns, shells, coaches, and animals, with a set of books one of the most popular.
Bonds and share certificates: bonds and shares have been issued since at least the seventeenth century and were often printed on vellum. Amongst the best known are the documents dealing with the South Sea Company in the early eighteenth century. Many of the bonds and certificates are lavishly printed in many colours, and the aim is to impress the subscrib-

Old advertising material is a popular collecting area, especially when it relates to the earlier days of well-known present-day companies.

Trade card of Chadburn Brothers 'optical mathematical and philosophical instrument makers' of Sheffield, dating from about 1850.

ers. In the United States and Canada shares were often made out to the bearer and not to a named person, and if the company is still in existence the share certificate could be valid.

Bookmarks: these were commercially produced advertising slip-ins in card, the work of skilled needlewomen, often using religious texts as the subject matter, or splendid silk Stevengraphs. Most were in the form of a thin rectangle, but among the shaped bookmarks were gloved hands, cricket bats, and cut-out figures. Some had a trick facility, such as pull-up sections.

Bottle openers: unlike corkscrews, a very basic object; the early ones were mostly of iron, later ones of steel or other metals, and all date from the time when beer bottles had fit-on metal tops and not corks. Some bottle openers were shaped to depict guitars, keys, etc, and many were issued by brewers and carry advertising material.

Boy Scout memorabilia: founded in 1908, the Boy Scout movement placed great stress on solidarity, emphasised by badges. County badges became universal from the 1930s. Periodical jamborees were also celebrated by badges, including pin-on types.

Calendars: issued since the nineteenth century, calendars have long been useful as Christmas presents and as opportunities for businesses to keep their names before their customers for twelve months. 1920s and 1930s calendars were largely pastoral, but in the post-war years there has been more of an emphasis on lavish photography, cuteness, and pin-ups, the best known of which are the Pirelli catalogues – in 1974 43,000 were issued, using a total of sixty models.

Charity boxes: used initially to collect for the

poor, and known in the 1880s as poor boxes, the charity box could have a long handle so that it could be thrust into a crowd. Made in many materials, such as tin and papier mâché, there is a good deal of ingenuity involved in enticing coins from passers-by. Perhaps the best known are the RSPCA free-standing dog models.

Cheques: in themselves there is little variation, but they were issued by dozens of small banks that were subsequently swallowed up by the giants or went out of business, so they have a modest historical interest. In 1896 there were 196 private banks and 67 joint-stock banks in England alone.

Coca-Cola memorabilia: one of the most promoted of all companies, Coca-Cola advertisments abound in the form of brooches, pin-on badges, trays, enamel signs and other promotional material. From about 1886 Coca-Cola was sold in cylindrical bottles with sloping shoulders, replaced in 1916 by the waisted bottle used today.

Comics: first issued in the nineteenth century to cater for the new literate working class, comics reached a peak in the 1930s when new ones were published almost every week. These included *The Dandy* and *The Beano*, bringing new life to a genre inclined to be prim and relying heavily on public-school humour (*Magnet* featuring Billy Bunter).

Disneyana: Mickey Mouse appeared in 1928, Pluto and Goofy in 1930, Donald Duck in 1934, followed by a train of celebrities, Snow White and the Seven Dwarfs, Pinnochio, Dumbo, 101 Dalmations and many others. These appeared as soft toys, moulded in terra cotta and other pottery, made in celluloid and plastic, presented as rug patterns, and made into mechanical tin-plate toys, such as the 'Mickey Mouse Organ Grinder' and the Mickey Mouse mechanical bank. The Disney organisation also published a massive amount of promotional material, such as books, posters, and magazines. Although most of Disneyana dates from the 1930s, Mickey Mouse and others are being made today, usually detected by anachronistic material and detail.

Film memorabilia: ranging from film star post-cards to Charlie Chaplin's hat, cane and shoes (£110,000 at Christie's South Kensington on 11 December 1987). Periodic studio sales supply an avid market. Items include props (a stand-in model for Boris Karloff as Frankenstein's monster made £16,500 at auction), costumes, and models. Collections of posters and front-of-house stills are periodically released onto the open market.

Garden gnomes: garden gnomes can date back to the nineteenth century, and have a certain mythological role as guardians. Carved rather than moulded gnomes are naturally preferred, as are those that are hand-painted or are carrying on some unusual occupation, such as spraying weeds.

Gramophone-needle tins: steel needles for gramophones were supposed to be used only once (through of course they weren't) and they were sold in small tins holding up to 300 needles. They were partly replaced by fibre needles which the user pared down to create a good point. As 78 rpm gramophones are still played by enthusiasts, needles are still bought mainly for use.

Matchbox labels: the collecting of matchbox labels is called phillumeny. Friction matches were invented in 1829, and in 1842 machinery was invented to manufacture the sticks or splints. Packaging in small boxes followed shortly afterwards. The range of matchboxes is immense, few of them of any great value, and often produced in foreign countries for the British market with amusing misspellings.

Menus: the preparation of menus could be an art form, especially for meals taken at prestige restaurants. The most collected are probably those related to steamship cruises and early air travel.

Milk bottles: milk was sold in bottles towards the end of the nineteenth century, but bottles were not greatly used until the 1920s. Most were clear glass but coloured glass was occasionally used. Many bore the name of the dairy, farm, or issuing authority, together with an appropriate logo. They were either stoppered, using a wire clasp and a crockery cap, or protected by a cardboard disc, often with a hole in the middle for the insertion of a straw. These discs have their devotees.

Oiliana: the collection of oilcans, pourers, oil bottles, enamel signs, advertising hand-outs, display cards, and everything to do with motor oil. As motor oils differ very little from one another, there was intense competition between the oil companies to establish that they and they alone had the key to happy motoring and there is a surprising wealth of material.

Packaging: a limitless area catering for limitless nostalgia and dating from the nineteenth century when brand names were being promoted with cynical ruthlessness and disregard for the truth. The materials vary from paper to wood and tin, and perhaps there is most interest in packaging relating to the early days of present-day companies.

Paper ephemera: posters, tickets, and similar items meant to be thrown away but which managed to survive. They are often collected on account of their design and the variety of type mounts used. Among the multitude of categories are official notices and election printing; police notices; rewards and wanted notices; booksellers' lists and leaflets; for sale notices; travel notices; entertainment notices; sporting posters; tickets of all kinds including travel, entertainments, functions, cloakroom and sporting; invitation and announcement cards; funeral invitations; exhibition cards; trade cards; tobacco labels; tea, coffee and grocery labels; pharmaceutical and perfumery labels; and hardware labels and stickers; plus paper bags with the name of the supplier printed on them. Some of these categories date from the seventeenth century; the earliest trade card is from about 1620. Early ephemera used a combination of letterpress and engraving.

At the NEW PLAY-HOUSE in MAY-FAIR.

DUring the time of the FAIR, will be Play'd, the True and Ancient Story of MAUDLIN *the Merchants Daughter of* Briſtol, *and her Lover* ANTONIO How they were Caſt away in a Tempeſt upon the Coaſt of *Barbary;* where the Mermaids were ſeen floating on the Seas, and ſinging on the Rocks, foretelling their Danger.

The D R O L L intermingled with moſt delightful merry Comedy, after the manner of an OPERA, with extraordinary variety of Singing and Dancing: By his Grace the Duke of *Southampton's* Servants.

The Place will be known by the Balcone adorn'd with Blue Pillars twiſted with Flowers.
VIVAT REGINA.

Playbills are an interesting collecting area. This one is undated. The long 's' shaped like an 'f' is not really a clue as it was used into the 19th century, but there is no question that it belongs to the period 1702–14, the reign of Queen Anne, indicated by the Latin phrase VIVAT REGINA (Long live the Queen).

Pop memorabilia: the first pop idols were Bill Haley and his Comets, the rock 'n roll band of the 1950s, but it was not until long after the arrival and demise of the Beatles that items connected with pop music began to be seriously and energetically collected, with drawings by John Lennon fetching more than £3,000, and original handwritten lyrics more than twice as much. Amongst other items were 'golden' discs, LP sleeves, photographs, autographed programmes, clothing, instruments, and letters – indeed everything that could be tied in with the members of the group, either individually or collectively. The interest also extended to their company, Apple, and a vast range of novelties including Beatle bubble-gum machines of the mid-1960s. Other celebrities, such as Elvis Presley, the Rolling Stones, and Jimi Hendrix, have joined the Beatles on this Parnassus, and their memorabilia are also diligently sought. It is a phenomenon centred around pop and rock music, and not jazz or other music.

Sheet music covers: music covers remained fairly plain until the early nineteenth century when lithography was invented. About 1840 colour lithography appeared, and thousands of titles were produced, especially for ballads, music-hall songs, and piano pieces, often beautifully executed by talented artists. The music was intended for domestic use. There was a deteriora-

tion in the 1880s with the use of half-tone and the employment of photography, but there was a revival after World War I when modern designers found a satisfactory and profitable outlet.

Spectacles: spectacles were worn probably in the thirteenth century; most early spectacles were no more than magnifying glasses, and glass technology was able to supply little else. Spectacles with side pieces were introduced in 1727, replacing the pince-nez type, and bifocals in 1785. Contact lenses were made in 1887, and sunglasses date from about the same time. Most frames were of steel or gold. The most common nineteenth-century type are 'granny glasses', sometimes bought today for use.

Sweet cigarette packets: chocolate cigarettes were popular from early in the twentieth century, before the introduction of sugary cigarettes, renamed candy sticks when cigarette advertisements became suspect. The packets depicted children's heroes from television and films.

Trench art: a name bestowed on souvenirs made by soldiers of two world wars in their spare time, with the quality of World War I

A rock 'n roll photograph featuring Elvis Presley.

items far exceeding those of World War II when there were more interesting things to do than make models of biplanes. The most popular items were smoking accessories such as lighters or ashtrays and vases made from shell cases.

War posters: vast quantities were issued by the warring nations exhorting the readers to do their bit, buy saving bonds, and shaming the reluctant ('what did you do in the war, daddy?'). Readers over sixty will certainly remember the 'Careless Talk Costs Lives' posters, plastered everywhere. These are worth about £100 each.

Whistles: ranging from children's tin whistles, through military whistles, police whistles, and referees' whistles to the fancy whistles in animal shapes and the bosuns' silver whistles of the eighteenth century. They can be made of a variety of materials including bone, ivory, gold, silver, jet, brass, tin, minerals, wood, pottery and porcelain. Whistles were often incorporated with other objects such as pen-knives.

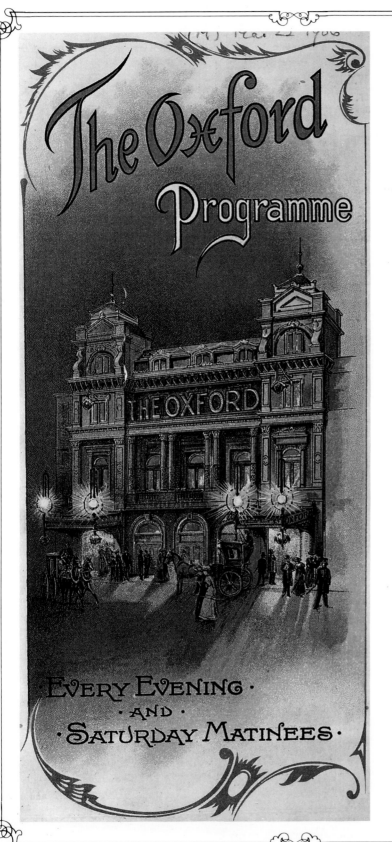

The Oxford Programme

THE OXFORD

EVERY EVENING ·
· AND ·
· SATURDAY MATINEES ·

Theatre programmes: interesting if autographed, or if for gala occasions, or if a now famous actor or actress appeared in a minor role, or if it relates to a theatre now closed, but mostly of concern only to someone who went to the actual show. An exception can be made for music-hall programmes, which have their own period panache.

Programmes are collected. The most interesting are music-hall programmes, as this one is.

COAL-SCUTTLE

With the widespread use of coal in the eighteenth century came the need for a suitable container, usually of copper, of helmet or scoop shape, perhaps with brass handles. These were workaday utensils, brought from the cellar, but about 1840 the coal vase made its appearance, with an ornamental cover and kept by the fire, being refilled from a bucket. The coal vase was of japanned metal and often of outrageous shape, such as a nautilus shell on coral, a Gothic font, or a tureen. The Purdonium box-like scuttle, which came in metal or wood with a liner, often with a slot for the shovel, was cheaper and made in huge quantities (and perhaps still is), as it is certainly the most functional of them all.

COIN GLASS

A drinking glass with a coin enclosed in one of the knops or protuberances in the stem, dating from the mid-seventeenth century. Other articles also had coins imbedded or enclosed, such as tankards.

COLONIAL FURNITURE

Most colonial furniture evolved in the eighteenth century, and models were European, though not necessarily those of the colonising power. In Latin America, dominated by the Spanish and Portuguese, there was local furniture unquestionably derived from English, German, French and Flemish models as well as from that of the occupiers. A characteristic of colonial furniture is that local woods were used and the native craftsmen continued to use time-honoured techniques, so that in Mexico and Peru silver was still used to adorn furniture, and in India and Burma straightforward pieces of furniture such as bureaux and desks were turned into convoluted nightmares.

COMBS

Made in wood, bone, horn, ivory and metal from ancient times, and from the early nineteenth century popular as hair ornaments, sometimes of gold decorated with cameos, gemstones, pearls or coral, though the most dis-tinctive are probably the art nouveau examples made at the end of the nineteenth century. Silver-backed combs from toilet-sets have often survived, whereas the mirror and the brush have either been broken or have been thrown away, and many hopeful owners believe that odd combs are in some way valuable when in fact they are valueless. One reason for this misapprehension is that women often own a silver toilet-set when they have never owned anything else of silver.

COMMEMORATIVE CHINA AND POTTERY

This is a peculiarly British genre, and probably the earliest examples are the blue-and-white delftware plates depicting the monarchs of the seventeenth century. In the eighteenth century there was a brief flurry of electioneering pottery, and in Liverpool there was a fashion for depicting nautical subjects on delftware. More important are the personalised items celebrating betrothals, marriages, births, christenings, popular from about 1750 onwards, cheap to do and effective. National, religious, sporting and other topical issues provided incentive to designers, some good, some bad, and the naive sporting

Late Victorian vase.

commemorative ware is the most valuable. The Napoleonic Wars brought forth a host of porcelain and pottery, honouring the defeaters and the defeated, and the Industrial Revolution was also celebrated. The favourite subjects were perhaps Sunderland Bridge (produced by Sunderland potteries) and the Iron Bridge at Coalbrookdale in Shropshire. Throughout the nineteenth century royal events sparked off the fervent monarchism of the potters, the various jubilees of Queen Victoria produced millions of individual items, the most-seen being plates. The most collected commemorative wares are Staffordshire pottery figures and groups, first handmade about 1840, later in moulds, and hand-coloured by armies of women and children employed by dozens of small factories in the Potteries. No subject was too trivial for these figures, known as flatbacks because their destination was the mantelpiece where only the front would show. There were heroes, criminals, sportsmen (boxers being the most important because they were easy to model), actors and actresses, almost anyone. Some of the groups were complex and are now very highly priced, but all retain their innocence and childishness. Towards the end of the nineteenth century the business was streamlined, the colouring was cursory and often placed in a token way, leaving most of the surface white. Although there was a brief flurry of interest in the Boer War and World War I, and the women's suffragette movement created a certain pottery interest, most commemorative pottery since has been concentrated largely on royal and sporting events, with cricket the most collectable and W. G. Grace the most highly featured personage.

COMMEMORATIVE MEDALS

Some of the 'coins' of ancient Greece and Rome were commemorative medals, and although there was a modest interest in commemorative medals in the Middle Ages the first real medal as such was cast in bronze in 1438 to celebrate the visit of a Byzantine ruler to Italy. Until about 1500 the Italians were the main issuers of commemorative medals, followed by the French, the Dutch, and the English (about 1540). Many of the English medals were political and patriotic, and one of the most famous was the Armada Medal. They were made in metals including bronze, silver, brass, and (rarely) gold. In the eighteenth century techniques for making them changed, and they were struck from dies in the same way as coins. Interest in them languished, and they became trivial, recording unimportant events, although there was a revival in propaganda medals during World War I, the best known of which is morally debatable British fake of a spurious German medal glorying in the loss of women and children in the torpedoed liner *Lusitania*. Some of the most interesting are those cast for sporting and local events, usually in bronze and often splendidly designed. These are available for a pound or two in considerable quantities and have yet to be codified or discovered.

COPELAND

A very important nineteenth-century porcelain producer, from 1841 onwards noted for its Pa-

Centrepiece by Copeland for a dessert service manufactured for the Princess of Wales (later Queen Alexandra).

rian figures and decorative panels for furniture inserts; it was the first English manufacturer to inlay porcelain with 'jewels'.

COPENHAGEN PORCELAIN

A factory with state monopoly was established in 1722, another in 1738, but the most famous was founded in 1774, producing high-quality hard-paste porcelain, the most notable of which was a service begun in 1789 intended for Empress Catherine of Russia numbering 1,602 pieces, each bearing a botanical painting. The style of Copenhagen was influenced by Meissen. The factory is still in existence.

COPPER

Used from Biblical times for domestic objects, copper was used less than brass because of its poisonous qualities, which were partly, but only partly, nullified by processes known as close-plating and tinning, which put a protective coating over the exposed copper (and which could wear off). Most copper objects derive from the eighteenth and nineteenth centuries and items before this, even if dated, must be treated with suspicion. Copper was regarded as a cheap substitute for gold and was used for decorative purposes in churches, sometimes enamelled or gilded. Among the more interesting eighteenth-century pieces are wedding gifts such as pots and pans, and kettles and jugs, with the initials of the lucky couple. The more collectable copper objects include warming-pans with perforated lids, eventually to be replaced by hot-water bottles, urns, coffee pots, kettles, measures, and watering cans. There are various implements such as skimmers, for removing impurities from the top of milk, and there are a number of quaintly named circular flat objects on a stick. The handles are usually of wood, occasionally of iron, and they often have a knob on the end or a hanging ring. Copper was much used in nautical manufactures such as diving helmets, and in decorative and nearly useful items such as crumb-trays and similar articles. It was a favourite metal in the art nouveau period, used for panels and decorative touches, often combined with oak. Being a soft malleable metal it is inclined to get battered, and fakers have used this tendency; when they try to reproduce the patina of old

copper they are inclined to overdo it or apply the 'finish' too evenly.

CORAL

Although usually red, coral can also be found in white, pink, brown and black, the last two from dead coral. Blue and yellow coral were once found, but no longer appear. Coral branches with bells attached were popular amongst mothers from the sixteenth to the nineteenth century – babies were given them to bite on to help them cut their teeth. Because it is easily carved it was used for jewellery in ancient times, especially in the form of amulets, and later also for statuettes, vases, snuff bottles, crucifixes, and chess pieces. Coral carving reached its peak in Italy in the seventeenth and eighteenth centuries.

CORKSCREWS

The basic shape of a corkscrew is a rod with a screw end attached at right angles to a handle, but throughout the years ways have been sought to extract the cork from a wine bottle with as little damage to the cork as possible, easing it rather yanking it out. Examples before the middle of the eighteenth century are rare, though it is difficult to date corkscrews, as various types persist, and value resides in the form the corkscrew takes, the material from which it is made, and any kind of decoration. The main alternative to the simple corkscrew is the double threaded type; the screw is driven into the cork, and a secondary action pulls the cork out. Sometimes the mechanism is enclosed in a tube, sometimes it is open. The first of the mechanical corkscrews was probably Henshall's Patent King Screw of 1795. Another form is the concertina corkscrew, with up to eight hinges. Many corkscrews of the basic form are fitted with a brush positioned at the end of the handle, to brush off encrustations and dust. Travelling corkscrews appear in the middle of the eighteenth century. The simplest consists of a rod with a screw end, with a ring, encased in a slender cylinder, which doubles as handle, slotting into the ring. Steel is most common, but ivory, mother-of-pearl, and porcelain are all used, in ascending order of value. Silver decoration and mounts are sometimes employed.

Ladies' corkscrews are often tiny, intended for scent bottles, and they enjoyed a short period of favour (1880s to 1914). Bar corkscrews are intended for heavy and prolonged use and have a clamp attachment. These were patented from the 1860s and are still in action in more or less their original form. Amongst the most collectable corkscrews are trade corkscrews, often used for medicine and inscribed with chemists' and pharmaceutical names, and there is a wide range of novelties, the most common of which is the simple corkscrew with a stag-horn handle. Often the corkscrew is one of a number of gadgets in an all-purpose assembly, which could include glass cutter, tin opener, and ruler; sometimes it is a hidden extra in a walking-stick or umbrella.

CORNER CUPBOARD

Very popular in the eighteenth century, the early hanging corner cupboards were often bow-fronted; these could be plain, lacquered, or painted with figurative subjects. Hanging straight-fronted cupboards could be open, glazed, or panelled, sometimes corner fitments rather than corner cupboards. The free-standing corner cupboards were a loftier design conception, sometimes in architectural style and made in pairs. Corner cupboards that may appear genuine may be artful marriages, using two distinct pieces of furniture. Some corner cupboards were made for a specific place and may not be right-angled. Pine was often used to match pine panelling.

COSTUME

Antique clothing is bought for wearing or for display, and is amongst the most vulnerable of all things collected or cherished, difficult to store without causing damage, space consuming, and subject to dirt, decay and insects as few other relics of the past are. The value of clothes depends not so much on age as on materials, colours, original buttons and fastenings, the standard of workmanship, and condition. There is very little earlier than the eighteenth century outside museums and private collections. Women's fabrics during the eighteenth century, light in weight, were silks and taffetas, velvet, satins and fine printed linens. Gowns were very

Some costumes are charming and collectable. Some are clearly not.

often hooped and worn with a petticoat. From the 1750s there was a fashion for the country look – milkmaid hats, tucked-up petticoats, tiny aprons, bonnets, and mob caps which fitted on the backs of heads. During the neo-Classical movement towards the end of the eighteenth century women's fashions became simpler, scanty, high waisted, with plain dresses, and no petticoats or corsets, though the number of accessories such as sashes, shawls and scarves increased. In the 1820s dresses became fuller, shoulders wider, waistline lower, and the petticoat returned. By 1830 the wasp-waist had arrived, with a petticoat made of a fabric called crinoline. The skirts became wider and wider, and had to be held in place by a frame, a fashion that continued until the bustle arrived about 1868, followed by the half-bustle and its variations. Throughout the Victorian period young girls wore white and pastel shades, their seniors subdued colours, and those in mourning black. Bright colours were considered racy. Eventually the bustle and other curious appendages were discarded, and a range of clothes for different functions appeared, for bicycling, tennis, golf, mornings, tea, matinees, and many others. Despite growing informality, the 'trailing' garments persisted until 1914. After World War I came a barrel-like outline with clothes swathed rather than worn, followed by experiments in various styles including the first mini-skirt, and a minimum of material for evening wear. New forms of clothing made their appearance, such as the pyjama suit or lounge pyjamas. Colours were garish, with silk, rayon, and gold and silver lamé. In 1930 evening gowns (the picture dress) descended to the ground, day dresses descended to below the calf, to rise again shortly before World War II, after which there was the 1947 'New Look' and succeeding permutations.

Men's clothing of the eighteenth century was elegant and formal, with the waistcoat an important element. Tight-fitting knee-breeches were worn. The coat had ornamental buttons, but was meant to swing open to display the waistcoat, and coats had no collars so that cravats and neck cloths could be seen at their best. The frock-coat was useful for all occasions, though the waistcoat (without a coat) was normal wear for servants and working men. The 1770s brought in skin-tight uncomfortable clothes, with small-cuffed coats with tight sleeves, and the dandies of the day wore high-heeled shoes, striped stockings and waistcoats, and carried long walking-sticks. In the 1790s tight pantaloons replaced knee-breeches, and boots, long and short, replaced buckled shoes,

"ECLIPSE" COMBINATIONS.

The above are made in Pink or White, of Elastic Woollen Texture, trimmed White Woollen Lace, giving a pretty and dainty effect.

	1st	2nd	3rd	4th	5th Sizes.
As Sketch—	10/6	11/6	12/6	13/6	14/6

Among the types of costume diligently collected is underwear. This advertisement is from the Queen *magazine of 1895.*

while coats were cut away in front and had long tails. Collars and cravats came up to the cheek. The fashions were so uncomfortable that men could not sit down. The top hat replaced the three-cornered hat. In the nineteenth century trousers became looser, the coat was padded at the sleeves, gathered at the shoulders, waistcoats and cravats were brightly coloured. Exaggerated shapes began to disappear, and the 'sack coat' appeared, three buttons but only the top one was buttoned, the distant ancestor of the modern lounge suit. Check, plaid, and striped materials were introduced in the 1840s especially for trousers. Head wear was more informal, with the flat tweed cap contending with the top hat. From the 1860s the deer stalker, hard straw hat, bowler, and cloth cap made their appearance. The waistcoat became merely part of a suit. As the nineteenth century drew to a close, formal wear, epitomised by the morning suit, was still stiff and starchy, but there was a trend towards informality with knee-breeches and stockings, white flannel trousers for sport, lounge suits, Norfolk suits, blazers and motoring wear. Shortly before World War I the sharp crease appeared in men's trousers for the first time. The 1920s brought in the tailored suit with turn-up trousers and wide lapels, worn with a soft shirt with changeable collars, the Fair Isle sweater for both men and women, pullovers and Oxford bags. With the collar-attached shirt the way to the future was open.

Some of the costume of the past is not interesting; pretty children's cotton-print dresses have been cannibalised for the material. Much Victorian clothing is heavy and drab, and very often black. Earlier women's clothing is necessarily fragile. But there is an enormous variety not only with the clothing but the accessories – hats, garters (often with mottoes and novelty clips), scarves, Paisley and Spanish shawls, handkerchiefs, gloves, stockings, and shoes. Underwear, corsets (those with patent devices being the most interesting), chemises, bodices and brassieres all have their collectors. Colourful men's items such as early waistcoats are in demand, as are the 'chimney-pot' hats of the early nineteenth century. Some old costumes are not what they seem; they may be theatrical costumes, made of cheap material, treated with spray dyes or enamelling, with decoration stuck on with glue, intended for a short life and impossible to repair or clean. Dressmakers' labels probably date from the 1860s; the presence of a couturier's labels such as Dior or Worth increases the value of an article (but it may have been transferred from something else).

COUNTRY CHAIRS

As a result of industrialisation, many agricultural workers uprooted from their native homes turned to furniture making, and moved to the expanding conurbations of Lancashire and Yorkshire. One of the best known is the Mendlesham chair, with turned legs and four

back rails, and the Derby chair with an arcade design. Country chairs were made for hard use, but this did not preclude imaginative design, some based on fashionable mahogany chairs, First recorded in 1724, the Windsor is the best known country chair, with a spindle or stick back, made mostly in ash or yew and with an elm seat, though all woods have been used including mahogany. Until about 1780 legs were wedged into mortise holes bored right through the seat, but after this the spoon bit was used, which had no point so that a deep hole could be bored without coming through the top of the seat. The customary stretcher was 'H'-shaped, but other shapes were used including the crinoline stretcher in the form of an arc. The splat was at first solid and vase- or fiddle-shaped, followed by pierced designs including the well-known wheel-back. The low-backed smoker's bow was introduced about 1830 and made almost without change for a century. The Windsor chair was introduced into America in the 1720s, and was first made in Philadelphia, later in Connecticut, Massachusetts, and Rhode Island, and as in England all convenient local woods were used. Cabriole legs are rare on Windsor chairs. There are numbers of Windsor-chair styles such as comb-back, bow-back, comb-and-bow-back, fan-back, loop-back, and rod-back and all refer to the spindle-and-splat layout. Although the main centre of production in Britain in the nineteenth century was High Wycombe, Buckinghamshire, Windsor chairs were made throughout the UK. Because of the wide variety of woods used, Windsor chairs are subject to selective woodworm.

COURT CUPBOARD*

A low two- or three-storey stand dating from the sixteenth century, and there are two basic kinds, those with an open base and those with a closed. The latter can often seem ungainly. In the seventeenth century each level of the open court cupboard was supported by sturdy bulbous forms of melon shape. Court is French for short, and the name probably given because the piece is usually low, below eye-level. It was used to display silver and other treasures. Because it has an old world air the court cupboard was revived in the 1920s and 1930s, this time with inappropriate as opposed to excessive carving.

COW CREAMER

Silver or ceramic cream jug in the form of a cow, with the tail looped over the back to serve as a handle. There is an oval opening in the back, covered by the lid, and topped by a bee, fly, or sometimes flowers. It was introduced to England about 1775 by a Dutch silversmith, but most were in pottery, sensitive by Whieldon in the 1760s, crude by the Staffordshire potters, who also did flat-backs for show, and possibly were used as advertising devices for dairies. Some potteries such as Pratt attempted to reproduce actual breeds, and lustre cow creamers were made in Sunderland and Wales. Porcelain cow creamers were made 1820–50 and are rare. Creamers with added extras such as milkmaids and calves are very desirable. The most vulnerable parts of the cow are the horns, and any prospective buyer should check that these are not replacements, and that the lid is a snug fit. Cow creamers, having their own quaint charm, are much reproduced, and are often difficult to spot, as the originals can be as fresh and shiny as deliberate fakes. Creamers are sometimes referred to as cow milk jugs, and it is more than likely that the liquid contained was indeed milk.

A group of Staffordshire cow creamers.

CRACKLE

Also called cracquelure, this was induced deliberately to ceramics to make the surface craze by adding a substance such as pegmatite to the glaze; first used by the Chinese. It is a textured finish much to the taste of modern studio potters.

CREAM WARE

One of the staple forms of pottery, developed in Staffordshire 1720–40 by using white clay and calcined flints, and within twenty years had begun to oust other tablewares, which were principally tin-glazed (delft) and salt-glazed (pitted surface like orange peel). Cream ware could be pierced, moulded, enamelled or bear printed designs, and was made by all potters, from the simplest to Wedgwood, whose version of cream ware in the 1760s was called Queensware. Another form, pearl ware, was introduced by Wedgwood in 1779. Naturally, white pottery always has been preferred for domestic use, and there have always been con-

Early 19th-century comic creamware jug, French enamelled condiment boat with bottles for oil and vinegar c1780, and a transfer-printed creamware jug, perhaps from the Leeds pottery.

tenders for the best, one of the most famous being Mason's ironstone china, patented in 1831, but a patent that was easily broken.

CRIMPING

Creating a wavy effect on the rims or lips of glass vessels. Much used in fancy Victorian coloured glass and in American glass.

CROWN GLASS

Whirlpool effect in window glass, deliberately produced from at least the twelfth century, and known more graphically in America as a bull's-eye. Despite its uselessness and its capacity to arouse annoyance it is still being made. Crown glass is a European term for English flint glass.

CURTAIN HOLDER

Sometimes called a hold-back, this was a decorative wall bracket, usually in brass, to hold back curtains at the sides of windows.

CUT GLASS

Glass made brilliant by cutting and polishing, practised by the Romans, but not introduced into England until the early eighteenth century. The practice was hampered by stern excise duties on glass, although Irish cut glass, not subject to tax, flourished. Expertise reached its peak in the nineteenth century, when cut glass could be razor sharp.

CUT-WORK EMBROIDERY

Dating at least from Elizabethan times, this involves cutting away fabric with the hole filled with geometrical patterns worked with needle and thread.

CYLINDER BUREAU*

The use of a sliding cylinder or tambour (fillets of wood connected horizontally by material) was a late-eighteenth century option to the hinged fall-front of the traditional bureau. It made the manufacture more complex (because the cylinder or tambour had to slide somewhere), but the object was marginally less useful because of the smaller writing surface. Eventually it led to the roll-top desk, larger and more functional if not so pretty.

DAVENPORT

An important Staffordshire pottery, founded in 1793. In 1820 porcelain was made as well as pottery. The firm, which also ventured into glass manufacture, was notable for its attractive blue-and-white pottery and its Imari-style ware. It was very prominent in the production of ironstone. After the 1830s it took its style from the less 'cottage' Derby factory.

DAVENPORT

Custom-built for a Captain Davenport in the 1790s, this desk with its forty-five versions is a cabinet with a writing slope, but all kinds of extras have been added, including pop-up sections, hidden compartments, slide-out compartments for the ink, and often a brass or wood gallery. Sometimes the desk top overlaps the base, and is connected with a plinth or the feet by elaborate pillars in the form of classical columns, nicely turned uprights, or an extravagant cabriole leg. A characteristic of the traditional Davenport is the set of real drawers down one side and a set of dummy drawers down the other. The highest-quality and perhaps more quirkish Davenports can top £5,000. A mean type of Davenport was made towards the end of the nineteenth century with a Davenport-style top and open base.

DAY-BED

A narrow bed with head, with or without a foot piece, with or without back, resembling a settee and introduced to England from Italy. A form of day-bed was made up of two chairlike sections with a stool between; others had two similar sections, one of which had an extension seat. In the nineteenth century the classical couch with outward-scroll ends was fashionable, and the *chaise longue* can be interpreted as a day-bed.

DECANTERS

First called serving bottles or jugs, decanters were introduced to Britain towards the end of the seventeenth century, before which wine was served straight from the bottle. Early eighteenth-century decanters had straight octagonal sides, and a tall neck, sometimes tapering, and about 1720 decanter bodies became indented (to expose the greatest area of glass to the ice in the wine-cooler). In the 1740s the 'shaft and globe' shape became fashionable, featuring a spheroid body and a long slim neck, and the glass was sometimes engraved, those with the name of the wine being especially collected. In the 1750s shouldered decanters, widest at the shoulders with a tapering base, came into vogue, and opaque and coloured glass with elaborate gilding and enamelling was used alongside plain glass. The mallet decanters of the 1760s onwards are self-descriptive, as are the 'Indian club' decanters of the same period. The most popular decanter throughout the nineteenth century, and even today, has what is known as a 'Prussian' body, with rings on the fairly short neck, and a mushroom-shaped cut stopper, though more typical of the nineteenth century were the heavy cut-glass decanters, often of massive proportions. About 1865 globular decanters with shallow depressions cut into the glass became fashionable, as did overlay glass (layers of coloured glass with areas cut to reveal the underlying colours). With the various artistic movements towards the end of the nineteenth century, there were a number of curious designs, with semiprecious stones inlaid into the glass and fancy silver handles and mounts. These were often one-offs, made to commission, a reaction against mass-produced pressed glass. Art nouveau decanters were not a success, but during the 1920s and 1930s the cocktail-party age resulted in some very dramatic angular and modernistic decanters, sometimes in bold contrasting colours. Ships' decanters are weighty with a wide bottom. Every antique dealer has a drawerful of decanter stoppers of all shapes and sizes, for decanters are apt to lose their stoppers or to acquire those that 'nearly fit'. Some are even jammed in with tissue paper. A slightly lop-sided decanter may indicate that a chip has been ground off. Interior stains may or may not come out; there is no infallible cure, though some swear by whisking lead shot around inside.

DELFTWARE

Earthenware coated with a lead glaze made opaque by the addition of tin ashes, named after Delft in Holland which in the seventeenth cen-

tury was an important centre for these products. Delftware was an attempt to reproduce Chinese blue-and-white porcelain in something that was not porcelain, but soon a distinctive Dutch style emerged. Delft also produced other ware in all styles, but it was mostly derivative, and eventually returned to just tin-glazed earthenware. Delftware (capital D) was made at Delft; delftware (small D) was made in most western countries.

DEMI-COMMODE

A commode being a chest of drawers, this was half a chest of drawers, made in the eighteenth century, and resembling a table with drawers beneath. It was sometimes designed to go with pier-glasses.

DERBY

From about 1750 the Derby factory was mainly concerned with making porcelain figures. The early potting was somewhat clumsy, but the decoration was superb, and from the start there was an emphasis on the ornamental rather than

18th-century delftware vase, possibly made in London.

Derby plate with hand-painted decoration.

88

the functional, with openwork baskets and pierced dishes and plates. Unlike most of the early English factories, Derby made comparatively little blue-and-white china. Amongst the products associated with the early years of Derby are rectangular butter tubs, covered salts and sauce-boats in the form of leaves. In 1770 Derby took over Chelsea, which became a decorating establishment. Although Chelsea-orientated work was made, with increasing influence of Sèvres, the proportion of useful wares produced by Derby increased, and the standard of porcelain improved. The firm had several owners, with consequent changes of emphasis, and in the early nineteenth century there was a phase in which poor-quality bone china was produced with Japanese-style patterns, with heavy colour and lavish gilding. Figures were reissued from earlier moulds. The firm closed in 1848. The present Royal Crown Derby Porcelain Company was formed in 1876. Its Imari-type ware was meant to be magnificent, and is.

DESK

The classic desk for hard sustained usage is the pedestal desk, two pedestals resting on a plinth rather than on feet with a capacious drawered top; when very large it is termed a partner's desk. While most pieces of furniture have undergone change, the pedestal desk has changed little since the middle of the eighteenth century except in the matter of drawer front design and the style of the handles. Most Victorian desks were of oak or mahogany, so those in other woods are more highly valued today. Towards the end of the nineteenth century there was a fashion for carved oak desks, with lion masks acting as pull-out handles, and with carved oak there is often a desire for complexity. So instead of a simple plinth-based pedestal, each pedestal was cut short and terminated in four legs, often with melon-type carving. Knee-hole desks, often used as dressing-tables and vice versa, are of less general utility, some of them being kidney-shaped, and tending to merge with the roll-top desk. During the Edwardian period there were some curious hybrids, neither a pedestal desk nor a writing-table but somehow a kind of dressing-table that has gone wrong. High desks, as used in banks or offices, are usually without much ornament, and the same

applies to children's desks. There is a very ambiguous area between desks and writing-tables.

DIE-STAMPING

For shaping objects between male and female dies, used from the sixteenth century to ornament items, and invaluable for the cheap production of buttons, furniture accessories such as mounts, medals, coins, etc, and from 1769 hollow household utensils such as saucepans. Cheaper than casting.

DINING-ROOM GLASSWARE

The dining tables of the seventeenth, eighteenth and nineteenth centuries glittered with silver, often complemented by the glass, whether drinking glasses, often of the most elaborate kind, decanters, winebottles, or the containers such as the salad bowl, a large circular or boat-shaped cut-glass bowl made since the late eighteenth century, sometimes on a stand, often with three feet. Salad servers were in silver or silverplate, and comprised a large spoon and a fork in the form of a cut-out spoon with prongs. The finger-bowl, for dipping fingers in at the dining-table, was usually of clear glass, but also made in purple, blue, red and green. The most used glass accessories were perhaps cruets, bottles for condiments in a cruet frame, made since the eighteenth century with open rings and central or side handles, sometimes with small raised feet. Later forms of the frames were oblong or boat-shaped. Cruets date from the seventeenth century. Bottles were mallet shape until about 1775, then cylindrical with a tapered neck for a short period, then urn shaped. Most bottles are translucent, but in the mid-eighteenth century opaque white bottles were made, as well as enamelled examples with bird and foliage decorations. The comport was a large glass round-topped stand with a substantial stem usually mounted on flared feet, popular from the eighteenth century onwards and intended for jelly or as syllabub glasses. Comports were also made in ceramics. There were also decorative centre pieces in glass, often with a vague functional use, or purely intended to reflect the light, such as the vases with hanging lustres. Mirrors, called plateaux, were placed beneath centre-pieces to add even more glitter.

The standish was a tray or box-like object now usually called an inkstand, used from the sixteenth century, its contents varying with changing writing technology but likely to include an ink pot, sand or cuttlefish powder (for sprinkling on the wet ink from a pounce box), a wafer box, sealing-wax, a taper stick (for melting wax) and quill pens. There was usually a penknife to cut the quills, and sometimes there was accommodation for a small bell. Standishes were made in most metals including gold and silver. The inkwell or ink pot of the seventeenth century was capstan-shaped, with a wide base tapering to a narrow neck, usually made of silver or pewter. The top was usually hinged and the ink was customarily contained in a removable china well. Office inkstands of the nineteenth century were often in the shape of a squat cylinder set on a disc with holes for the pens around the rim. Until about 1825 the quill was the standard writing instrument, and 33 million goose quills were imported in 1832. In 1810 the Bank of England alone was using more than a million a year; it is estimated that a clerk got through five a day. Quills could be resharpened with a penknife. The use of metal nibs was anticipated in 1822 when quills were cut into appropriate pieces and inserted into a penholder. A form of metal nib was first used in 1825, and in the Great Exhibition of 1851 there was an early form of fountain pen in glass, using capillary action, which was not proceeded with on a commercial scale. Early pen-nibs easily rusted, and children and young ladies made penwipers using half a dozen small circular felt mats stitched together. More sophisticated penwipers incorporated an upward-facing brush, set on a novelty stand: the shot pot was a glass bottle with a wide neck filled with lead sporting shot, into which the pen-nib was prodded. The penholder, which held the nib, could be wood, ivory, bone, or other materials, sometimes intricately carved and decorated, and could incorporate a paper opener or knife·or a pencil at the other end. Many had a cork section near the nib to keep the fingers free of ink. Rulers could be flat, usually made of boxwood, or round and made of ebony: they are still available for a pound or two and sought out by furniture restorers as a cheap source of ebony.

A silver-plated inkstand with cricketing interest, with the ink pots in the form of top hats.

DINING-ROOM SILVER

One of the great transformations took place in the eighteenth century. Civilised behaviour became the norm rather than the exception. This showed in many ways; in greater deference to women, in a new standard of elegance in furniture and furnishings, and in dining habits. It had not been many years since guests had brought their own basic cutlery, often just a knife stuck down the sock. Cutlery had evolved in a haphazard fashion, and only in the eighteenth century did knives, forks and spoons begin to match. Some of the dining-room silver was from a previous age, but some was new. Among the recent arrivals was the Argyle, a gravy server in the shape of tea- or coffee-pot with an inner container for hot water, thus keeping the gravy warm. The handle was usually at right-angles to the spout. Silver experts say that no mustard-pot exists prior to 1760. Before this date mustard was usually in powder form, and, like pepper, contained in casters. The first pots were 'blind', meaning that although the design for the piercing was engraved on the silver, the piercing was not carried through. The insides could be gilded, or there could be a blue glass liner. Mustard-pots could be in any shape – vase, oval, round, oblong.

Casters had been made from the end of the seventeenth century and came in sets of three.

A silver part table service, London 1853, comprising 17 each table forks, dessert forks, teaspoons, 18 dessert spoons, 8 table spoons, 6 salt spoons, 5 coffee spoons, 4 sauce ladles, 2 mustard spoons, one basting spoon, one butter knife, a sifter spoon and a pair of sugar tongs.

Up to about 1705 casters were cylindrical but in the early eighteenth century the pear shape was adopted, with the octagonal shape sometimes used. About 1715 the upper part of the body became concave and remained so until about 1745. The bun shape was also popular. About 1745 the lower part of the body developed a double curve, a feature that remained until the end of the century. In the same group as casters were salts. Early silver salt-cellars were prestige objects, which stood before the head of the household, though the salt container itself was small. Prior to 1700 salts were 'trencher' types (made from one piece) with a central depression for the salt and a skirt to the table, almost in ink-well shape. After 1700 octagonal trencher salts were popular, and between 1735 and 1785 circular three-legged salts, sometimes decorated with lion masks and elaborate feet, were used. About 1760 the pierced oval salt with a blue liner became fashionable, and has continued to be so. Boat-shaped salts appeared in 1785, followed by oblong tub salts.

Typical of the larger silver containers were

soup tureens. Originating from the 1730s, silver soup tureens were always very lavishly decorated, sometimes adorned with a design depicting the ingredients used, though the decoration was nearly always applied so that the inside presents a smooth surface for cleaning. A popular later design was the boat shape with elegant fluting and no legs. Elegant oval tureens with legs appeared about 1805. After 1730 sauce-boats were smaller, with handles opposite to the lips, made with a minimum of decoration and almost without change until about 1780 when sauce tureens (much like small soup tureens) became popular. There was a diversion for a time in the form of the helmet sauce-boat.

Vegetable and entree dishes were plain, and rarely seen before about 1760. The soufflé dish was in two parts, with the inner part for the oven and the ornate outer part, with two handles and three or four feet, for the table. The mazarine was a pierced dish for fitting in a larger dish and acting as a strainer. Serving spoons had an oval bowl, occasionally pierced, the earlier examples having a tubular stem and a finial at the end, though later serving spoons had patterns related to those of ordinary smaller spoons. These are one of the many utensils that have changed little over the years and bear alternative names, such as basting spoon and hash spoon. Silver dinner plates were made from about 1730 to 1820, when they fell out of use. These can be plain or shaped, and match other dining articles such as meat dishes and serving dishes, which were mostly oval. Some meat dishes, often called venison dishes, had a well at one end for the gravy and a ribbed base forming a cross, usually on two small feet with the depression caused by the gravy well acting as a third foot.

With the kitchens some distance from the dining-rooms, great efforts were made to keep food warm. The hot-water plate was a shallow covered silver or silverplated container of oval, round, or rectangular form, with an aperture so that it could be filled with hot water. The plate or dish was placed on top. Certain items were cooked at the table. The egg boiler was a metal container, usually cylindrical or ovoid, with handles at the side and a spirit-lamp beneath, between the feet. Eggs were placed in a frame inside. For easy access the lid was often in the form of hinged flaps. Fish was much eaten. The fish knife, used from the early nineteenth century,

had a blunt scimitar-shape blade with a haft of bone, ivory, or mother-of-pearl. There were several types of fish servers, one with two blades with a spring attachment so that it could grip, and a fish slice with matching fork. The fish slice was often intricately engraved and pierced, with a shaped blade and an often ornate ivory or silver handle. In the nineteenth century the fish slice could conform in pattern with the rest of the cutlery.

Among the smaller silver items used at table were grape scissors, which may look like ordinary scissors or proclaim their identity by vine-leaves on the handles, asparagus tongs, similar to large sugar-tongs, and the marrow scoop, a utensil with an elongated bowl and a narrow hollowed-out stem for extracting the marrow from bones. The sucket was a utensil with a spoon at one end and a fork at the other, usually quite plain with a flattish stem. It was made for succade, fruit that was candied or preserved in syrup. Knife rests were trestles connected by an axle. Glass knife rests were in the shape of dumb-bells, usually of cut glass but sometimes of coloured glass.

Sometimes called a slider, the coaster moved drinks on the dining table, fitted with small wheels or a baize-covered base. It was circular with a raised gallery, and sometimes had a wooden base. The galleries were often pierced or engraved, and there were circular rings cut into the surface of the coaster to keep the bottle or decanter stable in movement. The waiter was a salver, coming in all shapes and sizes, with variations on the square an early favourite. Armorial designs were usually the only adornment on eighteenth-century waiters, though the borders could vary enormously. Waiters and salvers were later far more ornate.

Drinking of course had its own dining-room silver. The wassail bowl was a two-handled bowl passed around the table for each person to drink from. The punch-bowl was usually wide and deep, resting on a plain foot rim, with handles that were often of the ring type. After 1730 they were more elaborate, frequently embossed with fluting, often supplied with a tray. They were also made in pottery and porcelain, sometimes decorated with nautical or hunting subjects. The punch ladle had a deep bowl, circular, oval, or shell shaped, sometimes with pouring lip. Handles could be of wood, bone, or ivory. Some punch ladles were made from silver coins hammered into shape. The quaitch was a Scottish drinking bowl of the seventeenth and eighteenth centuries, circular in form, fairly shallow, with two or three flat handles. The Monteith was a large bowl with a notched or scalloped rim intended to cool wine glasses, held by their feet in the notches, bowl down in cold water or ice. It was also made in ceramics. Most dining-room silver was made in Sheffield plate when it became available, and in electroplate in the mid-nineteenth century. Shapes did not change very much, though there was more decoration.

DOLLS

Dolls with jointed limbs date back to classical times, and there was little adventure until the seventeenth century. Dolls were among the trinkets brought to America by the colonists to barter with the natives, and records of these transactions go back to 1585. Eighteenth-century dolls were formalistic, and the so-called Queen Anne type have gesso plaster over a wooden head and prominent bulging glass eyes (without pupils). They have survived mainly because of lavish costuming. A doll could have several outfits and a large number of accessories, such as fans. In 1780 the wax doll appeared in England, introduced by an Italian, the family of whom supplied dolls to a London store until the 1930s. The Dutch or peg doll evolved in Georgian times, delicate and nicely painted, popular for many decades, with changing hairstyles (a centre parting came in in the 1840s perhaps in deference to the young Queen Victoria who favoured that style). Pedlar dolls came surrounded by their wares in miniature, and many trades were represented including haberdashers, fruiterers, flower girls, milliners, sometimes with accompanying men. Lively and naive, pedlar dolls are much faked. The most sophisticated dolls were made in France from the 1860s, with heads of porcelain, Parian china, or bisque. These were adults in miniature, but about 1880 there was a fashion for dolls depicting babies and young children, thus the name 'bébés'. The Germans entered the lucrative doll market in the 1870s, considered somewhat inferior to French makers, though making and exporting more because of better organisa-

Late 19th-century Armand Marseille doll made in Germany.

tion and more up-to-date production methods. Character dolls modelled on real children appeared, as did 'piano babies', portrayed crawling, lying down, or seated in natural poses. American 'kewpies', are similar, a corruption of cupids. Celluloid was very much used for early twentieth century dolls before being superseded by the huge range of plastics.

DOLLS HOUSES

Dolls' houses, formerly known as baby houses, predate 1600. The most familiar have a front consisting of a hinged door that swings away to reveal a series of boxes that form the rooms. Some were commissioned by the rich as miniatures of their own houses, with furniture to size. The best furniture was made from walnut, mahogany, and rosewood, and was jointed not glued, and precious items, such as the lids of enamel boxes, were used as pictures. Contemporary wallpaper was made in miniature, a useful dating guide. Dolls' houses for the mass market were made of cardboard with paper printed with bricks, tiles and slates pasted on the exterior. American children had brownstone houses, sand sprinkled onto a gummed surface. Miniature kitchens were made in the seventeenth century in Nuremberg, with fine metal work, meat carved from wood or moulded in plaster. Toy grocers' shops were used in America for promoting products with branded goods in small packs, bottles, and cans. Toy banks, post offices, railway booking offices, and garages followed, with many ingenious accessories, such as paper money, coins, stamps, tickets, and stationery, and these were regarded by parents, quite rightly, as valuable educational tools.

DOMESTIC CLOCKS

The first domestic clock was made from iron and known as a Gothic clock, a small-scale version of the church tower clock, mounted in a open-work frame. This was succeeded by the lantern clock, popular throughout the seventeenth century, mostly of brass, with a bell on top which gave the appearance of a helmet. It was weight-driven, wound up by a chain or a cord, and ran

Combination furniture was always regarded with amusement, but the clock that turns into a bed was not a possibility.

for about thirty hours between windings. It was known variously as a birdcage, a bedpost, or a Cromwellian clock. The first truly portable clock was the bracket clock, which not surprisingly had no bracket but carrying handles. Clocks were rare and they were transported from room to room when wanted. This was the standard clock of the late seventeenth and eighteenth centuries, spring-driven with pendulum and incorporating striking, alarm, and repeating mechanisms. Designs followed those of the long-case clock, with the sequence of woods — ebony, mock-ebony, marquetry, walnut, lacquer, and mahogany. Apart from the long-case clock, the fixed clock was the mantel clock, which came at a time when clocks were more common and there was no need to carry a bracket clock around. It remained a very timid object in Britain, but in France it became a major work of art in buhl (tortoiseshell and brass), ormolu, porcelain, enamel, bronze, marble and most other substances, with wood the poor relation. Chariots and horses, Venuses

THE ERA OF COMBINATION FURNITURE.
The Latest Thing in Folding Beds for Single Gentlemen.

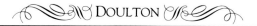

and Cupids, Napoleons in all moods, classical figures, all were incorporated in a complex mechanism that sometimes dispensed with the dial in favour of a rotating sphere with the hours marked on a circling band. The most famous mantel clock is the lyre clock, in the shape of a lyre, sometimes with a sunburst design on top. The culmination in show clocks was the garniture, or clock set, with the clock flanked by two ornate pieces in the same style. The nineteenth century had domestic clocks for every pocket; reproductions in cheap materials such as spelter and slate, wooden clocks from Germany and the United States, skeleton clocks where the framework was made from metal struts and the wheels were pierced to allow everything to be seen, exhibition clocks where the dial and movement were buried in a mass of inconsequentials, quaint clocks for the Arts and Crafts and art nouveau movements, culminating in the gimmick clocks of the twentieth century, sometimes incorporated into other objects. The most prolific clock perhaps of them all was the chiming oak mantel clock. Every surburban home had one, accurate, unpretentious and reliable.

Doulton Lambeth jardinière and two vases decorated in her inimitable style by Hannah Barlow and made sometime between 1880 and 1892.

DOOR FURNITURE

Term applied to anything that could go on or near a door, the most obvious being door knockers, finger-plates, escutcheons, doorstops, letter-boxes, knobs and handles, and perhaps bell-pushes as well. The most interesting is the door knocker, the earlier ones being of iron, often massive and in the shape of animal or human heads, sometimes matching the handles. Door porters were made in cast iron from the eighteenth century in the form of figures or half-bells, often with handles. Doorstops is a term strictly applied to glass balls up to six inches (15cm) high with a flattened base. Finger-plates could be very decorative, in almost any material, from ceramic to bronze, and during the eighteenth century were made by Wedgwood and other famous firms.

DOULTON

In 1815 John Doulton and John Watts established a firm at Vauxhall where they made salt-glazed stoneware, bottles, mugs and jugs with relief portrayals of windmills, hunting scenes, drinkers, etc. In 1826 they moved to Lambeth, where they later branched out into the ever-growing market for drain-pipes, lavatories, and chemical and sanitary ware of all kinds, while

still producing decorative and household articles. In 1877 another firm was taken over in Burslem for the production of good-quality domestic pottery, and in 1884 a new wing was added for the production of bone china. Amongst the most celebrated products was salt-glazed stoneware with incised decorations by individual artists, such as Hannah Barlow, who were allowed to sign their own names. This arose from an amazing co-operation between art schools and the pottery in 1864 when Doulton built an extension to the Lambeth works. Figures in naturalistic style, from miniatures to the huge, were also produced. Doulton was a pioneer experimenter in unusual glazes known by such names as *rouge flambé* and *sang-de-boeuf*, and the adventurous examples set encouraged young potters including the Martin Brothers. Doulton began producing faience (majolica) in 1872, with a warm earthenware body, and some pieces were painted overall with ornament based on Persian and sixteenth-century Italian originals. Royal Doulton is today often as-

The layout of a country-house kitchen in 1927. Of special interest is the complete dinner and tea service on the very low-quality dresser. The bread and flour enamel containers are now becoming collectable items.

sociated with the range of porcelain figures produced since 1913, of which there are more than 2,000 different models.

DOUTERS

Scissor-like objects with arms terminating in flat discs used to put out candles and known from the fifteenth century in silver, brass, and iron.

DRAM GLASSES

Known as nips, joeys, ginettes and gin glasses, these are very small tumblers used from the seventeenth until the nineteenth centuries and resemble elongated egg-cups.

DRAWING INSTRUMENTS

Usually in a cased set comprising dividers, compasses – sometimes several of different sizes – pens, rulers, protractors, etc. Presentation sets were made with silver or gold cases, but most sets are encased in leather or wood.

DRESSER

The dresser originated from the livery cupboard where the livery or portion of food for overnight

consumption by the master of the house was kept. The steward would fetch food and 'dress' it (prepare it) and serve. Dressers can have a superstructure or not. Many seventeenth-century dressers consisted merely of banks of drawers supported by stout legs, turned at the front, square at the back. Topless dressers continued, some sophisticated with cabriole legs. The superstructure of shelves came into general use about 1700. Whereas most 'country' furniture derived from London models, the dresser was evolved and developed in the country, often in what were remote places, such as Wales, where magnificent specimens were made. Because dresser-making communities were widespread there was endless variation; for example, cupboards in the superstructure of Welsh dressers disappeared, but across the border in Shropshire they remained. The pine dresser was mainly Welsh, though most dressers were made of oak, even the eighteenth-century architectural types. As with country chairs, certain types of dressers are described in terms of their origin or the disposition of shelving, cupboards and drawers, such as Cumberland dressers, Lancashire dressers, Anglesey dressers. Many of the dressers of the early eighteenth century were so sparing of ornament that, if signs of wear are ignored, they can be taken for Arts and Crafts dressers of the late nineteenth and early twentieth centuries. However, furniture-makers of these periods often preferred to adventure into reproduction, often bizarre and tasteless, with mean geometric moulding and 'old oak' panels.

DRESSING CHEST

A low chest of drawers, sometimes with a mirror on the underside of the lid, with perhaps a knee-hole front.

DRINKING GLASSES

The great age of English drinking glasses began in the 1670s when the secret of making clear glass was discovered. By 1695 there were 47 glass houses to cater for the demand. There is immense variety, with more than a dozen different types of stem, each subdivided. The stems often have protuberances known as knops, which come in various shapes and sizes each with their own names, as do the bowls. Among the best-known stem types is the air twist, spirals of air introduced into the stem, made by puncturing the molten glass. Opaque white glass could be incorporated into these spirals. Bowls could be plain, engraved, or stippled with dots. The decoration could be decorative, informative (telling the drinker what the glass was meant to hold – an apple design indicated cider), or political. Typical was the ale glass, a long narrow glass for serving ale, sometimes engraved with a hop or barley motif. The Jacobite glasses 1720–50 (much faked) had messages promoting Bonnie Prince Charlie. In 1745 the Glass Excise Act, supplemented in 1777 and 1787, made glass expensive, encouraging smaller lighter vessels and the migration of glass-makers to Ireland where there was no tax until 1825. Towards the end of the eighteenth century drinking vessels became heavier and the style of engraving became almost furrowing, with diamond shapes in high relief, brought to a pitch in the nineteenth century with 'prickly monstrosities', the triumph of cut glass. The introduction of moulded glass much affected individualistic glass-making, and the repeal of the Excise Act in 1845 made opulent drinking glasses available to all.

DRUG POTS

Sometimes called apothecary jars, these were intended for apothecaries' shelves and contained medicaments. Mostly made from delft since the seventeenth century, these could be vase-shaped, squat, globular or bottle-shaped for liquids; they could be plain, adorned with stripes, or have the name of the contents within a cartouche or fancy border. Polychrome designs featuring foliage appeared slightly later.

DUMB WAITER

This can have several meanings, including a stand with two or three circular surfaces of diminishing size around a central upright with tripod, or more rarely four-footed, base; a type with rectangular trays and four legs that stood at the end of the table; and a large revolving circular table-top on a square base which stood on the table, sometimes called a 'Lazy Susan'. Dumb waiters date from the eighteenth century and are customarily in mahogany.

DUMMY BOARD FIGURES

Introduced from Holland about 1620, and intended to hide an open fire when not in use, dummy board figures were life-sized figures of men, women and children realistically painted in contemporary, exotic, or mythological dress and distributed around the house to confuse the drunken and exasperate the servants, and often fitted with staples and hooks so that they could be attached to the wall at a distance of six inches (15cm) and throw realistic shadows. Dummy board figures were also features of tea-gardens, taverns, and pleasure grounds, and a favourite design was that of a sailor dancing the hornpipe. A sideline lay in dummy board dogs and cats, jugs and glasses, and bread and cheese, and dummy board figures were used outside shops as advertisements, kilted Highlanders representing the dealers in tobacco and snuff. Early dummy boards were made from oak and pine and were usually an inch (250mm) thick, but more fashionable woods such as mahogany were used in the eighteenth century, and the width of the wood was reduced to half an inch (125mm). Teak was employed for weather-resistant outside figures. A kind of dummy board figure was revived in the 1920s and 1930s, with the page-boy a popular design.

DUTCH FURNITURE

The importance of Dutch furniture is impossible to overemphasise. Joined panelling had been developed by 1400, important in making furniture lighter in construction and looks, linenfold decoration on panels was introduced soon afterwards, and the Dutch were among the first to reject carved oak in favour of marquetry and veneer. All these innovations greatly influenced English furniture, and especially significant was a series of Flemish furniture designs published in 1580 and widely available in England, where furniture was at a low ebb brought on by native insularity and prejudice. In 1660, with the restoration of the monarchy in England, Holland supplied England with trained craftsmen to teach English apprentices. The supremacy of Dutch furniture was partly due to the power of guilds, which enforced strict standards and disciplines. Important items in the seventeenth century were cabinets with a multitude of drawers, perhaps derived from Spanish models as the relationship between Spain and the Low Countries had always been close, and arched cupboards. Walnut and ebony were favourite woods, and rosewood was used extensively, unlike in England where it only appeared in quantity in the early nineteenth century. Seventeenth-century Holland, being a wealthy maritime power, could afford the best, both in materials and craftsmanship, and typical of the work was inlaying black marble with mother-of-pearl, the kind of technique only employed when simpler contrasts were commonplace. In 1685 refugees from French oppression fled to Holland and England, and French influences appeared. However, the new look of English furniture was also important, and the bureau bookcase made its appearance in Holland, while English chairs were shamelessly copied. Yet Dutch cabinet-makers still gloried in their expertise in serpentine and bombé fronts and in startling use of natural veneer figuring, and were still using motifs taken not only from their European neighbours but from trading partners in the Far East. In 1771 import of all foreign furniture was forbidden at the behest of the guilds. The Dutch cabinet-makers, thus left with the field free, enjoyed great prosperity, and created their own form of neo-Classicism despite their baroque traditions. Unlike the English, the Dutch incorporated lacquer and enamel panels into their furniture, including table-tops. The English Regency and French Empire styles had their parallels in Holland, with light colour woods fashionable (as in Germany). There was a tendency towards informality and simplicity, followed, as elsewhere, by revivalism and the mass-production of the second-rate, helped by the fact that the powerful furniture-making guilds had been abolished early in the nineteenth century.

EARLY EMBROIDERY

Stumpwork was a type of needlework in which some or all of the surface decoration was raised into relief on a foundation of wool or cotton wool, very popular until the seventeenth century. Crewel work was embroidery in thin worsteds, a term applied to the curtains and bed hangings of the second part of the seventeenth century, the designs being based on printed cottons imported into Britain. The 'Tree of Life' with waving branches was the most popular. The embroidery was multi-coloured or green, which has faded to a muted blue. Black work was Elizabethan embroidery worked in black silk on linen, used on pillow-covers, nightcaps, and bodices etc, often in conjunction with gold thread. It was sometimes called Spanish work, as it was believed the style originated in Spain. Much of the embroidery before the seventeenth century was lavish and had a three-dimensional quality, and often incorporated beads.

EARTHENWARE

The term applied to basic pottery, fired only until the particles jell together, the colours depending on the clay used, and not waterproof until glazed or fired at a high temperature.

EBONISING

Staining of wood to make it look like ebony, fashionable with the woodwork of early long-case clocks, (pear wood was often used), used for other pieces, and a craze in the nineteenth century when all kinds of furniture was ebonised, often in association with gilding. The wood used was usually close-grained. An ebonising effect can be obtained by using brown shoe polish.

EGG-CUP

One of the traditional starters for young collectors, egg-cups offer great scope. The hourglass shape has remained unaltered since at least the seventeenth century, whether in silver, pottery, porcelain, or other materials, but novelty egg-cups have been made in startling variety, as railway trains, as elephants, and indeed almost anything. The most interesting and valuable egg-cups are probably those produced by the great eighteenth-century manufacturers such as Bow, with delicate moulded decoration. Egg-

Mid-Victorian Aesthetic-style ebonised credenza with amboyna and walnut, demonstrating that ebonising could be used with stunning effect.

cups were often made in sets, and presented in an egg frame, which could be in the form of a cruet or as a novelty, such as a brooding hen.

EGGSHELL

A type of porcelain of very thin body, often white translucent, much seen in modern Japanese porcelain tea-services, which often have pictures built into the bottoms of cups, only seen by holding the cups to the light, and in quality at the opposite extreme to fine Chinese porcelain of the eggshell type made as early as the fifteenth century. Eggshell porcelain was made in English factories, including Minton in the nineteenth century. It is finished on a lathe.

ELECTROPLATING

Silver coating deposited on a base metal by electrolysis, patented by G. R. Elkington in 1840, and creating silver-like objects at little cost, rendering all other plating methods obsolete overnight. The same process applies to electrogilding.

ENAMELLED BOXES

Enamel is glass melted with metallic oxides as colouring agents, powdered and fused onto suitable surfaces such as gold, copper, ceramics and glass. Known in ancient times, there are various methods. *Champlevé* enamelling consists of a metal base cut away to leave troughs in which enamel paste is placed and fused; *cloisonné* involves the laying down on a ground of thin metal strips forming a grid, and the enamel is placed in these 'cells.' A variation, *plique-à-jour*, is where the base is removed after firing, leaving miniature coloured windows. *Basse-taille* enamelling is applying enamel over a base engraved in low relief. The English enamelled boxes were produced between 1750 and 1840, and were a more homely version of those made by jewellers and goldsmiths especially in France in enamel on gold. On English boxes a special paste was applied to thin sheet copper, fired, and the painting was carried out freehand or on a transfer-printed outline. Some of the work was clumsy and naive, some splendid and most professional. The most famous boxes were produced at Battersea between 1753 and 1756, and

they are therefore few in number, but are characterised by deep lustrous colouring. The boxes were round, oval, or rectangular and were made for snuff, patches, powder, or indeed any small object. Most of the boxes of this period were made in the Midlands, especially Bilston, Wednesbury and Birmingham, and the designers took their inspiration from books of engravings, motifs on china, and, of course, life. French pastoral scenes were very popular. Some boxes were in strange shapes such as swans, heads of dogs, and exotic figures. Boxes with extra pictures inside the lid and on the base carry a premium, as do those with 'secret' erotic scenes in an inner lid. Towards the end of the enamelled box period there was a coarsening of taste and a more slipshod approach, catering for the burgeoning seaside tourist trade. The colouring is pastel sweet, and there is a concentration on mottoes; 'A Trifle from . . .' followed by the name of the town is the most common type. Others bear sentimental messages. However, even the majority of these were 'hand done', unlike later imitations and forgeries where the whole picture was transfer-printed (look for the individual dots under a magnifying glass). Some of the fakes by the celebrated forger Samson are on a par with the originals, and have a collectability of their own. A clue lies in the use by Samson of details that would have been anachronistic perhaps eighty years earlier. Later continental boxes, which can be confused with the earlier English boxes, can be spotted because the central part of the three-piece hinge protrudes slightly whereas the English hinges were flat.

ENGINE TURNING

The process in ceramics in which an unfired article has geometrical or other repeating patterns bitten into the surface using a special lathe. A similar action is also carried out by silversmiths and goldsmiths on boxes and watches and other suitable articles. A degree of mathematical precision can be produced impossible by freehand engraving.

EPERGNE

Ornate and often complex and elaborate silver or plated centre-piece on the dining-table, with a variety of fittings such as bread and cake baskets, dishes, and condiment holders, vase-like containers and often candle sockets. During the nineteenth century it became a display piece rather than a functional object, with much use of elaborate filigree, a profusion of cut glass, and the use of coloured glass.

ÉTAGÈRE

Originally of French design, consisting of two or three graduated tiers, usually oval, supported by ornate pillars. They were often made in tulipwood, kingwood and inlaid satinwood, and were rich in ormolu. The term was often applied to the English whatnot.

ETCHING

Using acid to incise pattern on metal or glass. The surface is coated with wax or a similar substance, the design is drawn through exposing the surface, and acid is applied. First used probably to decorate armour, it was later used to make etchings, later still on glass and silver.

ETHNOGRAPHICA

A vast and complex area, including not only African tribal art but the most sophisticated artefacts from the Aztec and Inca civilisations, made at a time when Europe was hardly struggling out of the Dark Ages. African objects are among the best known because they were brought to Europe as plunder in the nineteenth century, especially by the British, the Belgians, and the French, and all who were establishing colonies in Africa. Missionaries were also a primary source of supply. Many are ceremonial and ritual figures and masks and artefacts to do with magic, often vigorously carved in wood, usually hardwood. Amongst the most interesting are European figures and groups, especially soldiers, carved by native craftsmen. It was believed by natives that if they had an image of their enemies they would be able to control them. Although much tribal art is expressive and finely worked, there is a curious absence of high-class ceramics, accounted for by the fact that the potter's wheel was not known and high temperatures needed for more than basic pottery were not available. Amongst the most widely collected objects are those from Oceania, mainly wooden, and including canoe-prow ornaments, head-rests, weaponry, and 'tikis' – small Maori images, often in greenstone, representing ancestors. An indication of the forthcoming interest in Oceanic ethnographica was supplied more than twenty years ago when the wooden club that killed Captain Cook in Hawaii in 1779 was sold for 1,000 guineas (£1,100), to the astonishment of the auctioneers. In all spheres of ethnographica fakes and forgeries are rampant, though objects which purport to be nineteenth-century (which in this context is antique) are no more than innocent tourist pieces carved in the same way and from the same woods.

ETUI

Small case of leather, tortoiseshell, pinchbeck, enamel, malachite, precious metal, shagreen, and many other materials to contain such items as scissors, snuff spoons, and bodkins. Made since the seventeenth century, and at its best in the eighteenth.

EXHIBITION PIECES

These are objects made especially for exhibitions to give an inflated idea of the range of the makers, who were so successful in promulgating this that later generations were persuaded that such exhibition pieces represented objects, par-

Many exhibition pieces were absurd. This 'Angel cot' was made in cast iron and exhibited at the Great Exhibition of 1851.

101

A piano made from paper mâché and exhibited in the Paris Exhibition of 1867.

ticularly furniture, used in everyday life. This caused problems to historians who could not relate this to what they knew of other aspects of Victorian life. The first major international exhibition was held at the Crystal Palace in 1851, though many of the later ones, such as the Exhibition of 1862, were much larger.

FAIRINGS

Porcelain figures or figure groups produced in Germany for the English market for about forty years between 1860 and the end of the century, usually bearing a saucy or whimsical motto (often spelled wrongly). From 1891 the makers were obliged to affix the legend 'Made in Germany'. Being simple, fairings are often faked; the rarer fairings fetch more than £1,000. The most common fairing is probably 'Last in bed'. Hollow-based fairings, sometimes in unglazed porcelain, were made by copyists.

FAKES AND FORGERIES

The annual turnover in antiques throughout the world is well in excess of £2,500m and it is conservatively reckoned that at least one eighth of that amount is accounted for by fakes. Fakes can be innocent. In China the marks on bronzes were often those of a previous dynasty, put there in homage. A genuine article can have detail added to make it more interesting or useful, and years afterwards these additions can be assumed to be part of the original article. A silver tankard may have a spout put on to turn it into a useful jug without any thought of fraud. A forgery is a deliberate attempt to deceive – but only when the intent is gain. A hobby-forgery only becomes heinous when it is pushed onto the open market. The law provides modest protection.

The Trades Description Act and the Misrepresentation Act are all very well, but an antique or a collectable is not a pound of sugar and in the end it can boil down to the opinion of a so-called expert who may very well be a pipsqueak dredged up from some obscure source who has his or her own axe to grind. The makers of the antiques of the past have often made it easy; potters have left their moulds lying around or let them be taken over by other potteries; they have been casual with their marks, either imitating others or being slapdash with their own, thinking that a quick squiggle is enough. And it was when honesty was the norm. How are fakes and forgeries detected? By knowledge, by being acquainted with the genuine article, by being able to distinguish between the equivalent of butter and margarine. It is important to use all the senses, as well as instinct. Someone who has been dealing with antiques for a long time knows when something is wrong; he or she may not know exactly what it is. It may be a certain lack of proportion in a piece of furniture, it may be a slightly anachronistic mark in silver, it may be a too shiny feel on a piece of porcelain or a too regular pattern of crazing on the surface, or there may be inexplicable wear on the rim of a glass, perhaps an indication that a chip has been ground out. But why shouldn't a chip be ground out? There's the rub. Why shouldn't a broken plate be glued together in such a way that it doesn't show? The only 'crime' is for someone who knows that it has been broken to pretend that it is perfect. Some articles are easier to fake than others, simply because there has been less work put into them. Carved objects are less suspect than moulded objects, intricate pieces are more likely to be genuine than simple ones. The cost of making a genuine-appearing four-poster bed would make the task uneconomical; the amount would probably be as much as the price obtained for the real thing. There is no point in putting out a black list, for everything with potential has been eyed with a view to skullduggery. Of course, this is a challenge. The question to be asked of any antique object is 'Prove to me that you are what you make out you are'. The question not to ask is 'Why are you so cheap?' Knowledge can be spread very thinly – even amongst people whose business is in antiques.

FAMILLE JAUNE

Chinese porcelain in which yellow is used with brownish-black outlining to depict characteristic designs, such as birds, flowers, and dragons.

FAMILLE NOIRE

Chinese porcelain where black covered with an iridescent greenish glaze is the chief colour combination. Not produced in great quantity as it was expensive to make.

FAMILLE ROSE

A predominantly rose-pink ceramic colour used on Chinese eighteenth-century porcelain in association with greens, blues and yellows with white for shading effects. Much appreciated in the West, and the Chinese catered for the demand using European motifs and exporting the ware in bulk from Canton.

'A faithful reproduction of a rare antique'. This claim is from an advertisement of 1923. So rare that no-one has ever seen a corner cabinet with a fall leaf and gate-leg underframe.

FAMILLE VERTE

Pre-dating *famille rose* by many years, a predominantly green colour scheme, in association with yellows, purples and blues and a very dominant iron-red, frequently as powerful as the greens. Gilding was sometimes used.

FANS

There are two types of fan, rigid or screen fan, and folding. The rigid fan dates back to ancient times while the folding fan is Chinese, brought to Europe by the Portuguese in the sixteenth century. The method of construction remained unaltered for centuries – sticks of ivory held together at one end with a pin or rivet, and a pleated leaf mounted on sticks. The first fans seen in Britain in the 1550s were clumsy, made of vellum cut and decorated to simulate lace. The first painted fans appear a century later, and provided work for many talented artists for many years, often on a par with easel painters. The design and picture could spread across the sticks as well. In the early eighteenth century Brisé fans came in, consisting entirely of sticks made from thin ivory and other suitable materials fretted and punched to imitate lace. To keep the fan in one piece, the upper parts of the sticks were connected by ribbon. The Minuet fan is a larger Brisé fan. The pictures on the silk or paper mounts varied enormously, the most popular being French pastoral-type scenes, though references were made to contemporary events and crazes such as ballooning. Advertising fans appeared in about 1750. From about 1770 gold thread, sequins, and netting were incorporated into fans, and from 1840 feather fans were fashionable, followed by a vogue for rigid Japanese and Japanese-type fans. Fans imported from China were known as Mandarin fans. Because of some of the materials used, many old fans turn up in a sorry and, worse, altered and faked state. Gauze and silk are very vulnerable and almost impossible to repair in a satisfactory way. The paper, often handmade in the earlier fan leaves, has worn better. Straw-work was also used, amongst the most vulnerable of all materials. Many fans were meant to be disposable. The sticks, too, are inclined to get broken, and, where a fan structure has collapsed, the leaves can be taken off and perhaps framed.

FEEDING-CUP

Usually a small plain saucepan-like cup with one or two handles and a straight or curved spout, used from the middle of the seventeenth century onwards and designed for feeding children or invalids. It could be made in silver, but later ones are mostly ceramic and of little interest.

FENDERS

Although the fronts of grates had bars to prevent coal from falling out, this was not enough, leading to the evolution of the fender and ash screen, with or without a sheet metal bottom. A fender without a bottom is often referred to as a curb. In the eighteenth century fenders were usually of bright steel, but the Victorians preferred brass or brass with other metals such as copper, and the fenders became very ornate and often massive. Towards the end of the nineteenth century the art nouveau movement produced some outstanding fenders, because it was a shape that lent itself to motifs such as writhing plant forms, tendrils, and the lily. Pewter was often used despite the fact that it has a low melting point. In the 1920s and 1930s the fender was also found to be a convenient vehicle for a display of modish decoration, often in block form and angular. The decoration is often embossed on sheet brass and copper over a frame of wood.

FILIGREE

Lace-like ornament made from gold or silver wire used for many purposes including jewellery, and giving its name to miscellaneous fine work not necessarily involving precious wire or indeed metals of any kind.

FILIGREE PAPER WORK

Narrow strips of parchment or paper rolled in spirals and scrolls, loops and cones, and glued at the edge to a flat surface, then gilded or painted. It was first used in the sixteenth century as a substitute for gold filigree but later taken up as a hobby and used to make panels as a substitute for pictures, to act as a frame, and to adorn other objects such as wax pictures, so that the paper filigree seems to be clothing. The most prolific period was from about 1775 to 1820, when patterns were issued in the ladies' magazines. Small articles such as tea-caddies were made with an open panel intended to be filled with filigree paper, and trays, ink stands, table-tops, fire-screens and even large pieces of furniture were decorated.

FINGER VASE

A vase with five tubular holders arranged like the fingers of a hand, made in the seventeenth century in delft and in the eighteenth in stoneware, and in the twentieth century as an art deco novelty vase.

FIRE BACK

A thick panel of cast iron placed at the back of the fireplace to protect the wall from the heat and to project warmth into the room. Made

As can be seen from the original caption to this early Victorian cartoon, fire-irons were often viewed as decorative objects, highly polished to impress visitors.

from the sixteenth century onwards and decorated in relief with coats-of-arms, mythological subjects and other themes.

FIRE-GUARD

A frame, usually of iron or brass, with a wire mesh to prevent spark damage, used from the seventeenth century. It is in two forms, rectangular and curved, the latter for the smaller fire.

FIRE-IRONS

Tongs, poker, and shovel, often of iron or steel, sometimes of brass. Eighteenth-century examples are larger than those which came later. Twisted-shank fire-irons were introduced in the eighteenth century. The shovel was replaced in modern times by the brush, and the whole hung together in a companion set, often in an inappropriate housing such as a suit of armour.

FIREMARKS

The emblems of insurance and fire offices made in lead and attached to walls of buildings to de-

THE DESECRATION OF THE BRIGHT POKER.
The alarm of a party, principally ancient spinsters, at a gentleman attempting to stir the fire with the sacred steel.

note to the world and to passing fire-engines that the displayers were insured by these self-same companies.

FIREPLACES

The primitive fire was laid on the floor, with a hole through the roof. When the Normans decided to live on the first floor (which was of wood) the fireplace was lodged in the wall, but by the thirteenth century the fire was brought forward, laid on a hearthstone with stone canopy to direct the smoke. The open wood-burning fire, with its attendant fire-backs and firedogs, was the quintessential warming device until the eighteenth century and the widespread use of coal. But in towns and cities where elegance was of the essence, marble was becoming popular, and the chimney-pieces were carved

A curious fireplace and a curious medley, with an array of blue-and-white dishes at odds with the Staffordshire trinkets on the mantelpiece. Notice the curious architectural device of having a fireplace within a fireplace.

with garlands, lion masks, with inlay and painting, and were often in the form of Greek or Roman temple doorways. Wood was also used, often extravagantly carved, with marble as a protective slip near the fire-opening, though this was superseded about 1776 with steel slips. The mantelshelf became a key feature in the chimney-piece, ideal for clocks and vases, and the central tablet below it was exploited. Wedgwood designed blue-and-white jasper cameos, medallions, and bas-reliefs for this space. The earliest chimney-pieces likely to be in circulation are Adam fireplaces of the late eighteenth century, usually of black or white marble, often inlaid with coloured stone, with the use of motifs such as urns, rams' heads, and vase forms. Small rooms had elegant but simple fireplaces. Adam designs were widely published and imitated, often in plaster, glued to wooden chimney-pieces. Scagliola was imitation marble made from lime, gypsum and marble dust, and much used. With the use of coal instead of wood, chimney-pieces could be much smaller, though often they were not, as the fireplace was the focal point of a room throughout the nineteenth century, and the floor area surround-

One of the modest and inoffensive 1920s fireplaces now being taken out and replaced or covered over. But some of these fireplaces can be of high quality with unusual materials and collectors' tiles.

ing the fireplace was widely valued as the best place for easy chairs and all kinds of odds and ends. Fireplaces could be made of any material, but marble was the favourite until the widespread use of coloured tiles in the nineteenth century, both as a surround and to provide a safe surface in front of the grate. Because of the structural quality of fireplaces and the effort needed to replace them, there is a tendency to hide them rather than replace them. If a smaller fireplace is wanted, it is often inset into a larger previous fireplace or aperture, as when a kitchen range is hacked out and replaced by something else. Many 1920s and 1930s tiled fireplaces have been unceremoniously yanked out, and replaced by natural stone, novelty substances, or wallpapered over in all-electric houses. Sometimes these are of high quality.

FITNESS FOR FUNCTION

This is the theory that items which function well and use materials with the maximum economy are necessarily beautiful. And vice versa. It was a philosophical concept propounded in the eighteenth century and elaborated by Emmanual Kant, the German philosopher. Advocates of the Arts and Crafts movement, such as William Morris, occasionally pursued it when they had nothing better to do. A variation on the theme was that of the theoretician Otto Wagner at a lecture in Vienna in 1894 who said that 'Nothing that is not practical can be beautiful'. It was not long before it was decreed that ornament was a crime. These ideas spread like a virus amongst designers of all kinds, especially industrial designers, and a habit was instituted of making objects that satisfied the criteria of the puritanical and austere non-smoking designers rather than the wishes of the users. This was particularly applicable to chairs, which could be stripped down to basics without the object falling apart and which could be made of modern materials such as bent plywood, plastics, and steel. The idea was taken up in a half-baked way by journalists, typified by an article in *Our Homes and Gardens* in April 1920 in which 'bad' articles, such as biscuit tins in the form of books, a log of wood, or a bag of golf clubs were ridiculed ('thoroughly bad boxes from every point of view') and 'wriggly ashtrays and a matchbox holder imitating the markings of crocodile skin' were compared unfavourably with plain boring undecorated objects. The pursuit of fitness for function could be dotty, as in the assertion in the article that glass chemical beakers ('tough and strong, though thin') would 'make very good vases for flowers, and are far more pleasing in shape than most of the vases one sees in the shops.' Much of the fitness-for-function furniture of the 1920s and 1930s is eagerly sought for, not so much for the ethos behind it but because it was well designed, though in some of the furniture there was not much to design. Fitness-for-function household chairs should be, declared the 1920s furniture-maker Percy Wells, strong, comfortable and easy to clean. Functional furniture has remained popular, epitomised by G-plan and Habitat, which are in turn derived from the Utility furniture of World War II and after, made to save materials, remind the buyers that life was hard and earnest, and easy to mass-produce for a consumer who had no other choice.

FLASK

Narrow-necked container of earthenware, leather, silver or pewter, it was often of leather over an inner container, with a silver cap in the case of travelling flasks.

FLAT-IRON

Evolved in the sixteenth century, probably in Holland, and made in brass. These were often ornately engraved and embossed, but those in iron and steel were more functional. The first British box-iron, heated from the inside, was patented in 1738. There were a number of inventions, especially in America, to improve the efficiency of the iron, including bellows. The sad-iron was patented in America in 1870 and had two pointed ends; this was being made until 1953. Although irons have been made in decorative forms including the swan, there is little variety generally, but there is a modest trade in them as doorstops.

FLATBACKS

Earthenware figures, often in matching pairs, mostly made in Staffordshire, and flat because they were meant to be mantelpiece ornaments and seen only from the front. There was a wide variety of folksy subjects, the most popular being the spaniel-type dogs.

FLATWARE

This name is given to sets of forks and spoons, as these objects were made from flat strips of metal. Two-pronged gold or silver forks were used in the Middle Ages for sweetmeats and fruit, and large iron two-pronged forks for meat were made from the fifteenth century. Three-and four-pronged forks came later. Sets of flatware came in with the fashion for elegant eating in about 1660, produced in silver, pewter, Sheffield plate, and electroplate. The patterns have altered over the years, the first being the trifid pattern, followed by the dog-nose, wavy end, and shield-end. The first pattern for which a full service (same maker, same year) was available was the Old English pattern from about 1760. The fiddle pattern (stem and handles shaped like a fiddle) came in about 1805; this evolved into the hourglass pattern with an emphasised waist. The king's pattern was popular and when Queen Victoria came to the thone it led to the queen's pattern; many of these patterns have become standard. About the middle of the nineteenth century genteel behaviour demanded specialised sets – fish services and dessert services (usually gilded to resist fruit acidity). The canteen of cutlery derives from this period. Some services could include sugar-tongs, grape scissors and other knick-knacks. The history of cutlery is the history of social behaviour; the custom of using a large knife and fork for the main course and smaller ones for dessert was not common until the end of the eighteenth century. Unlike spoons and forks, knives were produced by two industries, the cutlers who made the blades and the men who made the handles. Sometimes silver cutlery seems very heavy and it may be that the handle is loaded with resin to give weight. Fakers have been very busy in flatware, making a fork out of the bowl of a spoon. Silver marks are usually genuine. Transposed marks are more common on hollow-ware.

FLOW BLUE

A form of blue-and-white ceramic in which the lines are blurred, as though the pattern had been placed under water and allowed to run. Examples by Worcester are much sought after.

FOB CHAIN

Used from the seventeenth century, this was to attach a watch to the clothing. The best known type is the Albert, named after Queen Victoria's consort about 1845 and often in gold, stretching across a man's stomach from waistcoat buttonhole to waistcoat pocket.

FOOTMAN

Iron or brass four-legged trivet usually pierced. The front legs were often of the cabriole type, and there was often a hole in the top so that it could be carried around.

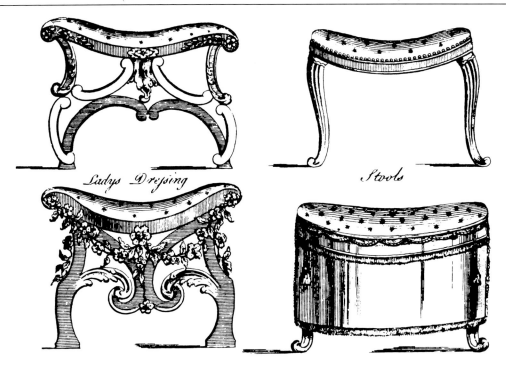

FOOTSTOOLS

Widely used in the nineteenth century with a pair considered necessary in each room, usually oval or rectangular, sometimes with squat cabriole legs. Walnut was a favourite wood. A variation was low and round with china knobs for feet, often ebonised with gilt banding and decoration. The coverings were often of velvet, bead work, or Berlin woolwork. The fender stool was low, and about four feet (1.2m) in length.

FORK

Early forks were two-pronged, small for fruit or sweetmeats, larger for meat. Four-pronged forks date from the fifteenth century, three-pronged from the seventeenth. Handles could be of ivory, amber, silver, tortoiseshell and other materials, with silver becoming predominant when the fork was teamed with the knife in a set. Specialised examples include the toasting-fork, usually of brass, with a telescopic handle.

FRENCH ART GLASS

From about 1870 French glass-makers sought to create something wholly new, taking glass and turning it into something exciting, often not like glass at all. The three main figures are Gallé,

Four typical stool designs from Rober Manwaring's The Cabinet and Chair-Maker's Real Friend and Companion of 1765.

Daum, and Lalique; the last-named continued into the art deco period and is well known for his glass car mascots. Glass could be enamelled, medievalised, layered in a most adventurous way (cameo glass), carved from the solid, or have bits of coloured glass pressed into it while still semi-molten, or built up in relief using pieces of coloured glass. *Pâte de verre* is the fusion of glass paste with metallic oxides. Because of the speculative nature of some of the techniques there was a high breakage rate. Most French art glass is signed, and if not someone will have added a signature or mark at some later stage. Many of the pieces were hated at the time. One English writer characterised art glass as being like 'spent dum-dum bullets'. The techniques were later commercialised, and the results are thousands, maybe millions, of 'characteristic' art deco vases, dishes, ashtrays, figures, paperweights, bowls, candlesticks – almost any kind of object that would reflect well on the up-to-date owner. Many of the methods were resurrected in the 1950s, and it is often a difficult task to determine between 1930s and 1950s art glass. Other major figures in the area

A typical grand drawing room, this one belonging to the exiled Napoleon III in 1871 after the Franco-Prussian War. The lay-out is the aristocratic type, with the centre of the room left free.

are Marinot, Eugène Rousseau, Léveillé, Décorchemont, Muller, Delatte, Arsall, Brocard, Cros, and Walter, each of whom had something to contribute to an art form that is always enterprising and never dull.

FRENCH FURNITURE

The cultural apartness of France and Britain is illustrated by their respective furniture. While British furniture was in a transitional muddled state from oak to walnut, with sometimes odd influences from Holland at variance with everything Britain had done in the way of furniture, French furniture was well proportioned, cleanly designed, elegant and refined. When Louis XIV came to the throne in 1661 these sterling qualities were retained, plus an added opulence. France was not a place for free-and-easy cabinet-makers. Until 1791 Paris furniture-making was presided over by guilds dating from the Middle Ages; from 1743 makers had been obliged to stamp their names on their work so there would

be no ambiguity. A diversion from normal good taste occurred about 1730 with the rococo movement, curves and asymmetry, but this died away as quickly as it had arrived and the revival of classical forms that swept England had an effect on French furniture as well. In the 1770s there was an emphasis on gentle lines, linear shapes, use of lacquer and marquetry, followed by a mahogany phase during which English furniture provided a stimulus. With their strong sense of identity French cabinet-makers did not copy English furniture, but incorporated un-English plaques and ormolu mounts. The Directoire period (about 1790-1800) was characterised by a degree of self-conscious austerity in response to Revolutionary precepts, with less veneer, ormolu, and marquetry, and this was followed by the Consular and Empire periods, running parallel with the Regency, with bold, sometimes massive, furniture. As in Britain, in the 1840s there was a desire for change, manifested in France with a fashion for dark woods such as ebony, oak and stained pear, inset with plaques and mother-of-pearl. The Second Empire (1848–70) was concerned with revivalism and comfort, with the upholsterer almost as important as the cabinet-maker, and the 1867 exhibition was dominated by upholstered chairs – *pouffes, crapauds, confidantes à*

FURNITURE DECORATION

Decoration can be applied to furniture in several ways. The wood can be carved, engraved or gouged, sometimes filling in with alternative woods or other materials such as brass; it can be inlaid, it can be painted, or it can be veneered. The wood can be overlaid with sections of other wood, such as moulding, or be topped off with mounts of metal. Self-contained decorative pieces, such as plaques, can be applied to surfaces. There is very little that can't be done, if there is a demand for it. Certain pieces of furniture, such as chairs, lend themselves to more decoration than others. The back alone can be treated in dozens of ways. The shape of a piece of furniture can be determined by need or fashion. Some fashions are attractive but have inbuilt disadvantages, such as the cabriole leg and the sabre leg be-

An Edwardian secretaire bookcase in 18th-century style, demonstrating the marvellous skills of the cabinet-maker of around 1900.

cause of the way in which the grain of the wood runs and the chance of the wood splitting with the grain. Certain forms of decoration, whether carved or inserted into the wood, reflect current fads, none more so than towards the end of the eighteenth century and neo-Classicism, and there is a type of tired decoration where clearly no-one is very concerned and it is merely a matter of 'filling in', doing something to plain wood. Nature abhors a vacuum, and so did many a cabinet- and furniture-maker. Among the motifs used have been:

knotted ribbons and bows
rising sun ornament
fan
roundel
fluting (using the gouge in parallel strokes)
scroll, used also for the feet of chairs
Portuguese bulb (inverted pear shape)
ram's head
reeding (reverse of fluting)
swag (fruit, flowers and foliage)
lunette (half moon)
lyre
echinus moulding (quarter-round section)
dentil (tooth shaped)
egg and tongue (ovoid and pinched-in horizontal triangle)
egg and dart (ovoid and arrowhead)
ogee (two curves, one concave, one convex)
paw feet
hoof foot
pad foot
patera (an ancient curved shape)
pear-drop moulding
husk (wheat ear)
herring-bone (used in banding)
lattice
lion mask

cabochon (ornament like polished uncut diamond)
astragal (half round)
ball foot
spiral turning (like barley sugar)
bead moulding (like row of beads)
bell flower
bobbin (used in turning)
chequer (alternate squares of contrasting colour)
club foot
spade foot (tapered square section)
split baluster (turned baluster cut in half)
cock beading (half-round moulding)
concave frieze (inward sloping)
convex frieze (outward sloping giving cushion-like appearance)
coquillage (in the form of a shell)
cupid's bow cresting (on top rail of chair backs)
cyma recta (moulding with two curves, upper concave, lower convex)
cyma reversa (moulding with two curves, upper convex, lower concave)
bell and baluster turning (bell shape above, baluster shape below)
anthemion (honeysuckle)
amorini (cupids)
acanthus leaf (as on Corinthian columns)
guilloche (interlaced ribbon enclosing circles)
ovolo moulding (convex quarter-circle section)
Prince of Wales feathers
palmette (branching palm tree)
vase
arcaded (a series of arches)
ball and claw foot (ball clutched by paw)
diaper (diamond shapes often with dots inside)
gadrooning (repetitive curved shapes usually convex)
baluster turning (lathe-executed bulging pear shapes of varying sizes)

Ram's head   Lion mask   Husk

deux places, indiscrets à trois places, canapés de l'amitié, some Anglicised, some not. At the same time, mass-produced furniture in the old styles, with no distinction at all, was being produced. As in England, there was a reaction against mechanical mediocrity, and crafts, societies, and schools of applied art mushroomed throughout France. The ultimate result of revulsion against the familiar and the second-rate was French art nouveau furniture, totally distinct from British furniture of the period. French art nouveau, said one English critic, was the essence of squiggle and worm. Today the correct words to use are 'casual, light-hearted, elegant, imaginative freshness' – and incredibly expensive. French furniture-makers rose to the challenge offered by the twentieth century, and their art deco furniture can be both eye catching and adventurous, with such materials as ebony, ivory and sharkskin used together, sometimes in tables with a black marble top. Tooled and lacquered leather was used as a veneer.

FROG MUG

Made from the eighteenth century onwards, this was an amusing piece of pottery in which a frog sits to be uncovered as the mug is drained, to hilarity all round. It is still a popular seaside novelty. The frog was also placed in chamber-pots.

FUDDLING CUP

A number of cups fitted together, usually by hollow handles, so that to drink one cupful it is necessary to go through the lot; made in delftware from the seventeenth century and by the Staffordshire potteries in the eighteenth.

FUNERARY WARES

Items buried with the dead, often unearthed by archeologists and, less publicised, by treasure-hunters, so that what are essentially museum pieces can slide onto the open market, available to all. They range from beads and tools to the magnificent objects made in bronze, silver, jade, wood and pottery for Chinese tomb burial. The pottery items are often unglazed terra cotta. The pottery horses so typical of early Chinese pottery and among the most sought-after relics of the past were intended as funerary objects.

FURNITURE ASSEMBLY

Furniture parts can be glued, screwed, and nailed, or joints can be used, in which the members are slotted in. Dovetailing is a technique of joining two pieces of wood together, usually at right angles, in which the ends interlock, the side angles so cut that the two pieces do not slide out. Most often used in the construction of drawers. A dowel is a cylinder of wood used to fix two solid pieces of wood together, and glued into place when slotted in. A mitre joint is used to join two pieces of wood at right-angles. The mortise and tenon joint is one of the basic woodworking joints, and involves slotting the tenon into a tight-fitting cavity, the mortise, and sometimes the joint is pegged, often a square peg from green wood so that it would hold solidly. Thus the phrase 'a square peg in a round hole', but it is inappropriate, as a square peg does the job better. There are a number of variations on the basic mortise and tenon, mainly to simplify the operation.

FURNITURE DETAIL

Banding is a border of a contrasting veneer. Cross banding is a veneer in which the wood is cut across the grain. Stringing is a line of inlay in contrasting wood or brass framing designs or acting as a border. The top rail or cresting rail is the top horizontal of a chair back. Splats are the vertical central sections within the uprights in a chair back. The slats in a slat-back chair are horizontal spaced pieces between the side uprights, as in the ladder-back chair. Stretchers are the horizontal members connecting the legs, giving them strength, important if the structure is heavy, but also used as decoration. Certain woods such as mahogany were strong enough not to need stretchers. Hipping is a cabriole leg extension where the leg continues at the top to a level above the seat. The two basic shapes of stretchers are H-shaped and X, with curved stretchers sometimes used, often known as cow-horn stretchers. An apron is an ornamental piece of wood, shaped or carved, beneath the seat rails of chairs or settees, on tables and stands, and on furniture of all kinds, sometimes added later to make a plain piece individual. Mouldings are the shaped edges of cornices, lids, etc. They can either be applied, or integral

17th century oak carving, probably from then.

(carved into the main body of the wood). The quality of the moulding is one of the best clues when determining whether a certain piece is 'right'. A fret can be applied or cut from the solid; if presented on a solid surface it is called blind fret. A frieze is the surface below a table-top or similar. A finial is a decorative knob or termination in the shape of an acorn, ball, pineapple, urn, etc. There are several different kinds of surface carving; scratch carving is the easiest, in which a shallow line design is scratched on the surface of the wood. Recessed carving is where the background is removed leaving the main section raised and prominent. The background is often stippled or given an all-over texture to contrast with the smooth pattern. A canted corner is a bevelled or chamfered corner on bureaux, chests of drawers and similar furniture. A chamfered panel is called a fielded panel. A stile is the upright of a frame, usually holding a panel. In furniture such as chests of drawers (known as carcase furniture) where there are no legs, there are two basic kinds of feet, bracket feet introduced about 1690, and bun feet used about 1650–1710 and revived in the nineteenth century. Where there are no feet at all, a plinth is used. Carcase furniture can be straight fronted, serpentine (in the shape of an

elongated S), bow fronted (a gentle curve), and bombé (swollen). Veneer can be applied directly, relying on the wood pattern or figure for the effect, or it can be quartered, applied in squares in mirror fashion to make a deliberate pattern. Tree branches can be used, resulting in oyster veneer. When grouped around each other these shapes resemble oysters, originally a Dutch fashion. Curl veneer is cut from just below a fork in the tree. The pattern on the wood is similar to that of a hair curl or an ostrich plume.

GADGETS

The *Chambers Twentieth Century Dictionary* definition of a gadget: '"a what-d'ye-call-it"; an ingenious device'. Gadgets abound in the world of antiques and collectables, languishing on a dealer's table waiting to be recognised. Some serve a purpose, often in a ponderous and not readily apparent way. A machine for tying up bouquets of flowers invented in the nineteenth century, with levers to raise and lower the flowers and push them this way and that, plus an arrangement to wind wire around the bouquet, is gadgetry for the sake of gadgetry. It was much easier and quicker to do it by hand. The addition pencil was intended for commercial use; it comprised a small plunger and a simple mechanism set in the body of a pencil that added in single digits. Some gadgets were, for the time, hopelessly inefficient. The nineteenth-century 'Eclipse' copying apparatus claimed 'clear black copies equal to lithography' at 500 per hour, but could not do one copy very well. The 'Indispensable' gumming machine of 1886 put as much gum on the operator as on the label. Some gadgets did work, and earned their inventors a fortune; an inverted glass bell to hang over a gas light to stop ceilings being blackened by fumes made its creator more than £100,000. The walking-stick that would convert into a pair of steps 'in the event of the owner meeting a mad dog' was patented in 1872. Dr Scott's Electric Hair Brush of 1883 and the Harness Electropathic Belt of 1891 would today come up against the acts dealing with trades description, as they did not even use electricity. Some gadgets were devised by mad people, such as the stilts patented for horses so that they could operate on steep hill sides. William Gillette was thought mad. He was a Sheffield cork salesman who discovered that with modern technology it was possible to produce steel strip a thousandth of an inch thick. So he invented the safety-razor blade in 1875, but it was not exploited until it was decided in 1895 that he was not mad after all. 'Ingenious devices' of the past have passed into the category of recognised antiques. These include puzzle jugs and Cadogan teapots (filled from the bottom), as well as intricate combination furniture, much satirised in the comic papers.

GARNITURE

Sometimes a set of vases for the mantelpiece, first made in China for the export market in the seventeenth and eighteenth centuries, sometimes a clock flanked by appropriate ornaments, some of which have long lost their clock and are treated as self-contained objects.

GAUDY DUTCH

Nothing to do with Holland, but a type of garish Staffordshire pottery in bright colours made for export to America.

GERMAN FURNITURE

As in all Europe early furniture was basic, but from as early as the fifteenth century ideas on furniture crossed frontiers regardless of wars and religious beliefs. One of the most important was the introduction of linenfold panelling from the Netherlands into other countries, including England and the German states. German styles were not all of a piece. Although oak prevailed in the north, the southern states were more adventurous, using softwood, necessitating inlay or painted surfaces instead of carving. Both north and south were open to the influences of the decorative styles of Italy, as well as of France and the Netherlands in the west, although certain articles of furniture were distinctly German, especially the exotic and magnificent cabinets made in the early seventeenth century in south Germany. Courtly taste reflected refinement, burgher taste, practicality and scale. A speciality of German furniture was a curious fleshy and flabby carving. Richer states, such as Prussia, prided themselves on their elegance,

and during the eighteenth century the influence of France predominated, though English taste was reflected in a liking for mahogany. But there was no simple pattern. German cabinet-makers picked the motifs they liked and incorporated them in their products. In Chippendale-like chairs of the mid-eighteenth century the splat was often topped by an armorial-type crest, unlike anything seen on English chairs, and carved oak remained popular when it had long been superseded elsewhere. In some cases, they outplayed the originals; walnut parquetry commodes based on an already complex French design had serpentine curves vertically and horizontally. Cabinet-making skills could hardly go further. Neo-Classicism had its effect on German furniture as elsewhere, and the French Empire style, severe, monumental, dominated the early nineteenth century until the arrival of the Biedermeier style, described by John Gloag in 1962 as 'a style of furnishing and interior decoration, exuberantly vulgar . . . popular among the new and tasteless rich classes of England. Opulently carved furniture loaded with embossed metal ornament caricatured the French Empire style, and black horsehair, frequently used for upholstery, contrasted vividly with gilt mounts.' Mahogany and oak were unfashionable, and walnut, birch, ash, pear and cherry were preferred. The style was characterised by simple straight lines, with leg and rail joints openly displayed. The aim – comfort with dignity. There was no monumentality and the tallest pieces were rarely above eye-level. The deep rectangular sofa with high back and ends on straight or sabre legs was a dominant piece. Rooms were arranged casually and often sparsely. Historians regret that this style wasn't taken further, but the Germans discovered their heritage, especially their own Gothic, followed by revivals of rococo and pretty Frenchified styles. Germany had its own art nouveau, too often in the shadow of the French art nouveau, but sometimes even more extraordinary and adventurous, parallel with one of the most important art movements of the twentieth century – the Austrian Secession. Between the wars Germany was in the lead in modernist furniture and design; there was nothing in France, England or America quite like the Bauhaus, perhaps the most important centre of design that has ever existed.

GILDING

Applying gold to surfaces by a number of methods including cold or water gilding (with size or on gesso), lacquer gilding, oil gilding, (using linseed oil, gum arabic, and mastic), fire gilding (powdered gold and mercury; the mercury heated and evaporated, the result ormolu), honey gilding, and amber gilding (crushed amber varnish with gold leaf). All methods except fire gilding use gold leaf. Liquid gold was used by Meissen in the early nineteenth century, gold dissolved by substances such as sulphur to make a paintable mix. The result was a kind of lustre highly suited to the taste of the time and much used in England and elsewhere after its discovery.

GINGERBREAD MOULDS

Dating back to pre-Elizabethan times, the variety of moulds was amazing including coats-

René Lalique (1860–1945) was perhaps the best-known European designer of glass. The budgerigar was one of his favourite motifs, and nude women proliferated whether or not thinly disguised as mermaids.

of-arms, birds, animals, highwaymen, pistols, letters of the alphabet, and famous personages such as Nelson. Birthdays and sporting events were commemorated in the form of gingerbread moulds. The wood used mostly was pear, very susceptible to woodworm, though boxwood, beech, apple, cherry and walnut were also popular. Most are rectangular, but there are also square and round moulds, while engagements were signalled by heart-shaped moulds.

GINGER JAR

One of the most popular of Oriental products, ancient or modern, a covered jar with a wide mouth, rounded body sloping in towards base, with decoration often of prunus blossom.

GLASS

Glass is made by fusing sand, quartz, or flints with soda-ash or potash, and it can be moulded, drawn or trailed (like slip in pottery), pressed, carved, or blown, a process discovered in Syria in the first century AD, but not known or ignored by many glass-makers throughout the world. Coloured glass is due to impurities in the 'metal' or mixture or through adding metal

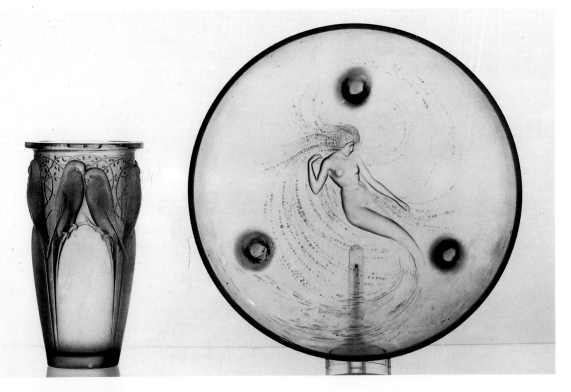

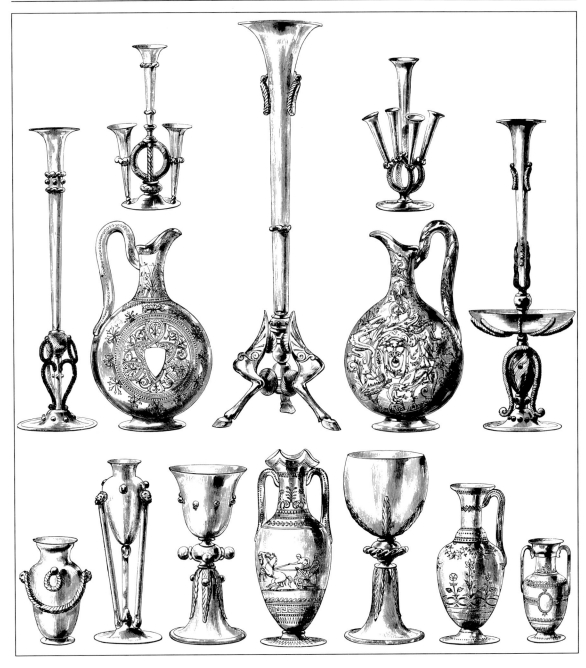

oxides. Typical of such glass is aventurine, in which flakes of copper or gold are added, known in ancient times, revived in Venice in the seventeenth century and often used in art glass towards the end of the nineteenth century. There are two main types of making moulded glass – blowing the 'gather' into a mould, or pouring molten metal into a shaped mould. Pressed is a step onwards from moulded glass. Molten glass in a mould is forced quickly into shape by the use of a plunger, withdrawn when

A selection of glass objects produced in the 1860s by Dobson of London.

the glass has set. The plunger has a smooth surface, so that the inside of the object being made is smoother than blown moulded glass. It was used in the final years of the eighteenth century to make such items as decanter stoppers, but the method was most widely exploited in America, first of all to make furniture knobs in 1825 and

Victorian glass claret jug with silver head dated 1894.

soon afterwards to make imitation cut glass. Only later were the merits of pressed glass – smoothness and regularity of texture – appreciated.

Unlike many other substances, glass can be melted and reshaped continually, can be regarded like a mineral (as the Chinese did, carv-ing it in the same manner as jade) or it can even be spun into threads. The Romans were acquainted with many of the techniques used today, but after the decline of the Roman Empire the quality of glass deteriorated. Until the fifteenth century it was usually discoloured due to impurities, and was only used for drinking vessels by the poor. The Venetians found that if they added oxide of manganese to the mix they could obtain clear glass which reminded them of rock crystal, a type of quartz, so they called this

glass *cristallo*. Today, crystal glass indicates hand-blown quality glass.

Germany was a pioneer in coloured glass; in the early eighteenth century deep blue and green glass of high quality was made. Ruby glass was made by dropping gold coins into the mix. Bohemia became predominant in coloured glass, evolving 'Hyalith', imitating natural stone, and 'Lithyalin', imitating marble. By the middle of the nineteenth century Bohemian glassworks were the most important in the world. A technique developed in Austria was *Verre églomisé*, double-walled vessels with scenes in gold leaf between the walls. Glass was also enamelled (from the fifteenth century) and gilded. English glass was cloudy and unsatisfactory until 1675 when lead oxide was introduced as a flux, and this led to the supremacy of the English drinking glass, with its endless variety of stems, with bulbous and pear-shaped knops, and bowl shapes. Knops containing air bubbles were drawn out and twisted into a stem containing a multiple spiral of air-lines. Threads of opaque white and sometimes coloured glass were later used. Cut glass was used from about 1730, and became increasingly elaborate.

Because of its extreme ductibility and versatility, glass has proved ideal for the adventurous. It can be layered (one layer on another, then cut into revealing the lower layer or layers, as in cameo glass), intricately engraved, etched with acid to produce textured frosted glass, dipped in water and then reheated to give the finish of ice, sand-blasted for mass-produced useful wares, scalloped, prinked, or have other materials pressed or embedded in it as in French art glass. The range of glass objects produced in the art deco period was immense, not only household wares, vases and decorative containers but boxes, car mascots, lamps, ashtrays, perfume bottles, inkwells, clock and picture frames, stained glass, huge panels for hotels, public buildings and luxury liners, and figures and natural forms of every kind.

GLASS WALKING-STICK

Chest-high shepherds' crooks were made in the eighteenth century in green bottle-glass, and in the nineteenth century examples were enriched with coloured spirals of red, white and blue glass, either in the glass or encircling it. These were made for decorating cottage parlours.

GLAZES

If fired to a temperature of about 1250°C, clay becomes impermeable to liquids. Before heat was controllable there was a lot of wastage, as articles melted or collapsed. By coating a vessel with a glaze it was possible to make it watertight at a lower temperature. Glaze is similar to clay, but a fluxing agent is added, such as lead, soda,

A pistol made from salt-glazed pottery with the characteristic orange-peel texture.

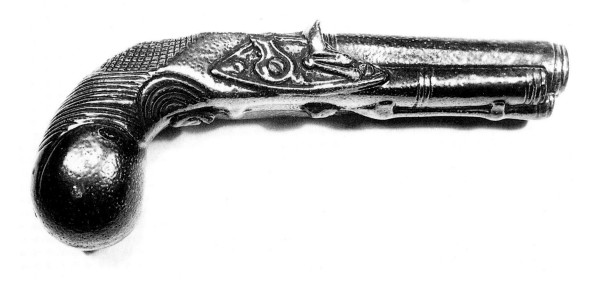

GLOBE

Of two kinds, the terrestrial and the celestial, the celestial has been made in one form or another for more than two thousand years though interesting terrestrial globes were obliged to wait until it was established that the world was round. Production of globes from about 1500 was simplified by the use of gores, pieces of paper of a special shape, which were printed and glued to a sphere, often of papier mâché. From the eighteenth century a pair of globes, handsomely mounted, was an essential for every gentleman's library. Pocket globes were very popular in the eighteenth century. A terrestrial globe is contained in a spherical case, usually covered with shagreen, while on the inside cover is pasted a map of the sky.

GONG

Either an Eastern instrument, often of great size, or a dinner gong on a stand, usually suspended from a wooden frame which is sometimes intricately carved. A gong can also be a spirally-wound steel wire in a clock on which the hours are struck.

GRAMOPHONES AND PHONOGRAPHS

The principle of sound vibrations being picked up by a thin membrane resulted in the telephone, the microphone, the phonograph and the gramophone. The phonograph uses a rotating cylinder and a stylus, the gramophone a disc and a stylus. The phonograph was invented by Thomas Edison in 1877 as a business aid but it was not successful, and it was taken up in Britain and named the graphophone. Edison returned to the scene in 1888, and his New Duplex and Concert phonographs were powered by a small electric motor, which in turn gave way to clockwork, first of all by Columbia in 1894 and then Edison in 1895. Millions were produced, and the phonograph survived for many years despite the coming of the gramophone, and as late as 1929 cylinders were still being sold. The gramophone was invented in 1887 and marketed in Germany as a toy. The discs were of coated vulcanised rubber, replaced in 1895 by shellac. Early gramophones were operated by

An early Victorian salt-glaze flask. Mr and Mrs Caudle were two comic characters created by Douglas Jerrold, editor of Punch.

potassium and calcium, which causes the glaze to melt and stick to the vessel. Silica in the form of silversand, ground flint or quartz is added. There are several types of glazes, such as lead glaze, known as early as the first century BC, which gives a rich metallic finish, tin glaze (maiolica in Italy, faience in France, fayence in Germany) produces a thick white surface, ideal for decoration, salt glaze is used with stoneware, and the lesser-known felspathic glaze, powdered rock and used with hard porcelain.

A Columbia gramophone in an oak case. Notice the curious carrying handle.

hand, but when the gramophone was taken up in America with the slogan 'The Talking Machine That Talks Talk!' a strong clockwork motor was supplied. In Britain the Gramophone Company began operations in 1898 and within two years was advertising 5,000 different discs. In 1903 12in (30cm) discs were introduced, and this type of record survived long after 1948 and the arrival of micro-groove discs, the sale of both being concurrent for many years. Throughout the twentieth century there were constant advances; the gramophone diaphragms (which receive the message from the stylus) were made from mica instead of metal or celluloid, and for extra fidelity and volume massive horns were produced, regarded as ugly and incorporated into a piece of furniture with the gramophone itself. These cabinets had grandiose names such as the Duncan Phyfe, the Aeolian Vocalion, and the Deccalion. Georgian furniture was converted to house gramophones. Electric recording and electrically driven gramophones coincided with the coming of radio, but the industry survived. The first automatic changers were introduced about 1935, about the same time as the radiogram, incorporating gramophone and radio. The record player of the

1940s theoretically rendered the gramophone obsolete, but not for some as there is a sterling body of gramophone enthusiasts who cherish the old 78 rpm records, some of which command very high prices, and play them on period machines. Early one-sided records are much sought after, as well as jazz and dance-band discs and records by artists such as Caruso. More recent vinyl discs by pop stars such as the Beatles and Elvis Presley fetch large sums, as do the sleeves provided with the disc.

GRATE

The framework with bars to contain coal when coal became the main type of fuel in the early eighteenth century. Early specimens were of iron, and plain, but as the century progressed the grate became increasingly ornate, often embossed and with shaped legs, with additions of brass and burnished steel. During the nineteenth century elaborate cast-iron grates were made, often with brass extras and finials.

HALL-STAND

The dictionary definition of a stand is 'a base or structure for setting things on; a piece of furniture for hanging things from.' The hall-stand answers both these criteria. It was basically a Victorian middle-class production; the rich had servants to take away the top clothes of visitors. It could be large and impressive, or it could be spindly, with bamboo often used, though oak was the favourite wood. There was usually accommodation for umbrellas with a drip tray, a mirror, and a glove box.

HAND-COOLERS

Suitable minerals carved into the form of eggs and highly polished, and one supposes that they were therapeutic rather than practical. Agates, marbles, and Derbyshire Blue John were popular. Hand-coolers are still being made today in cottage-craft areas. Darners for mending socks are often taken to be hand-coolers.

HARVEST JUGS

Earthenware jugs with naive motifs such as animals, flowers, birds, and ships scratched through a white slip to reveal the surface beneath. Sometimes stained a blotchy green, and made to commemorate harvests from the late seventeenth century almost up to the present.

HASTER

A high cupboard with an open metal-lined back dating from the eighteenth century. The back is sited towards the fire, and plates and other items in the cupboard are kept warm.

HAT-PINS

Pins between four and twelve inches long (10 and 30cm) used from about 1880 to anchor ladies' hats to their hair. Most interest lies in the pin heads, apart from a few technical innovations such as swivel joints and point-protectors, and the fact that some pins were made of silver and gold rather than steel. Heads varied from plain glass to jewels, wood to porcelain, and there were novelty hat-pins which incorporated peep-scopes with scenic views and hat-pins in

which the head was a huge lightweight sphere. The most adventurous designs were those of the art nouveau period, and these hat-pins are minor works of art. Hat-pins suffer from rust, but it is usually a superficial blemish, easily removed. Hat-pin holders were a necessary accessory. There are three main types – a vase with a pepper-pot top, a pincushion with a vertical stand carrying supports for the pins, and a stand with a perforated disc and a holder at the base for the pin points. The most expensive were of silver, but hat-pin stands were also made in plate, wood, bronze and brass, as well as porcelain and pottery.

HISPANO-MORESQUE WARE

Name given to tin-glazed earthenware produced by Spanish potters from as early as about 1200 when Spain was ruled by Islam. The ware was decorated with metallic lustre pigments, and the techniques used possibly originated in Persia. Hispano-Moresque ware was eventually superseded by more orthodox ceramics, but it had an important influence on European tin-glazed ware of all kinds and towards the end of the nineteenth century it was regarded with great awe by art potters.

HOOKAH

The traditional smoking apparatus of the Middle East in which tobacco smoke passes through water and is inhaled through a long flexible tube with a mouthpiece. Although originally made from a decorated coconut – one of the many alternative names for a hookah is a nargile, Persian for shell – examples were made in glass, metal, and ceramics, some of them in blue-and-white, made in China for the export market.

HORNBOOK

A sheet of paper containing the alphabet, perhaps numbers, and usually the Lord's Prayer, which was mounted on a piece of wood with a handle attached and covered with a thin protective layer of transparent horn. Used as a teaching aid from the sixteenth to the eighteenth centuries. These became obsolete with the increased availability of books.

HORSE-BRASSES

Flat or convex, often circular, horse-brasses were pierced, engraved, and stamped, and intended for attaching to the horse's harness, allegedly to ward off the evil eye, though they also served to advertise the occupation of the horse's owner and bring good luck. There is a plethora of crescents, moons, suns, hearts, birds, anchors, barrels and flowers, and, especially in the early days, playing-card emblems. Although used from the sixteenth century, when the brass was hammered by hand, most of the brasses seen today are modern and made for the weekend cottage industry. From about 1830 cast brass was used, heavier than the brass stamped from sheet metal and used from about 1870. Horse-brasses featuring celebrities such as politicians were widely used in the nineteenth century, and they sometimes appeared in connection with royal events such as jubilees or echoed patriotic fervour, as in the Boer War brasses. Horse-brasses are more appealing attached to old harness, which gives a kind of credibility. Modern horse-brasses are part of the tourist trade.

HUGUENOT STYLE

In 1681 following their persecution in France Huguenots or French Protestants were allowed to settle in Britain. In doing so they angered local craftsmen, but were gradually integrated. Some created a silk industry, others were in-

volved in precious metals, and they succeeded in ousting Dutch in favour of French influences, introducing new silver techniques and a novel range of decorative devices including acanthus leaves, ribbons, straps, and scrolls.

HURDY-GURDY

A musical instrument shaped like a violin and operated by turning a handle, which sets strings vibrating while the player picks out a tune on a miniature keyboard with his left hand. Used since the eleventh century in churches, then as a folk instrument under various names, and finally in the nineteenth century by buskers. It could be ornate with carving or inlay, or plain.

HUTCH

A simple box with one or two doors usually on legs used in the sixteenth and seventeenth centuries. If the wood is pierced it is likely that the particular hutch was intended to store food, but it is one of the basic containers given a host of names and used for a multitude of purposes.

IMARI

This Japanese seaport, a centre of export during the seventeeth and eighteenth centuries, has

Pair of modest quality 18th-century Imari plates.

given its name to perhaps the most popular and best known Oriental ware, characterised by crowded and sometimes overloaded porcelain, with chrysanthemums and other flowers, scrollwork, panels and people jostling for space. 'Brocaded Imari' in blue, red and gold provided inspiration for English porcelain and pottery factories including Derby, Worcester, and Spode, and, later, Minton and Mason. Realising its export potential, Imari-type ware was also made in China.

INDIAN FURNITURE

Furniture, apart from chairs and stools, played little part in the cultures of India, as life was lived at ground level, and even in the palaces of the wealthy there was an indifference to the kind of furniture the western world takes for granted, with perhaps cushions and a low table the essential items. The British presence did result in many Indians adopting European manners and modes, and Indian craftsmen created European-like furniture in the country's own distinctive woods for export and for the needs of occupying civilians and military, the most common object being the folding tables with a circular brass top (though these 'Benares brass' items are likely to have been made in Birmingham).

INRO

Japanese word for seal case, and from the fifteenth century used to carry the owner's seal for signature of documents and pigment. Later the inro was used to carry aromatic herbs or medicines in separate compartments. It was suspended from the girdle, or obi, by a cord secured by a netsuke. Wood covered in lacquer was the favourite material, though carved wood, ivory, porcelain and pottery, and bamboo were also used. For specialised use iron was employed. The finest examples come from the sixteenth to eighteenth centuries, and were decorated with gold or silver in delicate complex patterns, the favourite motifs being birds, beasts, gods, flowers, blossoms, dragons, and clouds, often depicted in an asymmetrical manner, often whimsical, often near-abstract. To specialists, the variety of the lacquer is of great interest, whether it is flat, raised, incised or carved.

INTAGLIO

A term used especially in jewellery and other fine work where the design lies beneath the surface of the gemstone, glass, porcelain, or other substance. The word can mean an engraved gem. It is the opposite of cameo.

IRISH GLASS

Glass-making was known in Ireland from the thirteenth century, and it was influenced by English glass-making until 1780 when Ireland was exempt from the tax that damaged the English glass trade. Skilled craftsmen left England to set up business in Ireland such as the Waterford Glass Works established in 1783. Irish glass was thicker and more deeply cut than English glass, and their specialities included salad bowls, lustres, chandeliers, drinking glasses, and decanters. In 1825 Ireland was abruptly brought into line with England regarding tax, and the glass industry was obliged to compete on an equal footing, which it did.

IRON

Known from 3500BC but rarely used until the Middle Ages when wrought iron was made, with cast iron being made in the fifteenth century. Techniques were crude, with difficulty in getting detail, so products were limited to stoves, firebacks, and similar robust articles made by sand-casting – casting metal in a mould made of quartz and sand with binding agents such as horsehair, which was contained in an iron frame with channels and air vents. The molten metal is poured in through the channels, solidifies in the mould, and the sand is then broken away and the casting is chiselled smooth. Vastly improved technical methods in the eighteenth and nineteenth centuries made iron a versatile medium that could not only be wrought and cast but stamped and rolled thin (so that domestic vessels could be made) and tinned (resulting in tin plate).

IRONSTONE CHINA

English pottery allegedly containing iron slag patented in 1813 by C. J. Mason, and made exclusively by him until 1827. The strength al-

It is often easy to overlook the brilliant craftsmanship of 19th-century metalworkers. This fountain is not in marble or indeed anything carvable, but in cast iron.

lowed for large objects not usually associated with pottery such as fireplaces and vestibule vases five feet (1.5m) in height.

ISLAMIC POTTERY

From the ninth century tin-glazed earthenware was made in Baghdad, probably in an attempt to emulate Chinese ware, and eventually the technique found its way to Europe. An independent school of potters flourished in Persia and Turkestan producing pink or buff ware decorated with slip under a transparent glaze, depicting birds and animals and with inscriptions.

Lustre painting, introduced in the ninth century, was transmitted to Spain, resulting eventually in maiolica (faience). Chinese influences on Islamic pottery continued through the centuries. One of the most important centres was Isnik, sixty miles (96km) from Istanbul, which began producing dishes, jugs, and ewers from about 1490 in blue and white, with greens, turquoises and purples from about 1525; work so distinctive that it was shamelessly imitated in Italy in the seventeenth century and in France in the late nineteenth century. Persia, a great centre of ceramics, suffered badly from the incursions of the Mongol hordes, but was producing blue-and-white ware from the fourteenth century. Tiles from the fifteenth century, made for the mosques and palaces, are especially outstanding. Lustre was revived in Persia in the seventeenth century, mainly restricted to flower and plant designs. Persian ware has a unique glowing quality impossible to define, and it is small wonder that it provided an inspiration in the late nineteenth century to English art potters such as de Morgan.

ITALIAN FURNITURE

Italian furniture-makers had never accepted Gothic as the natural style, and before the Renaissance, Italian furniture was of plain construction, painted rather than carved. As soon as the Renaissance spread, furniture reflected the new impetus, especially in the cassone, or clothes chest, the quintessential piece (as it was in many countries, England included). There were three types of cassone; painted, panelled, and carved, but carved in a sculptural rather than simply decorative or aimless way as in Britain. Walnut was the favourite wood, but by the 1470s nearly thirty different kinds of wood were in use. Other countries used Renaissance and thus Italian motifs from about 1500, France showing the most skill. A speciality of Italian furniture, especially of table-tops, was marvellous inlay using lapis lazuli, jasper, sardonyx, agate and other hard stones, work that has never been surpassed. The baroque was created in Rome, with softwood carved into naked figures, tritons and cupids with scrolls, leaves, and foliage, afterwards gilded, establishing a tradition of virtuoso wood-carving unknown elsewhere, though the furniture on which these decorations were used was often poorly constructed. As in all countries, Italy went through a lacquer phase, and in the 1730s its rococo was perhaps the most hedonistic of them all, with carved furniture assuming fantastic and, to outsiders accustomed to sobriety and good taste, dangerous shapes – 'Though much depended on the locality' – whereas Venetian furniture was outrageous, Florentine furniture was sober and Neopolitan furniture eccentric. The neo-Classical movement was hardly suited to Italian carving, and English styles proved an influence, with Hepplewhite chairs being faithfully reproduced in Naples. During the early nineteenth century French Empire furniture was imported along with French craftsmen, and these greatly influenced Italian furniture, and although Italy had a strong tradition for pictorial marquetry French influence persisted throughout the century, with the Empire style alone lasting into the 1840s. The Gothic revival played a minor part, and it was the great years of the Renaissance that inspired furniture-makers. Known as Dantesque, there was a fashion for X-chairs in red plush and heavily carved tables, but much of the everyday furniture was similar to that found in London and Paris, machine-made for the masses, over-bearingly vulgar for the rich, though in the villas and palaces of the ancient aristocracy eighteenth-century and earlier furniture predominated. An exhibition in Turin in 1902 created a tepid interest in the new forms of furniture, but in Italy there does not appear to have been the reaction against old forms that occurred elsewhere in the late nineteenth century. If there was an Arts and Crafts movement in Italy it kept very quiet about itself.

JACOBITE GLASSES*

English drinking vessels commemorating, with engraving, the Old Pretender (James Stuart 1688–1766), the Young Pretender (Bonny Prince Charlie 1720–88), and the Jacobite uprisings of 1715 and 1745. Among the designs are roses with two supplementary buds representing the Pretenders, verses of Jacobite song ending with Amen, portraits, and the words 'Fiat' (let it be done) and 'Redeat' (may he return). Miscellaneous motifs include the oak, oak-leaf, star, bee, butterfly, forget-me-not and other flowers, and the Prince of Wales plume, offering plenty

of scope for fakers who can use engraving tools on good-quality period glass.

JAPANESE FURNITURE

More than in any other culture, the Japanese way of life dictated the forms of their furniture, which was sparse, and rarely solid in the western manner because of earthquakes. Accustomed to sitting and sleeping on the floor, the Japanese did not need tables, chairs and beds of a European type. Writing-tables, book chests and cabinets were low and unobtrusive. Because of the practice of altering the interiors of their houses, the Japanese paid great attention to the screen, with frames of lacquered wood. The screen itself was strong paper. Free-standing furniture is predominantly lacquered, simple in form with surface decoration of outstanding beauty. Apart from shelved cabinets and kimono racks, Japanese furniture had little influence on the outside world.

JAPANNED FURNITURE

Imported lacquer furniture from the Orient was very fashionable in the seventeenth century (mentioned by Pepys), especially the Japanese, known as 'fine' or 'right' to distinguish it from Indian and Chinese lacquered pieces. Lacquered furniture was so popular that English traders sent out patterns and models of favourite English furniture to be made up by native craftsmen for the English market. An influential book, *Treatise of Japanning and Varnishing*, was published in 1688, and lacquered furniture began to be made in Britain, a trade helped by a law of 1701 which imposed heavier duties on all imported lacquer furniture. English lacquering was reckoned inferior to Japanese work, and sometimes what was sold as lacquering was merely varnishing. The vogue faded in the 1740s, revived towards the end of the century, received a fillip during the Aesthetic 1870s with the fashion for Anglo–Japanese furniture, and was a popular do-it-yourself hobby in the 1920s, with red lacquer the most common.

JAPANNED METAL WARE

Black or tin-plate iron, copper, or other suitable metals coated with lacquer and decorated in a pseudo-oriental manner. The leading early exponent was T. Allgood of Pontypool, who flourished in the 1680s, and whose products are known as Pontypool ware. Tin-plate iron was introduced in 1730 and made japanned metal ware very popular, the articles made including trays (especially), boxes, and tea-caddies. The trade was taken up by the larger manufacturers, especially in the Midlands, who sometimes referred to their work as 'fancy Pontipool ware', the change in spelling differentiating it from Allgood's ware. Heat-resisting properties were improved in the 1770s, and the output extended to tea- and coffee-urns and kettles. The English japanned metal ware was fashionable abroad, and quantities were exported to France and Holland, while French lacquered metal was imported. This is known as *tôle* or *tôle peinte* (painted tin), and very confusingly this name was also given to English japanned metal ware.

JARDINIÈRE

Can be used to describe a flower container, made of almost anything, or the stand on which the container is put or in which a receptacle is

19th-century Oriental bronze jardiniere.

inset. Or, if the occasion arises, the whole lot together.

JASPER

A variety of quartz containing iron oxide, and thus in reds, yellows and browns, used in drinking vessels and caskets often mounted in gold, silver or silver gilt and later in the eighteenth century as decoration in small articles.

JELLY MOULDS

Jelly, either sweet or savoury, has been known for centuries but not until the early eighteenth century was it decided to make different shaped moulds in the interests of presentation. The first moulds were made from salt-glazed stoneware in simple, usually geometric, shapes, and were for single portions, although larger moulds followed within twenty years or so. The main technical improvement on the simple mould came towards the end of the eighteenth century when a decorated wedge was pushed into the liquid jelly, so that when the jelly mould was removed the decoration showed through the translucency of the jelly. From 1830 onwards copper jelly moulds were used, tinned to prevent poisoning, and these today are very desirable, though the major potteries produced delightful

Wedgwood Pearlware jelly mould.

jelly moulds, often in a variety of whimsical and animaloid shapes. The dull brown jelly moulds were made for many years from the turn of the century; these were very cheap and many were imported from the Continent. Glass jelly moulds became increasingly popular from the 1930s onwards, along with enamelled metal moulds which were regarded as more hygienic. In their turn, glass and enamelled metal have been overtaken by plastic and aluminium.

JET

Fossilised wood found mainly at Whitby, used since primitive times for beads and fashionable from 1808 when the first workshop was opened. Although perfect for mourning jewellery, made fashionable by Queen Victoria (who was rarely out of mourning), jet was also used for general jewellery wear, suitable for carving, engraving, and mounting. By 1873 there were 200 workshops in the Whitby area processing jet. French jet is glass; Spanish jet is genuine but softer, and imported for the making of beads.

JEWELLED DECORATION

A term used in the ceramics industry, a misnomer as no jewels are involved, only enamel drops fused on gold or silver foil, introduced by Sèvres about 1781 and used in England in the nineteenth century by Worcester and Goss.

JEWELLERY

Jewellery has been worn as a sign of status and power, or for self adornment, since ancient times, and made from almost any substance. During the Dark Ages the usual item of jewellery was the brooch. During the fourteenth century precious stones began flooding into Europe, and techniques for shaping them and putting them into settings were developed, as well as gold technology. The Goldsmiths' Company of London received its charter in 1327. In France jewels became marks of rank, and rules were made by establishing what each class of society was to wear, and French influences appeared in England in 1396 when Edward II married Isabella. In the Renaissance pearls were worn in the hair or as necklaces, and the jewellery included pendants and rings as well as cameos. Low-cut gowns brought in a need for necklaces, and wide sleeves encouraged the use of bracelets. However, until the sixteenth century the more elaborate jewellery had been worn by men, and from that century diamonds became increasingly important as women's jewellery; new ways of cutting diamonds were introduced, and by the seventeenth century most gemstones were facet-cut. The 58-facet brilliant cut was adopted in the next century. Jewellery fashions echoed trends and supplemented the types of clothes being worn, and it was usual to break up and recycle items of jewellery when they became outmoded. Extravagant styles were followed by a degree of restraint. During the eighteenth century daytime jewels were modest, including the garnet and the topaz, but in the evening diamonds were worn. Paste, glass cut to emulate jewels, was greatly used, not as a cheap substitute but as a valid material in itself. During the nineteenth century much jewellery was made in the form of flowers and foliage, fruit, butterflies, birds, and especially hearts, and arranged so that large combinations could be divided into smaller pieces for less formal occasions, so that a tiara could become a necklace and two brooches. Flowers had distinct meanings; in 1856 a dictionary of 700 flowers and their meanings was published. Filigree flower and butterfly jewellery was popular from the 1860s, and earrings became fashionable in the shape of beetles, birds, fish, flies, horseshoes, as well as coal-scuttles and locomotives. The border line between precious stones (diamonds, rubies, emeralds and sapphires) and semiprecious stones was vague. The preciousness of diamonds was only relative; in 1867 the price of diamonds fell dramatically after their discovery in South Africa, which now provides 97 per cent of the world's diamonds. After the diamond the hardest gemstone is the ruby, used mostly after the

Victorian sapphire and diamond pendant.

By the 1890s diamonds had ceased to be luxury items. But the pearl necklace illustrated at the bottom of this advertisement cost £1,650 (thirty years wages for the working man).

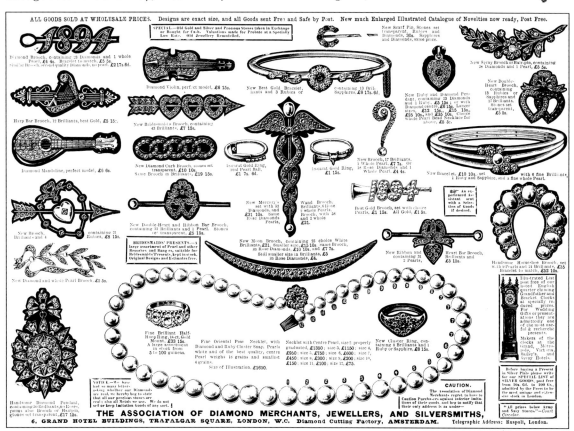

sixteenth century as it was rare, as was the opal until the nineteenth century when quantities were found in Australia. Opal, soft and usually cut in the round, is found in many colours; the black opal was discovered in 1905. Lapis lazuli, an intense blue mineral, was used from the seventeenth century. Garnets are a family of gemstones, one of the best known being the carbuncle. Turquoise is of a blue or bluish-green colour. Emeralds are often flawed, but the flaws themselves are valued; synthetic emeralds were made from 1946 in America. Marcasite (tiny particles of iron pyrites set in claws and pans) and cut steel (small faceted heads of steel on a thin back plate or on a chain, first produced commercially from 1762), valueless in themselves, were greatly esteemed, as were ammonites (tiny coiled fossils) and lava. Old styles were rediscovered, often re-presented in anachronistic and showy forms. The vogue for Egyptian motifs resulted in serpent necklaces, bracelets and rings. Towards the end of the nineteenth century small lace brooches and pins were rather more popular than the heavier type of jewellery and, with the growing independence of women, small sporting brooches became fashionable, portraying fox masks, hounds, horses, riding whips, and there were miniature gold bicycles, tennis-rackets and golf-clubs. Jewellery was ideal for art nouveau designers, with the accent on stylised forms. Art deco jewellery was influenced by the Russian ballet, Aztec and Inca motifs, popular Egyptiana (Tutankhamen's tomb was found in 1922), as well as echoing fashion. Much was geometric, a trend started at the beginning of the century, and unusual combinations were introduced such as onyx, diamonds, coral and platinum in one piece, or rock crystal, diamonds, rubies and coloured enamels. Jade, onyx and diamonds were used for drop ear-rings. The jewellery designers lavished just as much care on bangles of plastic, and necklaces of plastic and chrome. But there was always a distinction between what was fashionable and what was proper. There was always a role for diamonds and the string of pearls.

KAKIEMON

A Japanese seventeenth-century potter credited with the introduction in Japan in 1644 of painting in overglaze enamel colours and also a Japanese style of ceramic decoration, in which brilliant pure colours are applied often sparsely, often in asymmetrical patterns, on a milk-white ground. The most famous design is the 'quail pattern', two birds off-centre surrounded by stylised plants. Kakiemon ware had an immense influence on Europe.

KELIM CARPET

A type of carpet, not a description of its country or district of origin, this is a reversible, tapestry-weave carpet made using a specific technique involving weft threads of a specific colour worked to and fro in its own pattern area, with the next colour continuing the pattern from the adjacent warp thread. Between the different coloured areas there are slits, disguised by indenting the outlines of the patterns. Two widths were sometimes sewn together. Kelims, also called kilims, gilims, and ghilims, were made throughout the carpet-making areas of the Near East.

KETTLE

Originally a straightforward cooking pot, given a spout in the late seventeenth century, and from then on made in most materials from iron to silver, the most generally popular, because of the associations with cottages and the rural idyll, being in copper. The tea-kettle was used to pour the water into the teapot, and was often made of silver.

KETTLE STAND

A small table supporting an urn or a kettle, sometimes with a galleried top, occasionally with a metal-lined box-shaped top with an aperture for the kettle spout. There is usually a pull-out slide to support the teapot. Made throughout the eighteenth century, some of them are quaint. The stands were generally fitted with tripod legs.

KEYBOARD INSTRUMENTS

Early keyboard instruments include the virginals (very rare) and the harpsichord, which have a plucking action, and the clavichord, a striking action. The first grand piano was invented in

1709; the first square piano was introduced to England about 1742 and lasted about a century. Many have been converted to dressing tables, but they were made in huge quantities and they are still about, probably unrecognised for what they are. The upright piano came in a variety of sizes beginning about 1850 from the humble cottage piano to the giraffe piano (a grand piano on its side). Every conceivable space on an upright piano might be decorated; there was gilding, lacquering, ebonising, fretwork, pillars, candlesticks (often taken off and now sold separately), and expanses of silk. Better-class instruments were made of the show woods or lavishly inlaid with marquetry. Among the leading makers are Steinway, Bechstein, Broadwood and Blüthner. The name on the lid may be the retailer and thus of no importance.

KIDDERMINSTER CARPETS

Carpets were made since at least the seventeenth century, especially tough cheap rugs, and from 1735 double-cloth carpets were produced, the earliest type of machine-made carpet. This is made from two sets of worsted warp and two sets of woollen weft, woven on the draw loom in such a manner that the same pattern is on the front and back, though in reversed colours. This is called a Kidderminster carpet because of its type not place of origin. Jacquard looms, capable of weaving extremely complicated designs, and each needing only one operator, invented about 1805, first used in Paris about 1815, were introduced in 1825. The industry expanded greatly in the nineteenth century, with 1,000 looms in 1807 and more than 2,000 in 1838. Patterns and styles were unadventurous, but Kidderminster-made carpets have continued to be made in great quantities.

KITCHEN UTENSILS

In essentials, changing little over the centuries, summarised by vessels to cook in, vessels to contain food, tools to cook or serve with, and instruments involved with the fire. The con-

After World War I there was a shortage of servants, and houses were often arranged so that there would be little dusting and housework to do. One furniture-maker was nicknamed (Percy 'Dusty' Wells) because he made his furniture simple so that it was easy to keep clean. Whether the spartan kitchen of this illustration was to everybody's taste is doubtful.

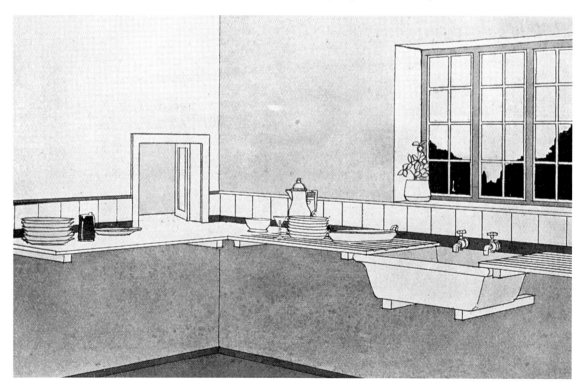

tainers include cauldrons, buckets, pots, pans, mortars and frying-pans. Food containers range from jelly moulds to plates, ewers, urns, dishes, and mugs, and the tools the customary knives, forks and spoons plus ladles and the array of instruments such as asparagus tongs, cheese scoops, fish servers, some of which occupy a hinterland between the kitchen and the dining-room. Numerous articles were used to arrange food in a satisfactory manner over an open fire, some of them extremely ingenious with arrangements of wires and pulleys. The main development lies in more suitable metals, iron and pewter being replaced or supplemented by tinned copper, with tin-plated iron from the 1730s and brass vessels appearing at the close of the eighteenth century. Tinned steel superseded copper in the early nineteenth century, and this in turn was often discarded in favour of enamelled iron in the 1850s, still much in evidence despite the use of aluminium. Prior to the age of plastics, many kitchen utensils were heavy and hard-wearing, and it is interesting to see old materials, such as iron, returning to favour.

KNEADING TROUGH

This is one of the many coffin-like objects in wood that have enjoyed a new lease of life as decorative objects. This particular container has sides slanting outwards towards the top, four legs, and can be recognised by the division into two sections, one for flour and one for dough. It had a detachable lid which could serve as a table. Although made in medieval times, troughs of all kinds, including the dough bin, are not amenable to alteration and were made without change into the nineteenth century.

KNIFE CASES

Dating from at least 1649, when the knife case was first illustrated, they catered for new sophisticated eating habits. The days when a visiting guest was obliged to bring his own knife and fork were soon to go for good. Matching sets of knives and forks were placed in cases designed to take a dozen of each, handles upwards. Spoons were soon added to the sets. It is interesting to note that table silver was not changed for each course of the meal but washed in the dining-room. The earlier knife boxes, made of deal,

were leather covered, with a velvet or chamois leather lining. Until the late eighteenth century the usual shape was with a sloping top and convex lid. Walnut and mahogany, the fashionable woods, tended to replace leather or shagreen. A vase-shaped case was introduced in the 1770s; the case was raised and lowered on a central stem, as it is difficult to hinge a circular lid. Knife cases were also made in satinwood with marquetry inlay, and lacquered, or in painted enamel. Silver and gilded brass mounts were often used. By the early nineteenth century a wealthy host's table silver could number more than a thousand individual pieces.

KNOCK-DOWN FURNITURE

Sometimes called package furniture, this is kit furniture, first made in Sweden in the 1940s, and assembled on site. As quality work was made at the time, it should not necessarily be dismissed out of hand.

KNOLE SETTEE

A settee with a high back and hinged arms which may be held upright or slanted. It was named after a unique specimen at Knole Park near Sevenoaks, Kent, and was immensely popular amongst the well-to-do in the 1920s and 1930s.

KOREAN CERAMICS

Although strongly influenced by Chinese models, Korean ware is often distinctive, especially the twelfth-century ware with a particular kingfisher-blue glaze and decorations, including small stars and flowers, inlaid into the surface in black or white slip. Unsophisticated brown glazed ware was valued sufficiently for it to be imported by the Japanese for their tea ceremonies.

LACE

Openwork fabric usually of linen but also of silk or gold and silver thread, first made in the late fifteenth century in Italy and Flanders. The word 'lace' comes from an old French word meaning noose, and can encompass many kinds of embroidery, crochet and knitting, but lace in its commonly accepted form is of two kinds, bobbin-lace and needlepoint. Bobbin-lace is made on a round or oval pillow held on the knees. The pattern is drawn on parchment, which is stretched on the pillow, and the design is marked out with pins. Around each pin a thread is looped, and the thread is wound round a bone or wooden bobbin, held in place by a groove. A separate bobbin is used for each thread. There can be two hundred, so the bobbins are differentiated by decoration or by coloured beads (one of the best-known types of lace, Honiton, uses about thirty beads). The bobbins are thrown and twisted around the pins, building up the lace. Needlepoint employs a single needle and a single thread and was first used as a decorative filling for small holes cut in the fabric. Needlepoint and bobbin-lace can be used in combination. There are many types of lace, usually named after their assumed places of origin, not always accurately. Of the pillow-laces, Chantilly is mainly black lace; Mechlin is characterised by rococo patterns outlined in a thread heavier than that used for the rest of the fabric, with pattern and ground made together, and Valenciennes, one of the finest and most costly, has delicate designs of scrolls and stylised flowers.

Antwerp lace is heavy, with a two-handled vase the dominant motif; many different types of lace were made at Brussels including *point plat* and, misleadingly, *point d'Angleterre*, typified by a hexagonal mesh. Bedfordshire lace was made also in Buckinghamshire and Northampton-shire. Some lace is delicate, some is robust and padded, such as the needlepoint lace *point de Venise*, or geometrical (*reticella*), also needle-point. About 1800 a machine was invented which made net, so the painstaking business of providing a background by hand was eliminated. It was not long before sophisticated machinery was making the actual lace, the centre of the industry being Nottingham. To alleviate hunger and distress a lace industry was started in Ireland, the makers of which proved adept in emulating the best lace, adding sham-rock and harp motifs. The Maltese lace industry was founded in 1833, the products being in silk, and usually incorporating the Maltese cross. The colour was customarily ecru (buff). Tape lace is thread tape linked by bars of fine needle-work. Tatting is coarse lace-making using ivory

A *section of intricate Victorian 1860s lace.*

or bone shuttles, used for edgings where fine lace would be too expensive or fragile, and is easily and quickly done. Decorated nets are laces having a regular open mesh, worked by running a needle in and out of them in regular patterns. Examples are filet (the most common), Limerick, Spanish Blonde, and Carickmacross. Filet was often used for lace pictures and for milk-jug covers with beads around the edge to weight them. Crochet is looping work done with a small hook, and not lace at all though fondly believed to be by the owners or execut-ants.

LACE BOBBINS

These are used in the making of pillow-lace, identifying the individual thread, each needing a bobbin. Up to about 1800, bobbins were usu-ally made of wood and were bulbous in appear-ance with a long neck topped by a knob. These are rare. Subsequently bobbins were slim, and made from wood, bone, pewter, copper, brass, ivory and, not very often, glass. Each bobbin is identified, often by beads strung along the length, known as spangles. A common spangle is made up of nine beads – two small clear round

It is often not realised how complex the processes were for many of the hand-made antiques, as seen in this picture of a pillow-lace (bobbin-lace) maker. Notice the lace-maker's globe on the table to give extra light from the candle.

glass beads, six square-cut beads of clear or pink glass, and a central bead with a coloured scroll round the centre. The bobbins themselves have different names depending on their construction; sometimes wood bobbins are inlaid with contrasting wood; spliced bobbins consist of two different woods or wood and bone; incised bobbins have grooves, dots and dashes cut into them, usually coloured afterwards; wired bobbins are bound with wire; the Mother-in-Babe is a bobbin inside a bobbin, similar to Cow-in-Calf, a bobbin in two sections, unscrewed to reveal a tiny bobbin inside; a two-section bobbin containing balls or beads is a Bird-Cage. Bobbins can be inscribed with names, and can be dated. Sometimes there are bobbins inscribed with convicted murderers' names and with the date of execution, apparently given away by murderers' relatives. With the revival of lace-making as a hobby, bobbins are again being made, but are usually plain and often not greatly prized.

LAMBETH DELFTWARE

Tin-glazed earthenware made from the early seventeenth to the late eighteenth centuries. Early examples have a pink tinge, later a greenish. There was a strong Chinese influence on the products of the earlier years, and later, Chinese motifs were intermingled with European. Lambeth made a variety of unusual delft, including puzzle jugs, hors-d'oeuvre dishes (a central compartment with four or five others around the rim), water-bottles with rounded bases, and interesting pharmacy ware, such as pill slabs and jars. Amongst the most attractive products are the large blue-and-white chargers. Delftware from other factories has often been credited to Lambeth, and no doubt vice versa, for there is no sure way of assigning the factory of origin.

LAMP-BLOWN GLASS

Novelty glass using rods or tubes manipulated under modest heat for the edification usually of a gawping mob, and the character of the pieces made reflect this. A fully rigged-up ship with the ropes represented by threads of glass is perhaps the supreme achievement.

LANTERN

Candle holder, enclosed or partly enclosed, protected from draughts by a thin section of horn, skin, or glass. Some lanterns were very ornamental, especially when intended for indoor use, such as in a hall.

LEAD

Used from ancient times for roofing, cisterns, garden objects; deadly poison and thus tinned if used for purposes other than practical or decorative. In 1770 a hardening process was developed, resulting in finer detail, and it was possible to make small items such as mantelpiece figures and containers out of it, although it was never so suitable as pewter (lead plus tin).

LEATHER

Used mostly for chair seats and backs, book covers, tops of writing-desks, chests, buckets,

134

clothing, and bottles (jacks). Techniques for decorating leather by punches and by painting were developed in the fourteenth century, and by the sixteenth century the centre of the industry had moved from Spain to the Netherlands, where embossing was used for wall hangings, table covers, and small decorative objects. Ornament could be applied using metal stamps (blind tooling) or impressing goldleaf under heat into blind tooling (gold tooling).

LEEDS POTTERY

Established in the 1770s, Leeds earthenware was noted for its colour, a rich cream with deep glaze, sometimes tinged with green. Pierced and basket-type ware was made, much was exported and, although other potteries were engaged in the same kind of work, Leeds was exceptionally delicate. One of its specialities was the plate with a border of interwoven twigs. Other products included transfer ware in red, black, lilac and green, black basalt, lustre, refined figures, red stoneware, and tortoiseshell ware. The factory went through several owners, and closed in 1878, although there was another Leeds-based firm that used the original Leeds Pottery moulds, thus causing confusion.

LIBRARY STEPS

It was not until the late seventeenth century that books were put into bookcases, but in the eighteenth century bookcases became huge. All gentlemen of note had their libraries, to reach the upper shelves of which was difficult without aids, ranging from a step-ladder to ingenious combination furniture, in which stools, chairs and tables opened up into steps. Sheraton produced designs with a rail and a book-rest 'so that a gentleman when he is looking at any book in his library may note down a passage from it without the trouble of going down again'. Some devices were simple; a stool tips on end to become two steps; armchairs divide into halves; a hinged table-top has steps on the under-side and pulls out to rest at an angle of forty-five degrees on the edge of the table while inside the table is another flight of steps arranged to form a continuation. The total length of the library steps would be about eight feet (2.4m). The most elegant were step-ladders with a handrail and

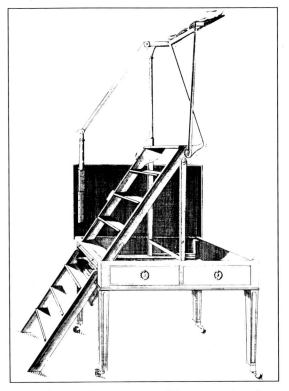

Design for a dual-purpose pair of library steps from Ince and Mayhew's Universal System of Household Furniture *(c1762).*

fitted with wheels or castors. Library steps should not be confused with bed steps, which are substantial, usually carpeted and enclosing commodes.

LIMOGES

Main centre of enamelling from the twelfth to the fourteenth centuries, with religious objects dominating. In the fifteenth century the painted enamel technique was developed; a speciality was the miniature portrait, and later the wall plaque. The factory faded at the end of the seventeenth century, but Limoges enamels were painstakingly faked in the nineteenth , both by the French and by the celebrated English faker Samson. Limoges was also a pottery and porcelain centre, established in 1736 and producing nondescript wares. A porcelain factory was opened in 1771 under the patronage of the king's brother, and acquired by King Louis XVI in 1784 to provide white ware for decoration at Sèvres, a project that did not work out. However, with the establishment of other factories Limoges became the main centre of porcelain production, mainly of the household type, in France and still is.

LINEN SMOOTHER

A plain or coloured glass device in the shape of a mushroom with a handle used in the eighteenth century for smoothing linen.

LITHOPHANE

A small rectangle of the thinnest possible unglazed porcelain on which is a moulded picture, only observable by holding up to the light. Although patented in Paris in 1827 it was a very popular novelty and made by factories throughout Europe. The quality of the design was often of the highest, and well-known landscapes were adapted for the quaint medium. From 1850 lithophanes were sometimes tinted.

LIVERPOOL DELFT AND PORCELAIN

Manufacture of delftware began about 1710 following the settlement in the area of potters from Southwark, London, though some Liverpool pottery dates from the seventeenth century. Transfer printing began in 1750, and other potteries sent their work to Liverpool to be decorated there. Designs were taken from books, prints, and paintings. Characteristic of Liverpool were tiles and curious brick-shaped vases. The ware was adventurous, somewhat coarse, bluish in tone, and is difficult to allocate to the various potteries, the best known of which is Chaffers.

LOBBY CHEST

Name given, probably by auctioneers in search of a new phrase, to a small chest of drawers designed, allegedly, to fit into small rooms. As most chests of drawers fit into small rooms anyway, probably a superfluous novelty.

LOCK

Used from medieval times; a technologically advanced piece of machinery which survived unchanged for centuries, only the setting

changing with Gothic decoration and coats-of-arms in the fourteenth century. Relief designs appeared in the mid-eighteenth century, shortly before the invention of the mortise lock (where the lock is inserted into the door rather than fixed on top), which brought in back plates, knobs, and escutcheon plates. In 1784 the cylinder lock using a rotating barrel was invented, leading to the Yale lock of 1848. All modern locks, including the combination, derive directly from the earlier types.

LOCKET

Oval, circular or heart-shaped object containing a miniature, hair, or a photograph, suspended from a ribbon or chain, made in all materials including gold and silver, often enriched with small gems.

LOCOMOTIVE MODELS

With the arrival of real locomotives, toy locomotives became popular. Tin-plate toys can date as early as 1840, provided without rails, and small brass trains were made about the same time. America made cast-iron locomotives and wagons from about 1870. As cheap clockwork motors were not available, motion was provided by boilers fired by methylated spirits (as used in toy boats). The wheels were serrated to give a grip on the surface. Birmingham began producing toy locomotives about 1870, some of them very large and elaborate with many exterior gadgets and, as the century drew to a close, locomotive models became more realistic, based on actual trains, and the details of the various companies were lithographed and pasted on the metal. Construction kits were marketed and, with the coming of clockwork, many famous companies entered the market, the first tinplate clockwork models rolling off the production line about 1880, made by Bing and Marklin of Germany. The most famous name is unquestionably Hornby, followed by Bassett-Lowke, whose products are valued very highly. After World War I there was greater realism, using castings, and electric trains vied with clockwork. There was a tremendous range of accessories. There is a clear distinction between toys and scale models, used in miniature railways, and about 1910 coal-fired boilers were

used. Non-working scale models were used as display items and are rare and valuable. Although locomotives are the most important kind of railwayana, there is great interest in platform signs and lamps, tickets, timetables, maps, train nameplates, even the brass locks from train lavatory doors, and anything to do with the individual railway companies.

LONG-CASE CLOCKS*

The pendulum was evolved in 1658, 400 years after the first mechanical clock; the longer the pendulum, the greater the accuracy, so the works (the movement) and the pendulum were housed in a long slender box – the long-case or grandfather clock. The first long-case clocks were in oak and veneered in ebony, with a small brass dial and a short pendulum. Ebony, being expensive, was counterfeited by stained and polished pearwood; and as furniture fashions changed so did the woods – marquetry from

Advertisement of 1908 for the Bassett-Lowke model locomotive.

about 1680, walnut veneer from about 1720, followed shortly by lacquer. Pendulums became longer, and the cases wider (to allow for the greater swing of a long pendulum) and architectural, with ornate top-pieces called caddies. The eighteenth-century mahogany clock might be termed the classic clock, restrained, and good-looking. As with the cases, dials altered, and not only did they indicate the time and maybe the date but the maker's name, a very important factor (but this is only the maker of the movement, not the case). Nineteenth-century clocks could be huge and monstrous, and play music as well as tell the time, thanks to an integral musical movement or tubular bells, which played the Westminster, St Michael or Whittington chimes. Bizarre long-case clocks were made in the 1930s, including some which incorporated an electric fire.

LONGTON HALL

The first factory in Staffordshire to manufacture porcelain, and one of the first to close, lasting only about ten years until 1760. The products of the first four years were primitive and crude, including so-called snowman figures, mugs, plates, dishes, tea bowls and saucers, teapots and sauce-boats. The underglaze blue was runny and unevenly applied and especially bright, and many pieces have an unfinished appearance. During the middle years potting became better and finish improved, and the work included leaf-moulded ware in the Meissen style – teapots, sauce-boats, tureens, dishes, jugs, mugs, bowls and open-work baskets. There was fine painted work including that by a mysterious personage known as the 'Trembly Rose' painter and first-class bird decoration, said to be un-equalled by any other contemporary English factory. Towards the end of the factory's life tea wares became more common, and blue-and-white rarer than coloured ware. Handles were inclined to be of the rustic twig type, and many of the patterns derived from those on Chinese porcelain. Much collected is transfer-printed ware in black.

LOUIS STYLE

A muddled Victorian expression for furniture that looked vaguely French.

LOUIS PHILIPPE STYLE

French furniture from the years 1830–48, de-rivative, concerned with reviving Gothic and other remote periods but with extra solidity and an emphasis on curvature and the flashy, with the use of porcelain plaques and bronze mounts.

LOUIS XIII STYLE

Strictly 1589–1643, furniture mostly walnut with spiral and baluster turning and the use of motifs such as cherubs, swags, scroll-work and shields. Carving, gilding, and inlay were all ex-tensively used, with the cabinet a prestige piece, often decorated with buhl work (tortoiseshell and brass inlay). Throughout the Continent, the cabinet was the most important piece of furniture.

LOUIS XIV STYLE

Dating from 1643–1715, the furniture was the ultimate in baroque, highly decorated, gradually becoming less oppressive with cleaner lines in the early eighteenth century.

LOUIS XV STYLE

From 1715–74, flowery, rococo, oriented to women's demands and requirements with an emphasis on curved forms and less formality, though the furniture was still replete with intri-cate marquetry and exotic inlay.

LOUIS XVI STYLE

Corresponding to the English neo-Classical style with use of such ornaments as husks, masks, various stylised flower motifs, and scrolls, increased use of mahogany but with metal mounts, which were not a feature of English furniture of the period.

LOWESTOFT PORCELAIN

Factory established in 1757 making unpretenti-ous coloured and blue-and-white soft-paste porcelain. From 1761 small boxes and other pieces were made for tourists often lettered 'A Trifle from Lowestoft'. Typical of its products are wickerwork designs, open-work baskets, and cabbage-leaf jugs. Its later pieces were more elaborate, often Chinese in style. The factory closed in 1802.

LUSTRES

Cut-glass pendants used from the eighteenth century and suspended from chandeliers, often surrounding glass table-centres in the form of a vase, usually coloured, with ruby red (cran-berry) the most popular colour. The term lustre applied in the trade to the pendants and the table-centre together.

LUSTRE DECORATION

A thin deposit of metal on the surface of ceramics, resulting from painting oxides on glazed surfaces, upon which the article is fired again, fixing the lustre, which can be of many

Sunderland lustre jug depicting on one side a frigate in full sail and on the other the celebrated Sunderland bridge, a popular subject.

colours. Known in Persia from the Middle Ages and brought to Europe via Spain, and used on all qualities of ware as it can be flashy as well as extremely subtle. The Sunderland lustreware is probably the best known.

MAIOLICA

Tin-glazed pottery, given the name maiolica because at one time the ware passed en route through Majorca. Known in Italy from the eleventh century. Also known as faience.

MAJOLICA

Not a synonym for maiolica but a specific product evolved by Minton in 1851 and introduced at the Great Exhibition, coloured with a clear glaze containing metallic oxides and becoming deservedly popular for very large objects, often meant for outdoor use in gardens (where they sometimes still are, untouched by 150 years of weather). Besides garden fountains majolica was also used for umbrella-stands, flower bowls, and animal pieces, often superbly modelled and utterly distinctive.

MANDARIN PORCELAIN

Jars with figure subjects in panels, made in China in the nineteenth century for the European market, and in pinks, reds and golds framed in blue scroll-work. Dutifully copied in England.

MARBLING

A method, originally Chinese, of emulating marble in ceramics by mixing different coloured clays and covering them with a transparent glaze, a process used in the manufacture of agate ware. Also painting wood to imitate marble, especially pillars and architectural elements, but not often used in furniture.

MARKS

Applied to all kinds of products, often in profusion. They can indicate the identity of the maker (either a firm, factory, or individual), date, the pattern number of the piece, sometimes even the price and, as in certain classical French furniture, proof that the item has passed the stern scrutiny of the furniture guild. Marks can be a token of reverence; Chinese potters marked their products with the signs for previous dynasties as a mark of respect and not with intent to deceive. Marks can be fakes, clever or fatuous. Even the great English eighteenth-century porcelain makers marked their wares with the marks and symbols used by Meissen and others. This may seem odd, and indicates a sense of inferiority, but none of the potters could visualise that sometime in the future there would be learned dispute on marks and imitation marks. The first consistent factory marks date from the 1570s in Italy. Early maiolica was marked if it was deemed sufficiently important, otherwise not. In 1764 in Holland there was a determined attempt to legalise marks, but this came to nothing. Genuine marks have been obliterated at all times from the date of manufacture to today, and others substituted, especially easy on the bases of objects. Marks on unglazed pottery can be scratched off with the point of a knife in a matter of seconds. A further complication lies in that genuine marks often differ enormously from one piece to the next. Unlike an impressed stamp, a workman's initial can vary immensely. Problems with marks occur mainly with ceramics, where there is no overall authority and nothing to stop a maker doing what he likes. An object lesson is provided by English silver, where all the information is provided, though, of course, such marks can be lifted from one article to another. There is no protection against the determined rogue.

MARQUETRY

An ornamental veneer in which different kinds of veneer are cut, placed, and glued on a furniture surface to represent flowers, plant life, and other natural forms, often stylised. It was introduced from Holland about 1675, and made veneer especially interesting. Veneer cut into geometric form is known as parquetry, but some use the term marquetry irrespective of its precise meaning.

MARY GREGORY GLASS

Nineteenth-century glassware of all kinds enamelled in white with figures, especially children, named after an American glass decorator, and made especially in Bohemia as well as America. Widely faked as are all nineteenth-century pretty-pretties.

MATCH HOLDERS

Match holders were used in the home, in public houses, in hotels, and all places where smokers congregated. The basic form was a flattened sphere made from pottery, porcelain, glass, wood, metal, and other substances, often ribbed to provide a striking surface. The earliest reference to a ceramic match holder seems to be a patent application in 1861. In the 1860s a Parian match holder was produced representing a sentry box with a sentry. The surfaces of match holders were decorated or bore advertising material. One by Doulton in 1897 to celebrate Queen Victoria's Diamond Jubilee advertised Foster's beers, and there were many celebrating Boer War heroes and events. 'Strike me and I will light' and 'A match for any man' were mottoes on match holders produced by the Devon art potteries of Aller Vale, Long Park and Watcombe. Wedgwood produced holders in basalt and jasper. Match holders were widely

produced in Germany, sometimes representing children, often with animals, sometimes with mottoes (particularly in French, so the market was the French smoker). Busts of famous people such as Buffalo Bill and General Gordon in iron and spelter, with the front of the base grooved for friction, were common. Glass, either plain or coloured, often had a silver rim. One of the most interesting patents taken out was for a match holder made from a horse's vertebra ('cleansed, bleached and suitably shaped'). Holders were also shaped from local materials, such as serpentine from Cornwall and Blue John from Derbyshire.

MAUCHLINE WARE

Wooden souvenirs usually in the form of boxes, napkin rings, string-holders, rulers, pincushions, darners, paper-knives and similar knickknacks, largely useless. Mauchline is the name of the Ayrshire town where these originated about 1820. The manufacturers peaked about 1860 when they employed more than 400 people, and although the company survived until the 1940s their products had long been old-fashioned. The first boxes were handdecorated with pen and ink, followed by tartan designs painted directly onto the wood. Sometimes portraits were included of celebrated Scotsmen, such as Bonnie Prince Charlie. Direct painting on wood was augmented by painting on paper and gluing the picture to the wood, but most boxes from about 1850 were transfer printed in black, often with views. These views, unchanged, were used well into the twentieth century. The firm also used ferns stuck to the wood and varnished over; a cheap substitute was provided by paper bearing a fern pattern. A minor diversion into lacquered boxes was made from about 1870, but they were of mediocre quality. The main task for collectors is to decide between direct painting and printing, not difficult as, if the picture is looked at under a magnifying glass, the individual dots resulting from the printing process can easily be detected. Collectors who build thematic collections – writing, needlework, domestic – will find Mauchline ware an interesting and financially undemanding source of material. It is often difficult to determine when a piece was made, often the case with traditional ware.

Medallion

Oval or circular object depicting portraits, figures, flowers, etc, which could be worn as jewellery, inset into furniture, or employed as a Persian carpet design.

Meissen

Alternatively called Dresden, perhaps the most eminent porcelain factory in the world, established in 1710 with red stoneware discovered by the resident alchemist in the Elector of Saxony's employ. The red clay was substituted by kaolin (china clay), and the first true porcelain was made outside China, first marketed in 1713. The earliest table ware followed silver models, decorated with floral motifs, and using enamels, gilding, and lustre. The first figures were based on those in ivory, and ivory carvers were employed at Meissen. Much chinoiserie was produced together with harbour scenes and armorial ware. Birds and floral designs became increasingly popular, also pastoral scenes, often in the French style. The figures became amazing, far ahead of anything being produced elsewhere in the world, with superb modelling and colouring. With the outbreak of the Seven Years War in 1756, Meissen suffered, being occupied by the alien Prussians, and it never regained its former supremacy. Towards the end of the eighteenth century there was an emphasis on neo-Classical styling, with copies of Wedgwood blue jasper. In the nineteenth century early successful figures were revamped to suit current taste, usually known as Dresden to differentiate them from the originals. Although there are many other German factories, Meissen eclipsed them all, though Nymphenburg made a superb white porcelain and is noted for its figures and figure groups. Faience (maiolica) was made in Berlin from 1678, and factories there produced an immense range of products, almost rivalling Meissen.

Metal Spinning

Shaping silver and other metal into teapots, bowls, and similar objects by making a core or chuck of wood, fixing it to a lathe and, while the lathe revolves, flat metal is pushed onto the chuck, taking its shape.

Microscopes

Microscopes, optical instruments for viewing very small objects, fall into two groups: (1) simple, consisting of one lens, and (2) compound, with more than one lens. The most basic of microscopes is the magnifying glass. Although the principle had been known for nearly two thousand years, the microscrope had to wait for its invention until the arrival of a suitable glass technology. The first powerful microscope (x 250) dates from 1660. Early simple microcopes were made mainly of brass with fittings of wood and ivory; compound microscopes had tubes of cardboard covered in leather or vellum. About 1725 microscopes were fitted with small movable mirrors beneath the 'stage' to illuminate transparent specimens, but the modern brass microscope dates from 1745. An improved image was possible in about 1760 by the invention of the achromatic lens, which did not leave a coloured fringe around the object viewed. Eighteenth-century microscopes are often ornate but technically flawed. The binocular microscope was introduced in the mid-nineteenth century. Boxed accessories are a great plus factor. Individual slides can be of great value, though the most common, a butterfly wing, is not.

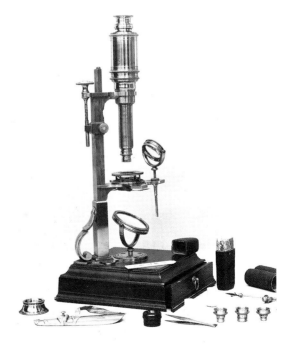

19th-century Cuff-type microscope with accessories.

MILITARIA

These comprise a great range of objects, such as armour, edged weapons, uniforms, medals, and firearms. Firearms are a grey area; some need firearms certificates for their possession. Armour was once the most spectacular piece of militaria; in the 1950s a good armour (not a suit of armour) could be bought for under £100, but when armour appears on the market today it is likely to be a composite set from different sources, though odd pieces dating from the English Civil War (1642–8) are within reach, such as the burgonet, a lobster-pot helmet with neck protection. A full armour includes protection for the legs; half armour does not. The introduction of firearms made armour obsolete about 1530 except for heavy cavalry. For a time soldiers did not wear helmets, but during the Napoleonic Wars decorative helmets of burnished steel, brass or copper were worn by the cavalry, and plumed helmets, issued in 1846, are worn today for ceremonial

occasions. The pickelhaube or spiked helmet was introduced in 1846 by Prussia, and copied by most armies including Britain. The Germans replaced it in 1916 with the well-known steel helmet; the British revived the ancient fifteenth century sallet. During World War II most of the world's armies used the helmets introduced in World War I.

As with costume of all kinds, uniforms are subject to decay, deterioration and dirt; no British uniforms are of great antiquity. Only in 1742 were they standardised. They were incongrous and unsuitable, and until 1836 even

Eleven Royal Staffordshire character jugs of World War I period representing King George V, Sir John French, Earl Haig, Lloyd George, Admirals Jellicoe and Beatty, Marshals Joffre and Foch, President Wilson of the USA, and General Botha (later South African president).

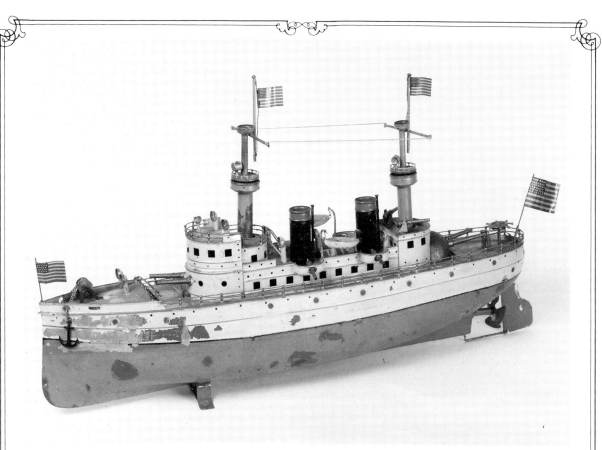

A Carette tinplate battleship of about 1905, intact but in a somewhat battered played-with condition, detracting from its value.

A pair of early Staffordshire figures depicting a soldier and a sailor.

the lowliest of soldiers wore gold and silver lace adornments, though the Crimean War made it necessary to evaluate uniform. Tropical uniform was white, changed to khaki during wars in India to make the soldiers less conspicuous to snipers; in 1902 khaki became the accepted colour except for ceremonial occasions. Headgear includes the broad-brimmed hats used in the English Civil War, a three-cornered hat modelled on civilian types, and a cylindrical hat, the shako. Forage caps of all kinds, including a stocking cap with a tassel at the end, a Scottish glengarry from 1874, and a type of balaclava from 1890, were worn off duty by other ranks. In World War I all ranks wore peaked khaki caps, followed in due course

by the much more convenient envelope-style forage cap and beret. Cap badges and regimental insignia are much sought after, especially if they relate to regiments that have been abolished or amalgamated.

Medals to commemorate a special event were first struck at the time of the Spanish Armada. During the eighteenth and nineteenth centuries they were widely issued (51,065 for one minor engagement alone, issued by the East India Company). The first general medal was the Waterloo medal of 1815. Most medals had clasps or bars for separate compaigns; the Naval General Medal could have 231 clasps, some for engagements involving a handful of men. Good conduct, long service, and I-was-there medals are of less interest than those issued for gallantry.

Until the coming of firearms there was a variety of specialised weapons, mainly edged –

A group of Britain model soldiers of 1907.

such as swords – and piercing – such as lances – and early weapons of this kind are often available at very little cost in 'excavated' condition. Swords were in two main groups, two-handed weapons and smaller ones for hand-to-hand fighting; development of the sword lay mainly in protecting the hand, twisting the straight cross-piece into an S, leading to a cup-hilt, often ornately engraved, still part of an officer's ceremonial equipment. The grip was often of shagreen bound with wire. The rapier was a civilian weapon rather than a military, as was the development of the rapier, the small-sword, the hilt often inset with gold, silver, and gemstones. The guards were often shaped in filigree or consisted of beads on wire. Curved swords of the sabre type were used for hunting and for naval service. Daggers were mostly personal self-protection weapons, or were left-handed weapons used in association with a rapier. A wide variety includes the Scottish dirk and the stiletto, but amongst the most desirable are Nazi ceremonial daggers and Commando daggers of World War II.

A pair of flintlock pistols of the early 19th century.

Bayonets were decidedly made for use and not for show; they were introduced in 1640, and are of limited variety, unlike pistols, produced by the craftsmen elite, the gunsmiths. Pistols could be primitive frightening weapons, such as the blunderbuss with a bell-shaped mouth, or they could be works of art, engraved, etched, damascened with gold and silver wire, and enamelled. Duelling and travelling pistols were encased in pairs with accessories such as cap tins, bullet moulds, and cleaning rods. Until the arrival of the percussion cap, the firing mechanism of a pistol involved the striking of a flint or similar material by metal using a strong spring mechanism to produce a spark that ignited powder to propel a missile down the barrel. The matchlock was introduced in the fifteenth century, followed by the wheel-lock, the snap-lock and the flintlock. Early pistols had stocks (butts) set almost at right angles; later the stock was almost an extension of the barrel. Some pistols were fitted with retractable blades.

Weapons fired from the shoulder were either smooth bored or rifled. Rifling, spiral grooves inside the barrel causing the projectile to twist in flight and ensuring that the bullet was a tight fit, gave accuracy. Rifling was known in the sixteenth century but only finally accepted in the nineteenth, and prior to the rifle (issued to the British Army in 1800) the musket was the main infantry weapon, first of all flintlock and from the 1830s percussion. Until the 1860s loading was down the barrel, and in 1886 the magazine rifle was produced. Some weapons were cobbled together ('composite' weapons), and this is especially true of some Asiatic and African firearms, where exquisite workmanship went hand in hand with suicidal technology. The main firearm accessory was the powder-horn or -flask; this could be a cow's horn, wide part stoppered, sharp end nipped off and plugged, or it could be a spring-loaded container releasing the requisite amount of powder. Flasks could also be triangular in shape, though from the eighteenth century there was a preference for pear-shaped flasks. Indian and similar powder-horns and -flasks were often exotic, made in silver and ivory and other materials.

MIHRAB

A conventional motif in Islamic rugs based on a prayer niche or mosque arch, which can be almost realistic or extremely abstract. The basic design element in the prayer rug.

MINIATURE BOOKS

Books measuring less than three inches by two inches (7.5 by 5cm) are reckoned as miniature books. The earliest were Bibles, prayer books, and other religious books, and although miniature books date from the fifteenth century, most of the ones available date from the eighteenth century and later and include almanacs and books of tables, although dictionaries are the

A pair of 19th-century Japanese bronzes flanking a mahogany serpentine-fronted toilet mirror of dubious date. The feet are not 'right' nor are the uprights holding the shield-shaped mirror.

most common. Some of the books are functional, others were issued to show off the skill of the printer or bookbinder, for some of the miniatures have fine leather covers. Children's miniature books date from 1744, and later included tiny books for dolls' houses.

MINTON POTTERY AND PORCELAIN

Founded in 1796 by Thomas Minton, reputed to be the inventor of the Willow Pattern, initially for the manufacture of pottery but from 1821 porcelain as well. Early wares were traditional with simple patterns and sprigs of flowers as decoration, but under a new French director Minton branched out, producing a marvellous array of adventurous work including maiolica, Parian, Sèvres-type prestige pieces as well as an enormous range of tiles, including encaustic, based on old manufacturing methods, and wall plaques, often of great power and complexity. Among the firm's most interesting products were those using the *pâte-sur-pâte* technique,

brought from Paris. Minton deserves more than a round of applause not only for its products (sometimes sneered at as being 'artistic') but for the marking of its wares, which include dates. Minton was one of the enterprising firms that moved with the times, adapting new techniques when they came along and reflecting current trends such as the Aesthetic movement and art nouveau. Perhaps the most interesting of all nineteenth century potteries.

MIRRORS

English mirrors date from 1665 when a glassworks was established at Vauxhall in London. Before the arrival of mirror glass, surfaces were made of polished speculum or bronze, used by the Romans. Glass mirrors were expensive and difficult to make, and thus were small, and until about 1750 larger ones were made by joining smaller ones together. Frames were very large and flamboyant to compensate for the small area of glass. Early mirrors had plain frames, but these became increasingly elaborate and the rococo movement in France had an effect on mirror design, but on very little else in the way of English furniture. Plain frames reappeared with the neo-Classical movement of the eighteenth century. A distinction must be made between carved wood and gesso (plaster of Paris mixed with size, often wound round wire to give a spacial effect). Gesso work is spectacular but vulnerable as it is affected by damp. Convex mirrors appeared in the early nineteenth century, as did mirrors inset with plaques. As Victorian glass was cheap, certain wall mirrors tended to be massive, with elaborate frames. There was a fashion for painting flowers on mirrors in the nineteenth century, which reappeared in a ghastly form in the 1920s. Overmantels could be very large, and were very popular in the nineteenth century, either with gilt frames or at the other extreme with scratch-carved cheap wood or ebonised surrounds. Girandoles, though they can mean an elaborate candle sconce or an American clock, can describe circular, oval and more rarely oblong mirrors flanked by candle holders. Pier-glasses were the narrow rectangular mirrors between the windows in grand houses. Amongst the most attractive mirrors are toilet mirrors, which came into vogue in the early eighteenth century. These are upright mirrors mounted on swivels between supports beneath which was often a bank of drawers or single drawer. These came in a multitude of styles and woods, with fluted, reeded, or carved uprights, and various kinds of feet. Victorian toilet mirrors could be very large. The cheval mirror was free-standing and was a tall mirror between supports and intended for the dressing-room. The supports and feet were often elaborately carved and before cheval-glasses were at all in demand these supports and feet were used to make sofa tables. Victorian shop mirrors bearing advertising have been reproduced and genuine examples are not common. Old mirror glass invariably shows signs of age with the silvering showing through; old glass is thin, and by holding the thumb-nail to it it is easy to detect – the image is closer than later glass. Silvering is expensive, and flaws may have to be lived with. Gilt frames can be revived or have superficial damage repaired quite easily, but it is important to determine whether the frame is gesso or wood. Intricately carved wooden frames can be worth several thousands pounds each, and should be left as they are or given to an expert to repair.

MOGUL CARPETS*

Carpets produced in India from the middle of the sixteenth to the middle of the seventeenth centuries. Techniques were introduced from Persia, and the producers were backed by the Mogul princes. The finest wool from Kashmir was used as well as silk, with gold and silver braiding, and Mogul carpets were characterised by a thick velvety texture and extreme naturalism in the flower and animal designs, totally unlike anything else produced at the time when natural forms, if they existed, were dealt with in an abstract or abstruse manner. In the same way, the Taj Mahal, constructed during the final years of the Moguls, is totally unlike anything else.

MONEY-BOXES

The first boxes for hoarders were of earthenware and date probably from the seventeenth century; the piggy bank (shaped like a pig) was established well before the close of that century. Another favourite shape was the fish (and fish and pig combined), with dogs, fowl, cattle, sheep, and people. An innovation was the cottage and castle money-box, a speciality of the Staffordshire potteries. The American metal mechanical money-box (or bank) appeared in the 1870s, in which the insertion of a coin results in certain exciting actions. The most common is the Sambo (1882) which rolls its eyes as a coin is dropped into its mouth. Novelty boxes were made in iron, steel, tin, and brass. The American mechanical money-boxes are being reproduced.

Dinky toy Austin taxi of about 1950.

MONOPODIUM

A furniture support comprising an animal's head and a leg, much used during the Regency period in England.

MORTAR

Used in association with a pestle, this was a vessel of bronze, bell-metal, marble, ceramics, etc, used for grinding or pounding materials, especially foodstuffs and pharmaceutical products.

MOTHER-OF-PEARL

The hard iridescent lining of certain shells, polished and used in furniture inlay and all kinds of small objects, typical of which were card cases. It was extensively inlaid into papier-mâché boxes, trays, and similar objects of the nineteenth century, the shining surface used as cloud colour or as flower petals in pictorial decoration.

MOTORING MEMORABILIA

Ranging from sparking plugs to veteran cars, from a pound or two to millions. Many items are bought to service older cars including rubber-bulb horns, dashboard instruments such as revolution counters, lamps of all kinds, carburettors, and high-tension coils, and handbooks are eagerly sought for, and indeed all books and leaflets of a technical nature. Amongst the most collected items are badges and mascots, one of the most valuable being the emblems of the French glass-maker Lalique particularly the Rolls-Royce 'Spirit of Ecstasy'. Mascots varied

greatly, sometimes supplied by the manufacturer, sometimes provided by the car owner; there was no restriction on their usage. Early AA and RAC badges, as well as those of more specialised groups and societies, such as the Brooklands Automobile Racing Club, are much in demand. All material no matter how trivial related to Brooklands is as gold-dust. Motoring spawned a host of novelties such as ashtrays, cigarette-and match-holders modelled on specific cars, scale models, chromium-plated decanters in the form of a car radiator, and plates and dishes in silver, pewter, and other metals engraved or embossed with car designs (some of these date back to the art nouveau period). Posters are sought for, especially those produced in France in the art nouveau style from the last years of the nineteenth century, and for enthusiasts who find such items beyond their pocket there is a modest vogue for back-window car stickers. There is also great interest in artefacts relating to garages, including old petrol pumps and enamel signs.

MOUNTS

Cabinet-makers' name for the metal extras of furniture such as hinges, locks and handles, but also used for metal edges and guards which protect furniture from damage and for bronze, brass and ormolu adornments on furniture.

MUG

One of the standard drinking vessels, made in silver, pewter, ceramics and other convenient substances, probably the most interesting being the vast range made in porcelain in the

MUSEUM PIECES*

It may be tempting providence to describe certain objects as museum pieces when a reader may have a room filled with them. In this category are items which are decidedly not everyday, though there may be nineteenth-century versions, even replicas, catering for the enthusiasm for the old and especially the Gothic. One characteristic of museum pieces is that most belong to the seventeenth century or earlier. But old objects are not necessarily valuable. Chinese bronzes more than a thousand years old are often surprisingly low-priced; odds and ends of Romano-British pottery are within the price range of a schoolboy.

Ecclesiastical objects are frequently to be found only in museums. When other items of the age were often crude and basic, great care and skill was taken with the fashioning of religious pieces, often using precious gems and metals. These include the pyx, a box for carrying a consecrated wafer to the sick, made in every conceivable material, and sometimes surmounted by a cross; the reliquary was a container for relics of saints and other holy people, made in many materials and shapes; the pilgrim bottle was a flask with a flat, rounded, body and a smooth, narrow, neck with a stopper, used in the Middle Ages for carrying water. Loops or rings were fitted to allow a carrying cord or chain to pass through for ease of carrying, and they were made in many materials including leather, pottery, silver and pewter. In the seventeenth century large specimens were made for display purposes. *Opus Anglicanum* was the name given to English ecclesiastical embroidery of the thirteenth and fourteenth centuries, acknowledged to be the best in Europe. Patens were silver or gold trays, as were communion plates. A lavabo was a bronze or brass vessel hanging above a basin containing water for washing the hands, a process associated with purification. The flagon was a large silver or silver gilt vessel for serving wine made from the sixteenth century onward. From about 1700 flagons were in domestic use for serving wine or ale. Ewers were large pouring vessels made from at least the thirteenth century. Sixteenth-century examples have an octagonal or round body on a circular foot, with the lid raised by a thumb piece on the handle in the manner of a tankard. Some ewers were in the shape of a human figure. Ewers were not used after the eighteenth century except on ceremonial occasions, but they were produced in the nineteenth century often in spelter and bronze as decorative objects. Chalices and communion cups were usually of silver with a deep beaker-shaped bowl, circular foot, and a knop in the middle of the stem.

Ceremonial and decorative objects of museum status include the ostrich-egg-cup, made in the fifteenth and sixteenth centuries, the egg sometimes painted and customarily set in an elaborate silver mount. The ostrich-egg-cup enjoyed great prestige as the egg was sometimes supposed to be that of the griffin or the phoenix. From ostrich eggs to Easter eggs, those produced each year by the Russian goldsmith and jeweller Fabergé for the emperor to give to his wife were made of a wide variety of precious and semiprecious materials, each of which contained a surprise for his rich patron – a statuette, a basket of gemstone flowers, or a set of enamel portraits. In the fifteenth century the rare and exotic coconut was mounted in silver and silver gilt, a practice that surprisingly continued into the nineteenth century. The wager cup was one of the many joke drinking vessels popular in unsophisticated times. Often made in silver gilt, it was a double cup usually designed as a skirted woman holding a swivelling cup above her head. The skirt turned upside-down acts as the larger cup. Both cups were to be emptied without spilling any. Wager cups were made in Germany and Holland from the sixteenth century.

The nef was a model ship in precious metals, used in the Middle Ages as a repository for the master's napkin, knife and spoon. By the sixteenth century nefs were table ornaments especially in Germany and Switzerland, where the ships could be fully rigged, accurate in every detail, and included a minature crew. Jugs, cups, and clocks were also made in the form of nefs.

Victorian optical toy, the praxinoscope.

Early ceramics and glass can come into the category of museum pieces. It is possible that such objects are about and simply not recognised, for few are adequately marked. Although pottery was made in Nottingham from the thirteenth century, the area is best known for the tygs (cylindrical drinking vessels with up to twelve handles) made in the sixteenth and seventeenth centuries. Old pottery may not be very valuable, but rare, and therefore qualifies as museum pieces. Some anonymous pottery was found in the grounds of churches and similar places and was known as abbey ware. Malling jugs belong to this group. These are tin-glazed pottery jugs of the mid-sixteenth century, and are named after West Malling in Kent, where there was an example in the local church. Wrotham ware was among the earliest English slip-ware, made from about 1612 typified by stamped white-clay decoration of rosettes, stars, and similar simple motifs. Drinking-vessel surfaces were often divided into sections divided by white slip. Contrasting coloured clays were sometimes used. Pieces were sometimes signed or initialled by the pot-

ters who made them. Metropolitan slip-ware pieces were orange earthenware dishes, bowls, chamber-pots, drinking vessels, and jugs decorated with white slip made near Harlow in Essex in the seventeeth century, and sometimes inscribed. A characteristic is a herring-bone pattern decoration. Without the inscription such pottery would be difficult even for an expert to identify, so typical was it of a certain kind of work. Some eighteenth-century pottery is distinctive enough to qualify as museum pieces, such as Jackfield ware, lead-glaze pottery known also as 'shining black', made by adding iron and manganese to both clay and glazes, and sometimes decorated with gilded vine leaves and grapes. Crouchware was a grey Staffordshire stoneware, claimed in 1829 to be the earliest of all Staffordshire salt-glazed pottery, so certainly pre-1730. Delft-field pottery was a Glasgow pottery producing delft from 1748, stoneware from 1766, cream ware from 1774, basalt from about 1785, and bone china for a short time until it closed in 1810. Perhaps not particularly valuable, but a museum piece because of the locality of the pottery. Much the same is true of Chesterfield stoneware, brown pottery characterised by reliefs of hunting scenes and drinking orgies made from the mid-eighteenth century.

Utterly untypical of anything at the time was Medici porcelain, first known makers of European soft-paste porcelain (1575), influenced by Chinese blue-and-white china. It was made for only a short time until 1587 and must be regarded as a brief expedition into vaguely understood territory. Wealdon glass is not likely to be encountered, but is significant in the history of antiques because the first English glass was made in the Weald of Surrey, Kent and Sussex in the thirteenth century. Window glass and domestic ware such as bottles and beakers were among the articles made. The Weald was forest when the glass-makers arrived; it was denuded by the time they moved out in the sixteenth century to other parts of the country. The use of wood for glass-making was prohibited by law in 1615.

Many early items associated with eating and drinking may be described as museum pieces, such as very early drinking ware, and containers such as the aquamanile, a ewer often made in animal shapes and used from the Middle Ages until the sixteenth century. The mazer was a medieval wooden drinking bowl, often made from burr maple and with a silver or gold rim. Sometimes a silver medallion is set in the bottom. It was rare after the sixteenth century. The standing salt was a large and imposing prestige piece in gold, silver, and silver gilt, used from medieval times until the middle of the seventeenth century, usually in architectural form and placed before the host or guest of honour at table. The tazza was a circular dish mounted on a stem or foot, with or without a rim, derived from a Venetian sixteenth century model in glass, popular in Elizabethan England in silver or silver gilt with ornate chased or engraved scenes. It was revived in the nineteenth century as a presentation piece. Inferior versions were made in brass and bronze and sometimes nasty alloys, and because of the wealth of modelling they are sometimes taken for objects of some importance.

As with all antiques, appearances can be deceptive, as museums, with drawers full of fakes

and misattributions, know very well. Unusual tapestries and carpets may be described as museum pieces, not because they are more valuable than classic Middle Eastern carpets but because so few were made, particularly in England. The production of knotted-pile carpets, the painstaking technique used in Persia and the other great carpet-making countries where there was a willing labour force, was not an economic proposition in England or the developing countries of the west because the process took up too many man- and woman-hours, but an attempt was made in the London district of Moorfields in the 1750s, though only the very rich could afford to buy the carpets. Robert Adam, the key figure in the neo-Classical movement, was responsible for many of the designs that were destined for a specific setting, with the pattern matching the interior features of the room such as the ceiling. Certain enterprises depended on foreign craftsmen, typical of these being Mortlake Tapestry, established in 1619 and staffed with Flemish weavers, producing work as good as anything in France and Flanders, but the standard dropped, and from the 1670s the weavers began to disperse. The factory soon closed.

Many antiques prior to the 16th century are museum pieces. These particular 13th-century encaustic tiles are in a museum, but surprisingly many tiles of considerable age are available at little cost.

eighteenth century, many of which were in gently bellied shapes. With the widespread use of tranfer printing and the undemanding nature of mug design, mugs of the nineteenth century were made in immense numbers and variety, sometimes with two handles so that technically they may be termed loving-cups. Among the designs were railway engines, convivial scenes, scenes after famous prints and pictures, armorials real and comic, animals especially dogs, well-known bridges such as the Iron Bridge at Coalbrookdale and the newly opened Clifton Suspension Bridge, and innumerable sporting scenes including cricket and cycling. There were also children's mugs produced in great quantities, a tradition that has persisted up to the present. Many were made by small Staffordshire potteries in a very basic form, but factories such as Doulton produced finely modelled and adventurous pieces, often with the decoration in relief.

MUSICAL BOXES*

The cylinder musical box was first made in the early nineteenth century and developed from the musical movements made for watches on the principle of tiny teeth being 'flicked' by a rotating pinned cylinder. Early boxes were plain and the spring mechanism was wound by a key. This was replaced by a ratchet lever. From 1860 the cases were more ornate, and later musical boxes were provided with extras such as drums and bells, often hidden under butterflies. Some boxes had interchangeable cylinders, thus increasing the repertoire. Serious cylinder musical boxes ceased to be made after 1914. The novelty musical box uses the same kind of mechanism as do other instruments, such as the barrel-organ, the serinette or bird organ, and the barrel piano. The disc musical box flourished between 1885 and 1914, and relies on a revolving disc with protrusions which strike keyed teeth. There are two basic models, the free-standing and the table model, where the disc is usually horizontal. The discs could be changed and popular songs could be put on disc overnight. Many of the free-standing models could be eight feet (2.4m) or more in height and often had a penny-in-the-slot mechanism for use in public houses. Sometimes musical movements, both cylinder and disc, were incorporated in clocks.

MUSICAL GLASSES

Sets of glasses of different sizes played by rubbing the rim with a damp finger, originating probably in the seventeenth century and an intriguing novelty in the nineteenth century, when they could be handsomely mounted in a case.

MUSICAL INSTRUMENTS

Some musical instruments are more interesting than others, such as the flute, which was made in a diversity of styles and woods, with boxwood being replaced in the early nineteenth century by ebony or crocus wood. Instruments such as lutes and citerns are mainly museum pieces, but guitars were produced in large numbers from the eighteenth century and were popular drawing-room instruments in the nineteenth along with the mandoline. Harps of various types were made from the 1780s, including harp-lyres and harp-lutes, as well as the Irish harp, but the much larger concert harp was the main type, usually in Gothic or Greek styling, examples of the nineteenth century especially those made by Erard being eagerly sought for by present-day harpists. The banjo was a very popular music-hall instrument in the early nineteenth century, and was considered rather dashing by young men; it was often highly ornate with mother-of-pearl inlay and ivory insets. Violins gradually replaced earlier stringed instruments such as the viol family, and were mass-produced in the nineteenth century, often with fake labels inside the sound-box. There is a specialised interest in violin bows. Brass instruments, including bugles and other military instruments, are often bought for use rather than for a collection, and their playability is often as important as their look or pedigree. Much the same is true of oboes, clarinets, and similar instruments; their development is often similar to that of the flute, with boxwood superseded by other woods and different arrangements of keys. Musical instruments should be approached with caution by non-musicians; they are not there to impress or be beautiful but to transmit sound. The violin with a rippling varnished back that might be likened poetically to veneer on a bureau may be rubbish; the harp with the strings dangling brokenly and great gashes in the gilt may be worth spending £2,000 on to get repaired; a flute

A musical box with interchangeable cylinders as well as extras including a zither function.

with the ivory flaking off may turn out to be a marvel of its kind. A gold-mounted woodwind instrument of the 1740s may be an aristocratic show-piece and useless.

NAILSEA

In 1788 a glasshouse was started for the production of crown window glass, followed in 1844 by sheet window glass and rolled plate glass from the 1860s, though the glasshouse is probably better known for its coloured novelties such as rolling-pins, canes, shoes, bells, top hats, model ships, pipes, and witch balls alongside jugs, bowls, and other useful objects. A characteristic of Nailsea was splashed-on, flecked-on, or striped colour, and glass of this kind is often assigned to Nailsea irrespective of the fact that it was made throughout the United Kingdom and also America and it is impossible to pin-point the place of origin. The glassworks closed in 1873.

NANTGARW PORCELAIN

A factory was established at Nantgarw, Glamorgan, in 1813, making glassy translucent porcelain with a thick glaze, but in the following year the firm moved to Swansea and in 1817 back again. The factory closed in 1822. Much of the production was table ware comprising tea- and dessert-services, though spill holders, taper stands, and pen trays were also made. A good deal of the work was decorated in London, of a more sophisticated standard than that carried out locally. The quality of the porcelain is rated very highly, but there was a high loss in the kiln, the shortfall in production contributing to the factory's short life.

NAUTILUS SHELL

The shell of a type of octopus that has the curious distinction of being in the form of a series of compartments, ideal for carvers who wished to impress. The outer shell is striped with yellow and orange, easily scraped away to reveal mother-of-pearl. The Dutch took over Chinese-style carving and decorating in the seventeenth century, and nautilus shells were mostly used for drinking vessels; if the carving and adornment were exceptionally good they were mounted. A carved nautilus shell worked by an Englishman featured in the Great Exhibition of 1851, but it was very much of a specialised hobby as nautilus shells are uncommon as well as vulnerable. Broken nautilus shells were used in the making of snuff-boxes and other small articles.

NÉCESSAIRE

A box, often highly ornate, for miscellaneous objects such as toothpicks, tongue-scrapers, earpicks, tweezers, powders, scent-bottles, and sewing implements. In purpose not unlike an etui, except that the nécessaire was a dressing-table object rather than something to take around.

NEO-CLASSICISM

A movement that swept across Europe and America towards the end of the eighteenth century, partly as a reaction against the exuberance of the rococo, partly as a result of the rediscovery of Greek and Roman culture spurred by excavations at Pompeii and other fashionable sites. In France it stimulated the Régence, Directoire and Empire styles, in Britain it was reflected in the Adam, Hepplewhite, and Sheraton styles, where motifs such as urns, masks, and stylised foliage were endlessly used on furniture, architecture, porcelain and silver. Neo-Classicism could be simple and elegant, as in Wedgwood's basalt ware; it could be lacking in warmth, as in some eighteenth-century furniture; and it could be heavy and humourless, as in some Regency furniture. Although the movement began to fade in the 1830s (some say earlier) the nineteenth century continued to hark back to its own interpretation of ancient Greece and Rome, best seen in such architecture as the long-departed Euston arch and the government buildings of Whitehall and in paintings. Classical motifs continued to be used on furniture, but without commitment, and often on objects the reverse of classical.

NETSUKE

Small carved toggles used to secure the cord which passed from the *inro* to the *obi* or girdle, and an essential fashion accessory for the pre-Europeanised Japanese male. The netsuke takes

the form of animals, humans, mythological creatures and other subjects, often quaint and whimsical. The main requirements are a smooth surface so as not to catch the cloth and holes for the cords to pass through. Sometimes the holes are disguised within the figure. Netsuke came into use in the sixteenth century, and were quite rudimentary until the seventeenth when talented carvers began work to create delightful art objects in ivory, bamboo, bone, cherry-wood, boxwood, and pine, and continue to do so despite increasing Westernisation. Many eighteenth- and nineteenth-century netsuke are signed by the carver. Sometimes there is inlay of amber, tortoiseshell, and black horn, and lacquer is also used. Wooden netsuke often have the holes lined with ivory. Netsukes have long been faked, by using moulded ivory dust, or by boring holes through otherwise unremarkable carvings. Moulded ivory does not have the striations and texture of solid ivory, and moulding lacks the bite of carving.

NEW HALL PORCELAIN

Established in 1782, the output of the factory was confined to useful wares especially tea- and coffee-services, often in imitation of Chinese models, the most common items being teapots, cream jugs, bowls, tea bowls, coffee-cups and saucers. Less common are mugs, cream boats, spoon trays, jugs and tea-caddies. After about 1790 there was a loss in individuality, with blue-and-white wares usually transfer-printed, usually with Chinese scenes of the willow pattern variety, often embellished with good-quality gilding. Characteristic motifs of New Hall are sprigs and festoons of flowers. From about 1812 the factory introduced bone ash into its products. The firm closed down in 1835.

NOAH'S ARKS

Carved Noah's Arks in wood were in use from at least the sixteenth century, and although these were crude, the accompanying animals were delicately fashioned in wood or, from 1740, *broteig*, a mixture of flour and glue-water moulded over a wire frame. In 1815 kaolin was introduced into the mix to stop insects eating it. Moulding often replaced carving, but by the middle of the nineteenth century twenty-four

factories in one area of Germany made nothing but Noah's Arks, some of them seaworthy, some of them containing as many as 400 different animals and humans, who were traditionally skittle-shaped (and remained so in the 1930s' children's cartoon strip *Ham, Shem, and Japhet*). A curious fillip was given to the industry in 1914 when Belgian refugees and wounded soldiers were encouraged to make Noah's Arks, the reason being that their involvement in this arcane art would not alienate British workers, who were not very much involved with Noah's Arks.

OBJETS DE VERTU

A thoroughly Anglicised word denoting a pretty trifle, encompassing snuff-boxes, scent-bottles, etuis, and indeed almost anything small and dainty. As with many saleroom-oriented pieces, it is difficult to know why such descriptions are lavished on items that have perfectly good names, though as a collective noun no doubt *objets de vertu* has its niche.

OCTANT

Navigational instrument evolved in 1731, superseding the cross staff (an upright with an adjustable cross-piece) and similar instruments, including the back staff, invented in 1594. A still earlier navigational instrument was the astrolabe, usually made up of three parts, a circular interchangeable base plate with a scale of degrees around the rim, an inner pierced plate, and a sighting guide (the alidade), made of brass and bronze. It was suspended from a ring. Until the invention of the octant, instruments used at sea either depended on a plumb-line or required the user to look in two directions at once. The inventor of the octant, Hadley, solved the problem with mirrors. Made in the form of a flat triangle, the octant has two mirrors, one fixed and half silvered, the other mounted on a moving arm (alidade). As with many navigational instruments, the object is to line up celestial features, in this case the horizon and the sun. The sextant, invented about 1757, was based on the octant but with added refinements, such as finer adjustments and a small telescope. It was made in brass, ivory and ebony, though unadorned brass was used from the last years of the

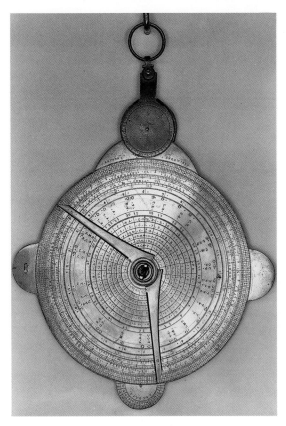

An astrolabe, one of the early navigation instruments before the invention of the octant.

eighteenth century. The quadrant was an astronomical and surveying instrument in the shape of a solid quarter circle in iron, brass, and wood. Astronomical versions can be more than six feet (1.8m) tall. The elements include a plumb-line and a pair of fixed sights, or a version with a sighting guide; used from the fourteenth century and a simple way of measuring altitudes, and employed by the more traditional surveyors well into the nineteenth century. There were also a large number of small navigational instruments, such as the nocturnal dial, a simple instrument for finding the time at night using fixed stars as reference points.

OIL LAMP

Early oil lamps were nothing more than saucers with a floating wick, but during the nineteenth century they became decorative objects, consisting of a base, a container for holding the lighting fluid (colza oil, succeeded by paraffin), a wick with a winding mechanism, and a glass chimney, with an optional shade around it. The shade, often of cranberry (red) glass, can be worth many times the value of the lamp itself. One of the most efficient was the Duplex, invented in 1865, which had two wicks side by side. Oil lamps had cast-iron or brass bases. The most attractive lamps are in the form of Corinthian columns. Miniature oil lamps, such as Tilley and Kelly lamps, are basically night-lights and, as they are still being made, it is difficult to date them. The better-quality oil lamps had porcelain winding buttons rather than brass. Oil standard lamps are not common, and were made of brass, wrought iron, and copper, often in combination. There was often a telescopic facility. These lamps ceased to be popular after about 1914, and many were converted to electric. Vestibule lamps were fitted with suspension chains and were widely used in public places, and bracket lamps were for use on walls and landings as well as on the front of pianos (though candle holders are more common), where the brackets are often ornate and pierced. None of these is very desirable, except with a view to conversion to electricity. Reading-lamps were a variant on the oil lamp and were often fitted with reflectors. Oil lanterns were used before the arrival of the battery lamp, and although car headlamps and ships' navigation lamps are highly collectable, oil lanterns as used by night watchmen or the police are not of great interest unless they bear interesting insignia.

ONYX

A hard stone used from antiquity, much used in the 1920s and 1930s for a variety of decorative objects, such as carved animals, plinths, and clock cases. The favourite colour was perhaps green. As with amethyst, rock crystal, and the Scottish cairngorm, onyx is a type of quartz, closely related to agate.

OPALINE

Modern name for translucent coloured glass, much used in the nineteenth century, often in imitation of porcelain. Sugar-basins, milk jugs and vases were made in great quantities for the mass market, being sold at fairs alongside Staffordshire figures and wooden dolls.

OPAQUE WHITE GLASS

Discovered in ancient times when calcined bone was used in the mix, revived in Venice in the fifteenth century where it was known as *lattimo*. The opacity varied from a milk-and-water quality to solid white, and it was gilded, painted, or splashed with colour. It was used in Europe to imitate fine china, and opaque white glass became a speciality of the Bristol glassworks in the eighteenth century. Among the products of Bristol and other glasshouses, impossible to distinguish from each other, were sets of vases, tea-caddies, candlesticks and toys such as snuff-boxes. In continental Europe framed sheets of the glass were enamelled to create paintings. Opaque glass was also used in the stems of English drinking glasses.

ORGANIC FURNITURE

Furniture put together from natural objects, not necessarily made by craftsmen. These included furniture, often intended for outdoor use, made from branches or roots of trees, or from rattan woven around a wooden frame. Experimental furniture of this type was especially popular in America, together with furniture made from animal horns.

ORIENTAL BRONZES

Bronzes were produced in quantity in China from the seventeenth century, and although Chinese bronzes can date from 2000BC these are museum pieces and not likely to be encountered. Chinese bronzes are traditional, and often are direct copies of ancient pieces, the makers even copying old marks. Figures are more desirable than vases or other decorative pieces, and amongst the most common objects, still within reach of those on a strict budget, are incense burners. The larger the object the higher the price. Japanese bronzes were not made in quantity until the nineteenth century when they were exported in massive quantities to Europe, and were well received on account of their subjects – animals, birds, and plants – sometimes inlaid with other metals. Japanese vases of the period are often overloaded with ornament, and are almost an exact visual equivalent of the products of the British potteries.

Unlike some antiques, the condition and quality of Oriental bronzes is more important than age, and crude bronzes of the Tang dynasty (618–906AD) are quite inexpensive (less than £200). There is always a tendency to brighten up drab bronzes, and this can be a mistake as old bronze takes on a distinctive patina, impossible to replace if taken off.

ORIENTAL IVORIES

Most ivory comes from India or Africa, but as early as 1000BC the Chinese were making ivory carvings. Most of the Oriental ivories seen today are nineteenth-century, and there are probably more Japanese ivories about than those from China, which only began producing in quantity in the early years of the present century. Old ivory, such as that carved in the Ming dynasty (c1600), can be detected by extensive surface cracking, caused by the oils within the ivory drying out. Japanese carvings are more popular than Chinese as they are more naturalistic and less stylised, but there are certain Chinese ivories that have a curiosity value, such as puzzle-balls with intricate interior carving, amazingly undervalued and still seen at considerably less than £100. The quality of much ivory carving is incredible, and the tradition is constantly maintained even though the supply of ivory will eventually dry up despite the huge stocks in Hong Kong. Large ivory pieces are worth considerably more than smaller items, mainly because of the work involved, wonder taking over from esthetic considerations, though there are exceptions, such as the Japanese netsuke. The Japanese sometimes used marine ivory, in most cases walrus, distinguished by a mottled paler grain; stag antler and bone can be confused with elephant ivory. Indian carvings are often cruder than those executed in China and Japan, and are less valued. One of the favourite Indian subjects is an animal group in a 'boat', following the shape of the tusk. Intricate pieces should be examined closely, as ivory is almost impossible to repair satisfactorily and even a skilled carver will have difficulty in matching colour and grain. Ivory varies enormously in hardness, and the teeth of various mammals and one reptile, the crocodile, have often been used by carvers. Sometimes the enamel has to be stripped off, sometimes not.

French 19th-century ormolu figure group on a marble base.

ORMOLU

From the French for ground gold, ormolu is gold and mercury, applied to bronze and brass surfaces and heated, disposing of the mercury and leaving a gold deposit. It is an expensive process (and injurious), and used mainly for furniture mounts, particularly in France, and for smaller items. What is often termed ormolu is not really ormolu at all, and true ormolu can be confused with electro-gilding, introduced in 1840. Gold lacquer was also a substitute, less successful because of its tendency to flake but superficially impressive. Among the pieces subject to ormolu treatment are clocks, inkstands, candlesticks and candelabra, fireside furniture, and vases.

All ormolu items from before the nineteenth century are expensive, including the British ormolu (1760s and 1770s) of Boulton and Fothergill of Birmingham.

OTTOMAN

Named after a low wide-cushioned Turkish bench, in England and France in the eighteenth century it was long low upholstered sofa, sometimes known as a Turkey sofa, but the term is flexible, and what is understood today by an ottoman is usually the box ottoman, with a hinged seat and storage space inside. Ottomans are sometimes constructed from plain chests, suitably upholstered. Circular or octagonal stuffed seats, often buttoned, also bear the name. The French *ottomane* was more specific, a small sofa often with an oval seat, with curving back and arms upholstered together.

OWL JUGS

Jugs with detachable heads serving as cups, made in slip-ware in Staffordshire in the late seventeenth and early eighteenth centuries, and from 1730 to 1770 in salt-glazed stoneware, sometimes with brown slip decoration. Owl jugs were also made in Germany in the sixteenth century, rather more elaborate with feathers in relief and armorials. Owls, like bears, had shapes that were convenient to turn into jugs. Consequently there are containers made today in the form of owls for the selfsame reason.

OZIER PATTERN

More obvious if the spelling is changed to osier (wickerwork). Repetitive relief decoration especially around the rims of plates simulating basket work, used at Meissen from about 1735 and subsequently copied throughout Europe, including Britain.

PALISSY WARE

Sixteenth-century naturalistic pottery depicting reptiles, snakes, lizards, snails and insects, often in dishes shaped like small ponds. Also made were dishes, ewers, vases, etc, decorated with Biblical or mythological scenes. Palissy ware, almost none of which survives, is known mainly from imitations that were made both at the time and later, both in France and elsewhere, including England. Fake Palissy ware was made on a large scale in France in the nineteenth century, and the curious preoccupations with reptilian life were an incentive for adventurous potters to pursue their own inclinations with regard to subject matter, especially in England towards the end of the nineteenth century.

PALLADIAN STYLE

A style inspired by the work of Andrea Palladio (1505-80), an Italian architect. Palladio did not design any furniture, and Palladian-style furniture is that which he no doubt would have designed had he got round to it and had he been living in the first part of the eighteenth century. Characteristics included much use of pediments, cornices, lion masks, paws, acanthus leaves, swags, massive yet restrained, lacking the exuberance of the Italian baroque but perhaps more powerful and self-confident. The most famous designer of Palladian-style furniture was William Kent.

PAKTONG

A Chinese alloy of nickel-copper with zinc, looking like silver with a yellow tinge, tough and not susceptible to corrosion. Imported from Canton, it was called 'tutong' and was used in small quantities for candlesticks and fire grates and other hearth furniture. Very similar to a nickel alloy first used in 1823 in Britain, an alloy later imported from Germany and given the name German silver, very suitable as a base for electroplating. In France German silver is called *maillechort*, in Italy *pachfong* (a reference to the original Chinese metal).

PALM STAND

Essentially a pot stand in Edwardian oak with four long legs, perhaps a pierced frieze beneath the top, and a shelf rather more than half-way down.

PAP BOAT

Small shallow boat-shaped container in silver or ceramics, dating from the eighteenth century, with tapering lip or spout at one end for feeding babies.

PAPER MONEY

An immense range of paper money has been issued from the seventh century in China and from the seventeenth century in Europe, the earliest examples of which were Swedish credit notes of 1661. British banknotes date from 1695, eighteenth-century paper money is rare but obtainable, but great quantities of notes were issued after 1810 by a multitude of small banks, later swallowed up by the larger. The last independent British bank ceased issuing notes as recently as 1921. Until World War I gold coins were used as everyday currency, and were then replaced by ten shilling (50p) and one pound notes. Collectors look for the various signatures on Bank of England notes (issued from 1797), and high value notes (£10 and upwards) are incredibly expensive. Pre-decimal ten shilling and one pound notes are about in quantity and worth little. All nineteenth-century foreign banknotes are worth several pounds each, with US Confederate notes greatly in demand, even if forged, as they were at the time and forever after, and there is a demand for European banknotes pre-World War I, especially those of Tsarist Russia. Post-World War I notes can be worth nothing or a small fortune, but there are paper money catalogues for those interested in pursuing this fascinating collecting area. Beginners should be wary of the German banknotes of the 1930s, when a million marks could buy a packet of cigarettes, as these are of little value. A plus for notes is crispness, specimen issues, printers' specimens (zero serial numbers, punched holes, embossed marks). As with postage stamps, 'paper money' may not be what it seems, but tourist novelties.

PAPERWEIGHTS

Glass objects used to hold down papers, first evolved in Venice in the early nineteenth century, spreading to France via Bohemia about 1845, where the finest were produced by three factories, Baccarat, Clichy and St Louis, mostly unmarked and widely faked and imitated and thus a minefield for the uninitiated. The most popular motif is *millefiori* ('thousand flowers'), though fruit, single flowers, insects, and other small objects are often used as well as portraits and views – almost anything that could be encased in glass. The cheapest paperweights use air bubbles as decoration. The classic paperweights are round and domed, but lesser works also appear as pyramids and rectangles. Many have prints, especially of views, glued to the bottom. There was a fashion in the US for moulded fruit shapes. The great period of paperweights is reckoned to have ended in 1870. Beware of paperweights that are lop-sided – they have probably been reground to get rid of chips or surface blemishes. The great majority of paperweights are unmarked, and glass rarely shows its age. Chinese paperweights made about 1920 use a coarse type of ochre-tinged glass, and today this may easily be confused with the kind of ageing process which takes place in certain other types of object.

A selection of 19th-century paperweights. The top four are French, the bottom left is Bohemian, and the bottom right was made in Birmingham.

PAPIER MÂCHÉ ('Chewed paper')

A composition of paper pulp reinforced with stiffeners such as size, evolved in the Far East, introduced to France in the seventeenth century and very popular in Britain from about 1750. In 1772 Henry Clay of Birmingham invented a process in which large sheets of paper were glued together, compressed, moulded and baked, but papier mâché was not produced on a really commercial scale until the early nineteenth century. To cut down on price hemp, flax, bark and plants were incorporated in the mix. Lighter than wood but inclined to get nibbled at the edges, papier mâché was ideal for lacquering, painting and inlaying, particularly with mother-of-pearl (a process patented in 1825). Quality objects were decorated with gold leaf. Decorating with bronze was evolved in the 1840s and known as the Wolverhampton style, useful for

A Victorian tip-up table in papier mâché.

landscape work. Contemporary paintings were copied until 1842 when the Registration of Designs Act came into force and stopped such piracy. Papier mâché was used for all kinds of furniture, including pianos, but is best seen in tripod tables, work-boxes, and trays, where some of the best painting was carried out. The most important manufacturer was Jennens and Bettridge, especially between 1825 and 1864. Between these dates their name was impressed. In 1856 there were fifteen manufacturers in Birmingham alone. A distinction must be made between hand-painting and transfer printing. Much of the work seen today is imported from Japan and easily recognisable by the range of motifs. A hint of bubbling can indicate a repair.

PARIAN

A fine unglazed porcelain known as statuary porcelain similar to marble in appearance and used for busts, figures, and figure groups, sometimes for decorative dishes and vases, with the hand a favourite design. It was produced at the Copeland factory in 1844, and many of the major factories including Minton, Wedgwood (which named their version Carrara ware), and Worcester made their own. Full-sized figures created a stir at the Great Exhibition of 1851. In the 1870s and 1880s there was a vogue for tinted Parian.

PASTE

Glass imitating gems, used from ancient times, depending for effect largely on underlying foil. Generally of indifferent quality until flint glass was used in the late seventeenth century. In the eighteenth century paste was acceptable in its own right and not as a counterfeit diamond, unlike paste in the nineteenth century, which was sometimes tinted and silvered (as in the manufacture of mirrors). A number of tiny paste pieces were more convincing than one large specimen, so brooches with unusually shaped components, such as animal shapes, were widely made. During the nineteenth century diamonds were much cheaper than earlier, available to women of relatively modest means, and paste was disdained as of no account whatsoever.

PATCH STAND

A small glass bowl on a stem used to hold face patches (adornments for ladies' faces emulating moles and beauty marks), very similar to a wineglass and made during the seventeenth and eighteenth centuries.

PATCHWORK

Patchwork started in America in the seventeenth century and reached Britain in the eighteenth. Templates are made from paper or card, often old letters, bills, or pieces of newspaper, and oddments of cloth are tacked on to

Parian figure of a girl.

them. The templates are then collected, arranged, and sewn to each other, the resulting patterned surface sewn onto a lining and backing material. This quilting was enormously popular as a social activity and quilting bees were common in America, especially New England. The patterns are associated with certain areas, and have been given imaginative names such as Birds in Air, Goose Tracks, Tree of Life or Moon over the Mountain. Printed cottons indicate a date later than about 1825, and machine stitching started in the 1860s. A Victorian cotton print does not indicate a nineteenth-century patchwork, for the making of patchwork is a favourite modern pastime, the creators of which frequent jumble sales and charity shops to try and find old materials. Because of the many hours of work involved – and many enthusiasts still use hand-sewing – even modern patchworks are very expensive.

PATENT METAL

Alloy of zinc and copper patented in 1832, sometimes called Muntz's metal after the inventor or yellow metal, occasionally used as a cheap alternative to ormolu.

PÂTE-SUR-PÂTE

Literally clay-on-clay, an expensive and hazardous process involving building up successive coats of slip, each of which is permitted to dry before the next one is laid. Modelled with metal tools, glazed, and fired. Invented by Sèvres in the 1850s and adapted by Minton.

PATTERN BOOKS

Pattern books offered patrons a choice and gave craftsmen models to follow, especially in furniture. An early example was *The Gentlemen's or Builders' Companion* (1739) by the architect William Jones, which contained designs for pier tables; a series of pattern books published between 1741 and 1746 by a Frenchman working in London promoted rococo. Batty (!) Langley's *Gothic Architecture Improved* (1742) encouraged not only Gothic (or Gothick) architecture but Gothic furniture as well. The most influential of all the pattern books was perhaps Chippendale's *Gentleman and Cabinet-Maker's Director* of 1754, with 160 engraved plates reflecting uninhibited delight in the exotic and the adventurous. Thomas Johnson's *One Hundred and Fifty New Designs* (1761) was also very important, so much so that it was republished in the nineteenth century under Chippendale's name, creating confusion. Also of great note was Hepplewhite's *The Cabinet-Maker and Upholsterer's Guide* (1788), followed shortly by Sheraton's *Cabinet-Maker and Upholsterer's Drawing Book* (1791–4), his *Cabinet Dictionary* (1803), and his *Cabinet-Maker, Upholsterer and General Artists' Encyclopaedia* (1804–06). Useful as all these were to their contemporaries, they have proved invaluable to historians of furniture, and it has been tempting to assign furniture that appeared in the pattern books to the actual authors of the books. If a piece of furniture was *proved* to be by Sheraton, its value would be astronomical.

PEDESTAL CUPBOARD

This was a round or octagonal bedside cupboard for keeping a chamber-pot, and was usually fitted with a white marble top and a hinged door. Mahogany was the favourite wood but maple, satinwood and other woods were also used.

PEDESTAL PLANT STAND

A heavily turned pillar, sometimes based on a classical column, usually with a plinth base. These have often been made up from the uprights of four-poster beds.

PEN WORK

A type of decoration on black lacquered furniture in the late eighteenth and early nineteenth centuries. The pattern was painted on in white and details and shading were added in black, with Chinese-type scenes popular.

PERSIAN CARPETS

The manufacture of carpets under court patronage began as early as the sixth century, although the earliest carpets of importance date from the sixteenth century, with geometrical and stylised motifs set alongside naturalistic flower and leaf designs, sometimes with birds and animals, dis-

tinguished by sophistication and subtlety. Throughout the centuries carpets were also produced by nomadic peoples, and there were many centres of production, each with its own speciality. The first Persian carpets to reach the west found their way to Poland, and were at first supposed to be of Polish make, so vague was knowledge of the Near East and its products. Carpets were both tapestry woven (such as kelims) and knotted pile; the Persians had their own particular knot, less a knot than a twist. A characteristic of Persian carpets is that straightforward pattern could be intermixed with naturalism and wholly integrated. Earlier designs were repeated in the nineteenth century, losing some freshness, and from the 1850s weavers concentrated on export. There was a deterioration in the 1870s with the introduction of modern dyes, which set in to such an alarming extent that in 1934 the Persian government forbade the export of inferior carpets. A large number of names are used to classify Persian carpets: Bijar (stout carpets with traditional designs); Feraghan (stylised flowers); Hamadan (strong coloured diapers); Herat (heavy carpets with a fish-type motif); Isfahan (vase motifs); Joshaghan (diamonds of flowers); Kara Dagh (some Caucasian motifs); Kermanshah (medallions, leaves and flowers); Khorassan (animals, birds and figures); Kirman (vase, flower leaf; later figures and birds); Meshed (rich colours, flower and animal themes); Niris (non-figurative); Saraband (pear-like motifs); Saruk (richly coloured); and Souj-Bulak (somewhat tribal).

PERSIAN POTTERY

Extraordinarily inventive, often so elaborate in design with a mixture of ornament and inscription that the pottery cannot readily be deciphered. Tiles and mosaics date from the fifteenth century with a colour scheme of blue, purple, yellow and green, contemporary with large dishes decorated in black on white. Blue-and-white ware was made from the fifteenth century, and there is speculation that this predates Chinese examples, for non-Chinese shapes are found. Lustre techniques were abandoned in the fourteenth century, revived in the seventeenth, the latter usually restricted to flower and plant motifs. From the sixteenth to the eighteenth century single-colour ware, in-

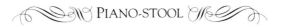

fluenced by Chinese models, was made, with decorations either in relief, applied in white, or cut through the coloured glaze to the white body. Most of the pottery is carried out with bravura and conviction.

PETROL LIGHTERS

Invented during World War I, early petrol lighters consisted of cotton wool, a wick, a cogged wheel and a flint, but in the 1920s they became transformed into decorative objects, made from a diverse range of materials, with mother-of-pearl for ladies' lighters one of the most popular. Heavy-based table lighters were made, often made to look like something else, such as a miniature drinks bar in chrome and plastic or a tennis-ball. An oddity was the lighter-watch made in the late 1920s in which a silver and gold lighter had a watch set in the side. Some of the more desirable lighters, such as the chunky and simple 'Zippo' of 1932, are being reproduced (though this is made clear on the body of the lighter). During World War II petrol lighters were made in slack times in aircraft factories, usually of brass. Butane lighters may be the antiques of the future, though this is doubtful.

PEWTER

Alloy of tin and lead or copper, sometimes hardened with antimony or bismuth, known to the Romans and used until the eighteenth century for most household wares, such as plates and drinking vessels, often being recycled so that less old pewter remains than one might expect. In the sixteenth century 'display' pewter was produced for decorative articles, especially in France and Germany. Pewterers' guilds, set up in the thirteenth century, set rigorous standards, but these were frequently broken and the marks on the pewter were often deliberately misleading. The shapes of pewter vessels often followed those of silver, and pewter was very much disregarded until the nineteenth century as a poor man's silver, except for small decorative pieces, and only in the art nouveau period was it treated with true respect. Sometimes too much respect, for pewter was so popular that it was used for totally unsuitable purposes such as teaspoons, which had a tendency to melt in the tea.

PHOTOGRAPHS

Daguerreotypes (1829–60) are on metal plates, often lavishly framed with much use of plush, and are frequently boxed or in folding-book form. Portraits are less interesting than landscapes, landscapes are less interesting than street or genre scenes. It was not possible to make prints off an original Daguerreotype, unlike the Calotype (1841–55, paper negatives and positives). Calotypes are much rarer and in huge demand, especially those by Fox Talbot, Hill and Adamson. Ambrotypes (1851–71) are negatives backed by black paper to give a positive, always increasing in value, as are tintypes as used by street photographers (1853–80), of poor quality but often of interesting subjects. After 1870 photography was no longer the province of the experts, and there are millions of photographs still about in antique shops, flea markets, junk-shops and even at boot fairs and jumble sales. Studio portraits of unknown people are worth nil, unusual for items that can be 130 years old, and the lavish albums in which such photographs were housed are often worth many times more than the entire contents.

Stereoscopic photographs were also issued by the million, and stereoscopes are still reasonably priced; stereoscopic photographs can be purchased remarkably cheaply. Their heyday was from 1851 to 1914. Family albums can be picked up cheaply and, although many of the photographs are of no interest, sometimes even the amateur takes time off from snapping the family to photograph everyday life (suffragette damage, coronations, air displays, contemporary transport). Most amateurs before World War II used Kodak or Kodak-type cameras, therefore the prints are small. Far more desirable are large format photographs (plate and half-plate); they were the products of professional and enthusiasts' cameras. Modern photographs, like those of the nineteenth century, depend largely for their value on the identity of the photographers.

PIANO-STOOL

Of various types, the most outstanding being the Victorian round-topped carved version, usually in one of the show woods such as walnut or rosewood. This was fitted with a swivel wind-up

A revolving Victorian piano stool in mahogany, a revolving bookcase in a mixture of ill-fitting styles, and an oak stool, probably 17th century.

mechanism, and was usually on tripod feet. Four-legged stools catered for either one player or two, and were made in a variety of woods. They had hinged lids, which were often upholstered.

PICTURE POSTCARDS

Postcards originated in Austria in 1869, picture postcards began as postcards with vignettes in the corner in the 1880s but picture postcards were not permitted in Britain until 1894. The collectable cards are those printed before 1914, especially cards depicting trains, trams, cars, buses, aircraft, shipwrecks, street scenes, accidents and catastrophes, and anything out of the ordinary and not posed. The most valuable cards are those of the art nouveau period, such as those by Mucha and Kirchner, though Louis Wain cat cards run them close. There is also a wide field in comic postcards, represented best by Donald McGill. World War I cards were printed in immense numbers and are rarely of

value. Many cards depend for their appeal on unusual features, such as being made from wood, leather, aluminium, silk, and even silver. 'Hold to light' postcards are those with a secret picture only revealed when held to the light, mechanical cards derive from Victorian Christmas cards and Valentines, and some postcards had fragments of fabric and other materials pasted onto them. There is a subsidiary interest in postmarks, especially if they relate to specific events, if they were carried by boat ('paquebot' cards), or even if they were village rubber-stamped.

PILL SLABS

Delftware in simple flat shapes such as oblong, octagonal, shield, or heart, made for seventeenth-century apothecaries to shape their pills, and usually with one or two holes so that they could be hung up when not in use.

PINCHBECK

Alloy of 90 per cent copper and 10 per cent zinc resembling, but not necessarily faking, gold, invented by a clock and watchmaker of that name who died in 1732. Used for snuff-boxes and other small objects and for jewellery. Unlike gilded metals, pinchbeck was the same colour all through.

PINXTON

A short-lived ceramics factory established in 1796 by W. Billingsley, a potter who moved about a good deal, working at Derby in his early career and later starting another ephemeral factory, Nantgarw. Perhaps an early asset-stripper. Pinxton wares were attractive, a speciality being a small sprig, a cornflower or a forget-me-not, on a white ground. Billingsley left the firm in 1801, taking his trade secrets with him, and after he had gone the quality of the products deteriorated until the factory closed in 1813.

PIPE-RACK

Originally a stand for clay pipes, which could be in the form of a circular platform on a stem, pierced with holes to hold the pipes, an open frame, or an iron basket in which the pipes were placed horizontally so that they could be baked in an oven and cleansed. The pipe-rack later became a test piece for amateur carpenters, often ornate and involving convoluted fretwork. Sometimes ceramic ashtrays were made in the twentieth century with a moulded depression to take a pipe on its side.

PIPES

Smoking began in the sixteenth century when tobacco was introduced from America. Clay pipes were used, the earliest of which had flat bases so that they could stand upright on a table when not in use. During the reign of Queen Anne long-stemmed pipes known as aldermen were smoked, and about 1780 spurs were applied to the bowl. The churchwarden was a long curved pipe of the nineteenth century. No wood had been found that did not catch fire, and the only other materials were meerschaum and porcelain. Meerschaum was first used for pipebowls in the 1770s, splendidly carved, and highly prized after they had been 'well smoked' whereupon they assumed additional colour and lustre. Much of the meerschaum was imported from Turkey, and mostly carved in Germany and Austria. Up to about 1850 the bowls were large, but they became smaller. The stems were

of ivory or wood. About 1750 porcelain was used for pipes in Germany, but it did not prove an ideal substance, for the oils from the tobacco percolated to the bottom of the bowl and spoilt the flavour. So an extra reservoir was provided in the form of a Y, made of many kinds of substance, such as wood, metal, bone, horn or china. The mouthpiece was usually of horn and connected to the stem by tubing covered with a woven material. The whole ensemble was made very decorative, and the bowls were decorated with a great range of subjects, with tiny representations of famous people, infamous murderers, scenes of the chase, mythological subjects and views. The modern everyday pipe dates its inception to 1859 when a root from a shrub called *bruyère* was used (the name later anglicised to briar). This root proved to be the ideal material, though briar pipes are by their nature functional and they do not much differ from each other.

PIPE STOPPERS

Pipe stoppers or tampers have been used since the seventeenth century when pipe-smoking became popular. Early ones were small because tobacco was an expensive luxury, and most were of brass, which remained the favourite material, though wood, bone, gold, silver and glass have also been used, nothwithstanding the unsuitability of many substances. Porcelain stoppers include prestige products from Chelsea and Derby. The most common sort are miniature cast figures, especially of fictitious characters from Shakespeare and Dickens, but female legs were popular in the nineteenth century as well as tools of the various trades. There were novelty stoppers with moving parts, and stoppers could form part of a corkscrew set, while some stoppers were made from well-known ships and trees, difficult to authenticate. A pricker, to break up the coagulated tobacco in the bowl, was sometimes provided with the stopper. Stoppers can be taken by the uninitiated to be figurines, and vice versa.

PITKIN FLASKS

American ribbed glass flasks, especially amber and green, with swirled coloured patterns, made between about 1780 and 1830.

PLASTICS

One of the earliest plastics was Parkesine, a mixture of cellulose nitrate and castor oil (later replaced by camphor), displayed to the public in the Great Exhibition of 1862, and used for buttons, toys, combs, knife handles, brushes, and even medallions. It lasted until 1868, and items made from it are rare. Celluloid resulted from a shortage of ivory in the 1860s. An American manufacturer of billiard balls offered a prize to anyone who could come up with an ivory substitute. Celluloid was patented in 1871, and became so overwhelmingly popular that it acquired a small 'c'; celluloid was ideal for buttons, combs, brush handles, typewriter keys, knobs and dials, and toys. Flexible, long-lasting, and strong, it was prone to discoloration and was flammable. A less dangerous substance was sought for and the answer was cellulose acetate, first produced in 1926. Bakelite was discovered in 1872, first manufactured commercially in 1910, and proved a sturdy practical substance, ideal for the handles of cooking utensils because of its resistance to heat; it was moulded into ashtrays, knobs on wireless sets, and novelties of all kinds. Customarily it is brown, and bakelite has a devoted army of admirers and collectors. A mixture of casein (sour milk) and formaldehyde was patented in 1900, and went under a variety of names. In Britain it was called Erinoid, in America Aladdinite, and it was used mainly for knick-knacks and accessories – buttons, buckles, brooches, hair-slides, combs, parasol handles, pens, knitting-needles, cigarette boxes, and lighters. Occasionally it was employed for larger articles, such as bowls, but these are not common. Urea formaldehyde resin was known in 1897, first used commercially after about 1928 and marketed as Beetle, Scarab, Aldur and Plaskon. It was light, heat-resistant, and colourful, and used for lampshades, electrical equipment, toys and novelties. In sheet form it could serve as table-tops or panelling.

PLATE

A general name for silver and gold, later applied to imitative wares such as Sheffield plate and electroplate. It therefore only has a definite meaning in its context.

PLATE PAIL

A mahogany bucket-like object with a handle for carrying plates from kitchen to dining-room, usually circular with an open section for taking the plates in and out.

PLATE WARMER

A device often of iron made in various shapes to put by the fire to warm plates. One type was a wrought-iron revolving stand on a tripod base with upright bars to hold the plates secure. Another was an arrangement of crossed wooden or metal rods which formed a double tripod, one on top of the other.

PLYMOUTH

The first factory in England to make hard-paste porcelain, and the experimental nature of 'real' porcelain resulted in a high kiln loss. The factory opened in 1768 and in 1770 the founder moved to Bristol where there was a stronger potting tradition. The most common objects made were mugs, sauce-boats, bowls, cream boats, coffee-cups and leaf-like dishes for pickles, but plates are rare. Designs were Chinese influenced. The glaze was often imperfect and has a pitted appearance, and firecracks are not uncommon. The blue-and-white ware, which is rarer than polychrome, has a blackish tinge.

POKER-WORK

A popular hobby in the nineteenth and twentieth centuries, involving tracing a design on wood with a hot iron, and sometimes seen on table-tops.

PORRINGER

Two-handed bowl with or without a cover made from silver, plate, or pewter from the fourteenth to the nineteenth centuries. The handles are often flat, in the form of 'ears'; these sometimes differ in the same piece, with a hole in one of them so that the porringer can be hung up. The shape of a porringer varied, and the term was often used for other bowls. A popular form in America.

PORTLAND VASE

Perhaps the most famous piece of decorative ware in existence. Made in cameo glass by the Romans, it is a two-handled blue urn cased in white opaque glass in which mythological figures are carved in relief. Smashed by an 'inebriated lunatic' in 1845, it was restored, using a Wedgwood ceramic copy made 1786–90. Wedgwood made an initial 'edition' of twenty-nine, and other copies followed, some of them bowdlerised (nude figures were draped). In 1929 the repaired original vase was put up for sale, but the bidding only reached £29,000 and it was withdrawn. It was bought by the British Museum in 1946.

PORTUGUESE FURNITURE

In the sixteenth century Lisbon was the richest capital in Europe. In 1580 Spain claimed the Portuguese throne, so Portuguese furniture, in its heyday predominantly influenced by Italy and France, was now open to increasing Spanish influence as well as that of the Orient, Portugal's principal trading outlet. In 1640 Portugal recovered its independence, and its furniture, especially a type of high-backed chair, began to influence Spain. With the recapture of Brazil from the Dutch in 1654, quantities of Brazilian wood such as jacaranda and pausanto, not often seen in Europe, were imported and vied with native walnut and chestnut. An important feature of Portuguese chairs was the use of leather and studded nails, used in a way different to that employed in Spanish and English leather-backed and leather-seated chairs. The chest was also important, as well as the cabinet, initially derived from Spain but seasoned with Dutch features such as raised geometrical panels. A curious feature of Portuguese cabinets is that they are set on lions couchant instead of feet. A result of Portuguese conquests is the distinctive Indo-Portuguese furniture, European in style with Indian and Oriental decoration. Portugal's enclave in India, Goa, was one of the richest cities in the world and the inhabitants demanded the best and most lavish furniture that money could buy. During the eighteenth century English furniture style, the most important in Portugal, was re-created in Brazilian hardwoods, permitting crisp carving and thin legs without the need for stretchers. Chippendale-style furniture was copied and made more exuberant, but furniture of the late eighteenth century was reproduced more exactly. A typical and original Portuguese eighteenth-century piece was a version of the chest of drawers with four banks of drawers, serpentine front, and with scrolled bracket feet. In the early nineteenth century, French Empire styling was practised, heavier and cruder than the original models, but liberation from the French in 1811 brought English furniture back into fashion, with a fondness for a Sheraton type. But due to dynastic marriages there was now a German influence, and plain simple furniture of the Biedermeier type provided a restful interlude until Portugal, like France, Germany, and Britain, discovered its past in an orgy of revivalism and fake antiquarianism.

POT LIDS

Hard pottery lids on pots containing bear's-grease (for slicking down the hair) and miscellaneous products, first made using labels and later transfers, often coloured by hand and depicting an enormous range of subjects, often superbly designed and presented. Mostly made by F. and R. Pratt, Staffordshire potters. Much collected, and much faked, with some very clever crazing on the glaze.

POT-HOOK

The simplest of metal devices for hanging a cooking pot over a fire, sometimes a mere S shape, sometimes fitted up with a ratchet mechanism for adjustment. A Scottish variant was the jumping rope, a chain and a hook. Much fireplace furniture was made of iron, and it is sometimes difficult to judge the age of pot-hooks and similar objects.

POT-POURRIS

Containers for sweet-smelling herbs in silver and china popular in the eighteenth century. Pot-pourris were made in porcelain by the Derby factory, amongst others. Provision was made for the scent to permeate by either piercing, as in the cover of the silver examples, or by a kind of trellis in the porcelain types.

There are two kinds of porcelain, hard-paste and soft-paste. Hard-paste was first made in China in the seventh or eighth century, and first made in Europe about 1710 at Meissen and thence spread throughout Europe. Usually porcelain was glazed, but if unglazed was called biscuit or bisque. Porcelain could be painted before being glazed, or after, in which case it was fired again. Soft-paste porcelain was a type invented before 'real' porcelain was discovered, and as losses in the firing process were heavy, soft-paste porcelain is less common. In the middle of the seventeenth century China began producing porcelain for overseas markets, and the blue-and-white Canton ware, not greatly rated by the Chinese, was shipped in bulk as ballast for ships transporting silks and tea. The first coloured Chinese porcelain to make an impact in England was *famille verte* with a range of brilliant enamel colours – copper-green, purple, blue, red and yellow. This was succeeded in public esteem by *famille rose*, pastel colours with the emphasis on pink. The

Pair of raised anchor Chelsea porcelain strawberry dishes c1752 painted in the Japanese Kakiemon style.

Chinese potters did work to order, often copying armorial designs with astonishing precision; the English potters did work in the Chinese style, a compliment to the begetters of true porcelain. Of all the factories the most famous at the time was Chelsea (1745–70), noted for its luxury items; Bow (1749–76) concentrated on everyday domestic china, and probably had the largest output of blue-and-white in Britain; Worcester was the largest factory, beginning in 1751 and pioneering transfer printing in 1757; Longton Hall was a small concern which lasted about ten years until 1760; Derby began with figures, expanded, and in 1770 took over Chelsea. Liverpool porcelain is a general name associated with several factories, of which Chaffers is the most prominent. Caughley was another small factory, and one of the shortest lived was Plymouth, the first to make hard-paste porcelain, in production for two years before the owners moved to Bristol. The small New Hall factory of Staffordshire was mostly concerned with tea- and coffee-ware. Lowestoft (1757–1802) made only soft-paste porcelain, and factory marks of Worcester and Meissen were imitated, not unusual in the eighteenth

century when marks often served to confuse rather than inform, and still do. The products of the British eighteenth-century factories often bear a family resemblance – simple, refined, functional, sometimes derivative, often technically maladroit. Except for the figure work, strongly influenced by continental models. Technical advances were constantly being made. Spode introduced bone china, by adding bone ash to the mix, and advances in pottery technology made the borderline between porcelain and pottery increasingly vague, so that we have ironstone china from 1813 (which is not porcelain but pottery) and semi-porcelain from Spode. Some of the most delicate work was done in pottery and not porcelain, such as Wedgwood basalt (black) and jasper (blue). Meissen (founded in 1710) produced work of a sophistication rare in Britain at the time (though not later), as did Sèvres (founded in 1738), which had a monopoly protecting it from competition until the French Revolution of 1789; it began to produce its unrivalled biscuit figures from 1753. As techniques became mastered there was an emphasis on colour, intricacy, elabora-

Four Naples porcelain figures of classical women.

tion, and beautiful hand-painting especially for show-pieces and luxury items. Factories strove to outdo their rivals and make something new, such as the *pâte-sur-pâte* technique of Sèvres introduced into England by the Minton factory in 1870, or the pierced work from the Worcester factory. Some of the work of the art potteries from 1870 onwards is amazing. In a consumer society eager for novelty there was no end to ceramic adventure, and this has continued throughout the twentieth century. What were considered revolutionary processes in their day are now commonplace. The most incredible and complex designs can now be transferred by photographic methods onto porcelain. 'Collectors' plates' as advertised in the colour supplements are works of outstanding technical skill, though there may be some question about their status as works of art. If only a few survived there is no doubt that they would be accepted. As with many artefacts, value is often dependent on how many there are of them.

POTTERY AND PORCELAIN COTTAGES

These could be either purely decorative or they could serve a purpose, such as pastille burning to produce a pleasant aroma. Examples date from the 1750s by the potter Whieldon. Pastille-burner cottages (and castles) were at their peak from 1810 to 1850, and during World War II they disappeared from the open market as American servicemen found that they were delightful souvenirs to send back home. Other homesteads, some fantastic with turrets, minarets, and towers, were intended as candlesticks, spill holders, money-boxes, and multi-purpose containers with a detachable roof. Many well-known potteries were making pastille burners including Coalport, Worcester, Minton (often fitted out with a goldfinch on the roof), Pratt, and Spode. Solid cottages were often miniature replicas of real buildings, and similar novelties are made today and may, if unmarked, be confused with nineteenth-century cottages. More confusing are modern Coalport cottages made using the original moulds, and although these are fully marked, leaving no room for ambiguity, these marks can be filed out. The finger-tip test is often better than sight alone.

POUNCE POT

Made from the eighteenth century in glass, silver, brass, plate and pewter, this was a desk-top item to sprinkle powdered pumice on writing-paper to stop the ink spreading. As with most desk-top articles it could be plain and simple, in vase, cylindrical, or baluster shape, often little different from a sugar caster, or it could be fancy, in the shape of birds or animals. It was rendered obsolete overnight by the invention of blotting-paper.

PRATT WARE

Although established in 1812, the firm of Pratt was most famed for the terracotta vases and other decorative objects with detailed scenes painted in bright enamel colours often in the form of friezes produced from the 1840s and for the pot lids of the 1850s onwards. The factory also did a line in Toby jugs.

PRAYER RUG

Small carpet carried around by Moslems so that at the appointed hour they can make their devotions. The Mihrab (prayer niche or arch) is an important feature, often depicted in abstract form. Because of hard continuous wear old prayer rugs are often much worn, and modern rugs with a modicum of usage are often taken to be older than they are.

PROPELLING PENCILS

The practical value of a propelling pencil must always be in doubt and, although its use obviates the need to sharpen a pencil, there is no gradation in the writing stroke and leads always have a tendency to snap. It is not surprising that many propelling pencils are purely novelties, and are disguised as Egyptian mummies, pitchers, oars, tennis-rackets, golf-clubs, railway engines and lanterns, and indeed almost anything where a tube can be incorporated. The first propelling pencil was patented in 1822, and there are only a limited number of ways in which a lead can be pushed up a narrow cylinder, the most common being a spiral turning action. Many propelling pencils contain a chamber at the end to hold spare leads, and others are combined with other writing equipment such as penholders (at the other end), rulers, bookmarks, paper-knives and tiny balances. One of the more interesting novelties includes a peep-show attachment. Although the early propelling pencils are made of silver, a variety of materials has been used including bone, wood, all kinds of base metal and a range of plastics, some of them simulating something natural such as tortoiseshell. It is difficult to date propelling pencils, though the novelty types are easier than others.

PUZZLE JUG

The puzzle jug, a drinking rather than a pouring vessel, is perforated around the top and the liquid is drunk from an inconspicuous tube. It was sometimes necessary to stop some of the apertures with the fingers. Popular from the Middle Ages, it was made throughout the eighteenth century by famous potteries as well as small-scale easily-amused potters, and it was popular well into the nineteenth century.

QUILT

Padded bed-cover made of a layer of wool, flock or down sewn between two pieces of material. The stitching is often geometrical, but can be done in arabesque or floral patterns. Corded quilting involves inserting cords under the surface of the covering material, kept in place by rows of parallel stitches. Made from the seventeenth century, brought to an art in America in the form of the patchwork quilt.

RAZORS

Until the 1880s the cutthroat razor, sharpened on a leather strop, was used, though for safety's sake a guard along the blade had been patented about 1850. The 'Hypetome' or beard plane was produced in 1851. The American Home Safety Razor of 1891 claimed that it was impossible to cut the face, but the modern wet razor dates from the throw-away steel blade developed by William Gillette. In 1931 the Schick Electric Razor was put on the market. Cutthroat sets have continued to be sold long after theoretically they were obsolete, and they are still used by barbers who find that the modern usurpers do not give such a close shave.

RED STONEWARE

Originally made in China, red 'porcelain' (which it was not) was made at Delft from about 1672. It became very fashionable in England in the 1690s and it was made at Meissen during research into the fine art of porcelain-making. It was popular in America from the seventeenth to the nineteenth centuries and was known as redware, often lead-glazed and decorated with slip.

RENAISSANCE STYLE

Revival of interest in and rediscovery of the ancient world and its artefacts from the fourteenth century in Italy and then throughout Europe, transforming the way of looking at the world and changing attitudes to art, architecture, and not least the home environment. The Gothic style was gradually ousted, though it took a long time, and persisted in furniture for centuries. A certain austerity was replaced by the luxuriant, with rich fabrics, the import of

Oriental carpets, marble, bronzes, and strong colours and patterns, often disposed symmetrically.

REPOUSSÉ

A term used to describe embossed work, mostly on metals where the surface to be worked is hammered and shaped from the reverse side.

RIDGWAY POTTERY AND PORCELAIN

A prolific Staffordshire pottery, founded in 1792 and producing blue-and-white pottery and other wares, including porcelain, and which was eventually in serious competition with Minton. Very large items including fountains were made, and although 'sanitary vessels' were exhibited at the Great Exhibition of 1851 the firm is perhaps best known for its Cauldon ware (one of the factories was sited at Cauldon Place, Shelton), much of it exported to America, particularly the blue-and-white 'Beauties of America' service, with prints of famous American buildings. Views of American rivers later followed. The concern was eventually taken over by Coalport.

RINGS

Rings are something other than jewellery. Bracelets, necklaces, brooches and pendants may be worn for other reasons than self adornment, but not in most cases. The scarab rings worn by the ancient Egyptians typified death, resurrection and immortality, and the gold rings worn by the Roman emperors were symbols of power. Roman rings could be inset with emerald cameos and other designs. Medieval rings are rare, Renaissance rings aimed at classicism, with cameos and intaglios, but in the seventeenth century precious and semiprecious stones were set into rings, mostly gold and silver. Platinum was discovered in Russia in 1823. The wedding-ring is traditionally of plain gold; Queen Elizabeth II's wedding-ring is of thin Welsh gold, totally without ornament. Posy-rings can date from medieval days; they bore mottoes and pious verses. Ecclesiastical rings were gold, usually set with an amethyst or a sapphire, in form not unlike a signet-ring, while rosary or prayer rings had ten small protrusions to remind the wearer to say ten *Ave Marias*, and a stone for one Lord's Prayer. Talismanic rings were engraved with characters, sometimes in Hebrew or Greek, and were intended to save the owners from dangers. Poison rings were fitted with a receptacle and a projecting pin; some were suicide rings, to save the wearer from torture. Container rings could hold tiny portraits, or hair, which was also often a feature of mourning-rings, though mourning-rings could be a plain band with an 'In Memoriam' dedication, often in black enamel on gold. Serjeant-at-law rings were in use until about the middle of the nineteenth century, and were presented to judges and other barristers (which was what a serjeant was) by a recently-promoted lawyer after being wined and dined by his fellows. Watch rings, a poor alternative to the wrist-watch, are long obsolete, unlike the gemel ring, twin rings which could be worn separately or joined together as one.

ROCK-CRYSTAL

Besides giving its name to crystal glass, rock-crystal, a colourless quartz, was used for the making of cups, salts, caskets, jewellery, and watch-cases, a time-consuming process as rock-crystal is a very hard substance.

ROCKINGHAM POTTERY AND PORCELAIN

A factory was established on the Marquis of Rockingham's estate in Yorkshire in 1745, making simple brown ware. In 1787 Leeds Pottery took a controlling interest, but in 1806 the firm was acquired by two men with enterprising ideas who ran the factory until its closure in 1842. A distinctive brown glaze from manganese oxide was introduced about 1806, given the name of the firm. Amongst its more unusual products was the Cadogan teapot, moulded green-glazed ware in cabbage-leaf shape, caneware jugs, and pastille burners in the shapes of castles and cottages, but all rendered insignificant by the Rhinoceros Vase, made in 1826, 3ft 9in (1.14m) high, with the cover topped by a gilded rhinoceros. Porcelain was made from 1826. Such was the fame of this factory that in America earthenware with a mottled brown glaze is known as Rockingham ware.

ROCOCO STYLE

Airy, light, elegant, this style succeeded the baroque, and is characterised further by bright colours against white and gilt, naturalistic motifs, often of a leafy or floral form, and a leaning towards asymmetry. It first appeared in France in the 1690s, rather than in Italy the home of so many movements, and was taken up rather slowly, not having a full impact until the 1730s. Enthusiasm was then often excessive, with natural curves being exaggerated into a kind of corpulence. In England rococo was regarded with suspicion, and in furniture its effect was minimal except in decorative objects such as mirror frames. Porcelain was in the process of being developed, and rococo themes and figuration proved ideal, especially for the German factories and through them, by imitation, those in England. Rococo was in its turn replaced by the move towards a more severe classical style, but throughout the nineteenth century it continued to emerge, often in unfamiliar forms.

ROGERS POTTERY

Established in 1780, the factory produced transfer-printed blue-and-white pottery with adventurous designs depicting zebras, elephants, and exotic places as seen by the Staffordshire mind; it was much exported to America. The factory closed in 1836.

ROLLING BALL CLOCK*

A novelty clock, in which a ball rolling down grooves places weight on a pivoted table which, as it oscillates, provides the driving force. Devised by theorists seeking the chimera of perpetual motion in the seventeenth century, the best known example was made by Congreve in 1808, and is made by clock makers today to special order. The rolling ball clock is not an example of perpetual motion; it has to be started off externally.

ROLLING-PIN

In wood a familiar, rather dull object; in glass often exotic, made in the early nineteenth century in brightly coloured glass by Nailsea and others, especially in opaque white, purple, blue,

amber, and green. They were made for the gift market, and sold at markets and fairs, engraved or painted with amorous pledges or religious mottoes and exhortations. Their ultimate destiny was no doubt to be hung up over the cottage fireplace, and there is some doubt as to whether they ever were used for rolling pastry.

ROLL-TOP DESK

Twin-pedestal desk with bureau fitment with interior drawers and pigeon-holes. The top is slatted, and this type of utilitarian no-nonsense desk was much used in the nineteenth and twentieth centuries as basic office furniture.

ROMAN POTTERY

Although many early items are in museums or private collections, this does not apply to Roman pottery and more specifically Romano-British pottery, which was made in great quantities and is available at low cost, though whether specific items are genuine or small red earthenware objects of dubious ancestry is open to question. The most notable Roman type of

18th-century side table with strong rococo influences, quite rare in English furniture and restricted mainly to mirrors and console tables.

pottery is *terra sigillata*, a ware covered with a red gloss. The Romans knew the secrets of lead-glazing, and produced handsome vessels with a yellowy-green glaze. In the Eastern provinces of the Roman Empire pottery was made with a turquoise glaze, and exported to other parts of the Empire.

RUSHLIGHT HOLDER

Usually of iron and free-standing or made for the table, this is a lighting device in which a length of rush pith, dipped in tallow, is fitted into an adjustable clip. Some rushlight facilities have facilities for holding a candle. Rush gave out a weak and insipid light but it was cheap.

RUSSIAN FURNITURE

Russian eighteenth-century furniture was strongly influenced by French, English, and less often German models, imported and copied, often with significant differences, loading surfaces with inlay and using gemstones in a bravura manner as furniture decorations, and using malachite as an inlay on English-derived eighteenth-century furniture. A truly Russian achievement was the cut steel furniture produced at Tula up to 1796 and known as Tula furniture. But this too was influenced by the work of Matthew Boulton at the Soho Works, Birmingham, though the use of incrustations of silver, pewter, brass and copper on steel was wholly Russian. Early nineteenth-century furniture was also after western European models, though the Russians showed a preference for light-coloured woods and Russia, too, went through a French Empire phase and a taste for revivalism, perhaps less so than Britain and Germany because of the absence of a rich industrial middle-class avid for new things. The turn of the century enthusiasm for adventure was muted in Russia, perhaps because more momentous things than in the west were happening and about to happen.

RUSTIC FURNITURE

There are several meanings; one a term for honest country furniture of the Windsor-chair type; another is a term for furniture made of wood that is picked up and roughly pulled together; and rustic furniture can mean furniture which looks as though it is picked up and roughly pulled together but which, in fact, is artfully assembled for use in hermitages, arbours, and country-house follies. Several pattern books to help in making such furniture were published in the eighteenth century. In the nineteenth century rustic furniture was simulated in cast iron and other materials for garden use.

SAMPLER

An embroidered panel, dating from the seventeenth century and made well into the nineteenth, originally worked in a variety of stitches to act as a reference guide, and to demonstrate the skill of the needlewoman or, more likely, needlegirl. This led to the creation of charming pictures incorporating pious mottoes, the letters of the alphabet, numbers, and a thesaurus of animals, birds, buildings and anything else that appealed to the mind of a twelve-year-old, and usually carried out using one specific stitch, which became known as the sampler stitch. Samplers were done on a tough linen ground, and bore the maker's name, age, and the date of completion (which was often unpicked at a later stage to keep the needlewoman's age secret).

SAMSON

The most famous and persuasive maker of reproduction porcelain, especially Chinese porcelain, eighteenth-century Sèvres, and Meissen, now himself almost as much collected as the originals. Samson (1837–1913) has a lot to answer for; he demonstrated how easily experts are fooled.

SATSUMA

With Imari the best known of Japanese ceramics. There are two kinds of Satsuma, simple earthenware for home use, and gaudy tin-glazed ware for export and taken to be the very essence of Japan. Attractive small objects such as incense burners and winebottles were made in the early nineteenth century, but the greatest demand in the west from the 1850s was for 'Brocaded' Satsuma, a crackled cream-coloured ware decorated in gold and enamel, sometimes artificially aged for the ignorant European by using tea, sulphuric acid, and smoke.

SAUCEPAN

Originally silver, with pear-shaped, rotund, or cylindrical body, with jutting-out handle, sometimes of wood, with perhaps accompanying spirit burner and stand, it has developed very little to become the mundane kitchen utensil of today. Large saucepans were fitted with lids. Small saucepans were often used to heat brandy, and have names such as pannikin or pipkin.

SCAGLIOLA

Imitation marble, using marble chips as a basis, bound with isinglass and plaster of Paris to form one of the first substitutes, used from the eighteenth century for furniture as well as for floors and pillars, though painted wood was often preferred to simulate marble columns.

SCALES AND BALANCES

Scales and balances are of four kinds: equal-armed balances, unequal-armed balances, spring balances and automatic machines. In equal-armed balances there is usually an up-right, but not necessarily, for goldsmiths' balances are suspended and folded away in a container with weights and tweezers. The first precision balance dates from the 1770s; the horizontal beam was triangular for rigidity and lifted off the vertical when not in use, either by using a cranked lever inside the vertical rod or a system of pulleys. An indicator in front of the scale was supplied to give precise readings. Wire was used to suspend the brass pans. Accuracy was ensured by enclosing the balance in a glass case. Balances with the pans below the beams are called scale beams; those with the pans above are old-fashioned shop scales, often made of cast iron, with brass pans or marble weighing surfaces. Unequal-armed balances are represented by the old type of public weighing machines (with weights added along a bar) and weighbridges. Spring balances can be suspended, such as laundry scales, or can be below the pan as in kitchen scales or postal scales. Automatic weighing machines date from the end of the nineteenth century, and work on the principle of the displacement of a loaded pendulum. The weights themselves, usually of brass, can be very decorative, especially continental examples.

SCANDINAVIAN FURNITURE

In 1666 the Great Fire of London meant massive rebuilding; the wood came from Norway, then joined with Denmark, and profits from it created great prosperity. Iron ore was imported from Sweden. Not surprisingly these close trading links encouraged imports from Britain to Scandinavia, in particular furniture, though English furniture had been popular for many years before 1666. This furniture was copied, often exactly, so it is often difficult to find Scandinavian features, except for a tendency to simplify or change proportions. There was also a tendency, for reasons of economy, to copy oak and walnut originals in birch, ash and deal, leading to a reduction in crispness. Some characteristics were retained when those in the furniture of the country of origin had long been dropped, such as the cabriole leg. In Denmark the import of foreign chairs was prohibited in 1746, so the Danes had no opportunity to keep up to date with latest fashions. A good deal of furniture was imported from the Netherlands in the eighteenth century but, just as England had been influenced by Dutch furniture in the seventeenth century, so had the Netherlands been by English furniture in the eighteenth. This hybrid is described as 'Anglo-Dutch' in Scandinavia. The French influence on Scandinavian furniture was mainly restricted to that used by courtly and highly-placed circles. With the Napoleonic wars the influence of English furniture lessened, and German models were taken and simplified. There was also a home-grown Empire style, with mahogany furniture contrasted with light birchwood veneer instead of gilt metal, followed, as in most countries, by a frenzy of revivalism, but it was never so pervasive in Scandinavia as elsewhere, and a tradition of craftsmanship was retained. The result was that there were always furniture-makers creating good unpretentious furniture, a tradition that continues.

SCENT-BOTTLES

Made from the thirteenth century in Italy in glass imitating agate and other stones, later clear glass bottles of the fifteenth and sixteenth centuries were simple in form and decorated with beads or trails of glass. Milk glass was used in Germany, often decorated with figurative designs, barrel-shape scent-bottles were produced in France, and opaque-white and blue glass scent-bottles were made at Bristol. During the eighteenth century scent-bottles in ingenious, often naturalistic forms were made throughout Europe in porcelain, often of the highest standard, as well as by the English factories especially Chelsea. Many enamel scent-bottles were made by Battersea, Birmingham and the other Midland factories, decorated similarly to snuff-boxes and, indeed, catering for exactly the same class, only this time for women rather than men. The two-ended scent-bottle in coloured glass was a popular product of the nineteenth century, and often had silver caps. Gold and silver scent-bottles were made from the sixteenth century onward, often elaborately worked and enamelled.

SCHWARZLOT

Painting in black enamel on glass and ceramics, first used on glass before being applied to ceramics. Developed some time in the mid-seventeenth century and used by Meissen and other factories throughout the eighteenth century. When the enamel is applied thinly, the colour can be sepia rather than black.

SCONCE

Wall light comprising a bracket candlestick with a polished back plate or mirror to reflect the light, made from wood, brass, silver and other suitable materials, popular from the late seventeenth century and sometimes known as a girandole.

SCRATCH BLUE

Eighteenth-century salt-glazed stoneware, decorated before firing with incised designs such as birds or flowers or inscriptions, into which a mixture of clay and cobalt was rubbed. Existing specimens come from the years 1724–76.

SCREEN

Covered frame, the most popular and useful form being the folding screen used from the Middle Ages and becoming increasingly elaborate from the sixteenth century, with lacquered screens imported from Japan and later copied. Leather, often elaborately tooled, was much used, and in the nineteenth century plain screens were sold and were decorated with scraps (cut-out pictures). Lacquer screens reappeared in the 1920s. Specialised small screens for protecting delicate complexions from the heat of a fire were popular from the eighteenth century, coming in two forms, the pole screen, an adjustable screen that slides up and down an often ornate stand, and the cheval screen, on four feet. As with the cheval mirror, the feet of cheval screens have often been used to make more desirable pieces.

SCRIMSHAW

A term of American origin describing any kind of craft carried out on board ship, especially a whaler, and mostly applied to carved marine ivory, such as the teeth of the sperm whale, the killer whale, and the elephant seal. The walrus was also used. The implements used were files, jack-knives, chisels and sandpaper (sometimes sharkskin was used instead of sandpaper), and the most notable item produced was the busk, engraved with designs and lines of verse, which was worn by women as a foundation garment. The engraved scrimshaw was called a graphic. The earliest scrimshaw was made of wood, and a tobacco box is in existence dating from 1665. Scrimshaws were made both for souvenirs and to supplement mariners' income; among the useful objects made were boxes, knitting and embroidery items, kitchen equipment such as ladles, games pieces and pastry crimps. The scrimshaw is very widely faked, often in a more naive style than the originals, many of which were painstakingly and professionally executed.

SEALS

An engraved stamp for making impressions on sealing-wax, set on a mount which could be a bird or an animal, animal or human heads, or a clenched fist, though a simple shaft was often sufficient. A fob seal was worn on the chatelaine from the early eighteenth century, the small mount being of gold. From the early nineteenth century the heavy desk-top model was preferred. The seal could be made of any material that could be finely engraved with a monogram or other device, and amongst them were agate, black onyx, bloodstone (perhaps the most popular), cornelian, jasper, lapis lazuli, and sard. Amongst the materials used for the shafts were gold, pinchbeck, ivory, hardstones, silver, brass, steel, coloured twist glass (as used in wineglass stems) and in the 1840s *millefiori* (thousand flowers) as used in paperweights. Seals were less employed when the introduction of the penny post in 1840 led to the evolution of the gummed envelope, so that it was no longer necessary to seal every letter. The mount was sometimes in the form of a ring, thus the seal ring, but sometimes seals have been stripped off their mounts to make these rings.

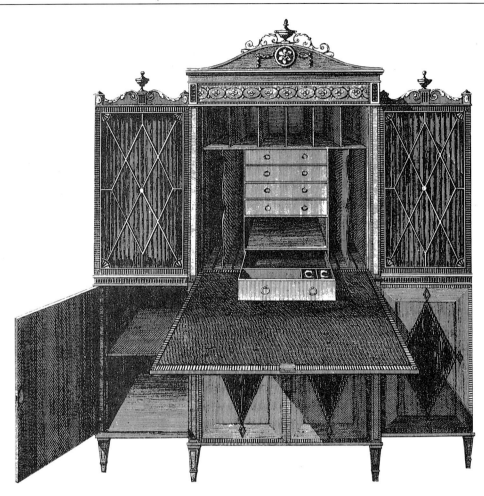

SECRETAIRE*

Originally a French word for a piece of writing furniture, it has now been Anglicised, and it shares with scrutoire and escritoire the charm of mystery. A secretaire is a bureau, with pigeon-holes, drawers, and compartments. The secretaire bookcase ranks with the bureau bookcase as the ultimate triumph of the cabinet-maker. A secretary is the American name for a bureau.

SETTEE

Originally a wide seat with arms designed for two or more people, often in the form of two chairs side by side, it was rather ungainly when compared with the fully upholstered settees that appeared about 1770. Settees echoed general furniture styles, and in the nineteenth century the settee was ideal for intricate carving and exotic shapes, with the most famous of all the

'A Gentleman's Secretary' from Sheraton's drawing book.

varieties being the buttoned-back *chaise longue*, or single-ended settee. About 1880 the languid curves of the *chaise longue* were succeeded by a more austere form, in which the sinuous design of the back was replaced by a row of spindles with the head piece becoming a hump. Velvet was succeeded by imitation leather. Some unusual settees were produced about 1900 with art nouveau shapes and motifs, and these included the cosy corner, designed for the corner of a room. The drop-arm settee could turn an ordinary piece of furniture into a temporary and uncomfortable bed for unexpected or unwelcome guests, and throughout the twentieth century there were successive revivals, probably more so than in any other kind of furniture. These included the chairs-side-by-side settee. The settee

The upholstered chairs of the 1920s and 1930s were noted for comfort rather than looks, and many of them could be turned into beds or settees. The Minty chair which 'took years to develop' could be taken apart, hardly an example of between-the-wars high technology.

en suite with armchairs brought, in the 1920s and 1930s, extreme shapelessness along with great comfort, although some of the examples, especially those in uncut moquette, have charm as well.

SETTLE

Dating from the Middle Ages, the settle is a long bench with a high back and arms or sides at each end. The base is often built as a long chest with the seat hinged at the back to give access to storage space, or it is open, with up to eight legs. Although earlier settles are carved in the vigorous traditions of no-nonsense old oak, most settles have a panelled back and sometimes a panelled base. The bacon settle is usually very tall, with cupboards in which to hang bacon. The settle was an ideal piece of furniture for nineteenth-century revivalists, who produced spectacular painted pieces, and it was ideally

suited to art nouveau treatment with copper and pewter panels. In the 1920s the settle, with a somewhat lower back, found a niche as a hall seat.

SÈVRES

Unquestionably the best-known French porcelain factory and, with Meissen, the most famous in the world, and deservedly so for, although it had the inestimable advantage of being state-backed and was thus able to take full use of the inevitable monopolies granted, this would have amounted to nothing had the products been indifferent. Founded in 1738, soft-paste porcelain was made exclusively until 1768 and occasionally until about 1800. The greatest period was between 1751 and 1815. In 1756 the factory was moved to a new building, and in 1759 it was taken over by the king, who had the best of both worlds, being the best client and the ace salesman, selling products from his own quarters at Versailles to courtiers and other hangers-on who, not surprisingly, were eager to buy. Sèvres catered for the luxury market and, unlike English factories, did not have to depend on mundane household wares. Among the products were restrained pieces in the rococo style including vases and sauce-boats, as well as flowerpots, perfume burners, pot-pourris, and a marvellous array of figures. Ground colours of brilliant enamel marked a departure from the customary white backgrounds of earlier French porcelain. Absolutely distinctive were new colours invented by Sèvres including *gros bleu, bleu céleste, jaune jonquille,* and *rose Pompadour,* often combined with lavish gilding. Among the best known objects were the biscuit figures, endlessly copied by all, produced from the 1750s. Hard-paste porcelain necessitated a new range of colours, and there was a move towards simpler forms but richer colour combinations; jewelled decoration appeared, and plaques were made for the adornment of furniture. In 1793 during the republican fervour the factory was declared state property and much undecorated porcelain was sold, often bought by painters (including English ones) and decorated in their studios. The staff was reduced, production nearly stopped, but in 1800 a talented administrator was brought in, new luscious colours were introduced and Napoleon became one of the main patrons, revelling in what might be termed, taking the word from fine art, 'grand machines.' After 1815 fussiness crept in, and the factory was reorganised in 1848, with more attention to the porcelain and a trend towards paler colouring. Eighteenth-century designs were revived and there was much imitation of Meissen and Chinese products, including eggshell porcelain. Lavish as well as simpler Chinese-influenced products were made throughout the nineteenth century, and Japanese china was also emulated. There were constant experiments in materials, and new types of stoneware and soft-paste porcelain were introduced. Unlike some other factories, Sèvres made its own contribution to the art nouveau movement and later produced individual art deco ware, but during the twentieth century most attention has been paid to recapturing the magic of the eighteenth century, with copies and revised versions of early works. Although there were many fine porcelain manufacturers in France, some of which shamelessly copied Sèvres, Sèvres set the tone.

SEWING-MACHINES

It was not until 1830, despite many false starts, that the French made a sewing-machine that actually worked, and in America an inventor evolved a machine that would make a lock stitch, the first stitch not to imitate a hand stitch. The production of successful sewing-machines depended on the availability of interchangeable parts; each machine had to be identical with the next one produced, and this was only possible with mass-production techniques and quality control, which the Americans had in abundance. In 1851 Isaac M. Singer patented the first truly practical sewing-machine, widely advertised, and the sewing-machine industry pioneered instalment purchase. The potential was immediately seen, and a patent war broke out, resulting in an eccentric variety of machines, shaped like Greek temples, dolphins or cupids, some elegant, some curious, but all having an overhanging arm carrying the needle mechanism, a continuous thread, and a handle to turn or a treadle to operate with the feet. Many were equipped with a wide range of accessories. Early sewing-machines were open with the works displayed, but they were soon covered in, with hand-painted flower and similar motifs

and inlay on the casing. The wooden domed covers were also very decorative. The ornate cast-iron stands of treadle machines have been topped with marble and sold as occasional tables for more than twenty years. Old sewing-machines, long neglected, are often rusted up, and are virtually valueless.

SGRAFFITO

Decorations on pottery using a pointed instrument to draw through a coating of slip to reveal the underlying body.

SHAGREEN

Shagreen can be untanned leather, treated when still moist by trampling seeds into it, resulting in the characteristic granulated look. Or it can be sharkskin. Both are used for a variety of products including covers for flasks, small boxes, tea-caddies, telescope tubes, etc.

SHEFFIELD PLATE

Is copper rolled between and fused with films of silver; a process discovered about 1742, and initially used for buttons and other small objects, but its potential as a cheap substitute for silver was seen about 1760. As with all substitutes where there is an expensive ingredient, the proportion of this ingredient, in this case silver, was reduced over the years from 1 in 10 to 1 in 60. Although Sheffield plate tended to displace silver, it had disadvantages; it could not be engraved as the copper would show through; the edges in objects, such as plates, were inclined to show the copper in the middle of the sandwich (solved by lapping, applying silver wire to the edges). Electroplating about 1840 rendered Sheffield plate obsolete, but it continued to be made until about 1880. As the silver wears off and the copper begins to show through, Sheffield plate takes on a unique glow, and it is probably more attractive now than it was when it was a second-best to silver.

SIDEBOARD

The sideboard is a mid-eighteenth-century piece of furniture, designed for gracious living, and envisaged by Robert Adam to be flanked by urns on pedestals, one for iced water, one for hot washing-up water. The pedestals themselves contained a wine store and a plate warmer. The eighteenth-century sideboard was elegant, mahogany with or without inlay, with usually six legs of slender tapering form in two groups of three. There was a central drawer, with two side cupboards. The basic shape was retained in the early nineteenth century with turned and fluted legs preferred, but about 1830 the sides of the sideboard descended to the floor, and from the 1840s the centre section was built in also, so that to all intents and purposes the sideboard became a side cabinet, with (when it might be labelled a chiffonier) and without a back piece. Some had the flattened arches so much a feature of early Victorian carcase furniture. The solid sideboard was ideal for oak exhibition pieces, richly and profusely carved, and also for experimentation in Gothic, Aesthetic, Arts and Crafts, 'Quaint', and art nouveau styles. Some sideboards were austere, essays in the vertical, others were phantasmagoric with acres of dashing inlay and massive decorative hinges. The main new feature was the massive mirror in the back. However, during the 1900–1914 period some admirable reproduction eighteenth-century sideboards were made which, at first glance (and sometimes at a second), can be taken as original. Until about 1930 perhaps the most popular kind was 'Jacobethan' (old English without being too particular), and being almost indestructible they are still used. Many of the 'fitness for function' furniture makers tried their hand at the sideboard, but many of these products are inclined to be worthy but dull.

SIGNS

Always of interest whether they are the wrought-iron type used from the Middle Ages, painted wooden boards for pubs and shops, or the enamel types, much reproduced. When the bulk of the population was illiterate, the trade or profession was denoted by a device, such as a boot for a cobbler, sometimes presented in profile or even in the solid.

SILHOUETTE

A portrait in profile, popular from about 1770 and a cheap substitute for a portrait before the age of photography. It was a considerable industry with special chairs being constructed for the sitter to keep him or her motionless. The silhouette could be solid black or bronzed, or adorned with inner detail or clothing, and could be on paper, plaster, ivory, glass or any suitable surface. Small silhouettes were done for miniatures and toys, such as snuff-boxes, as well as for jewellery inserts. Silhouettes were used on ceramics, commemorative and novelty ware, throughout the nineteenth and twentieth centuries; and were very popular on children's ware of the 1920s and 1930s.

SILK

A natural fibre, used in China from at least 1000BC and exported to Europe from about 200BC. A silk-weaving industry was started in the Near East about AD200, eventually to flourish in Spain and Sicily in the tenth century. By the Middle Ages Italy and Spain were the main centres, the lead passing to France in the seventeenth century and thence silk weaving spread to other countries including Britain, the main site being Spitalfields. It has been widely used in textiles, clothing, and for needlework, as well as for silk pictures.

SILVER

A brilliant white metal, too soft to use by itself. Known from earliest times when it was far more valuable than gold (which could be picked up in quantity in streams) since silver needed mining. From the fifteenth century it was much used in continental Europe and Britain for coinage, domestic vessels, and for display, and it was sometimes gilded to prevent tarnishing and to simulate gold. From the seventeenth century, domestic silver became a symbol of status, and still is, though often in an unconscious way, with even the unaware holding on to something quite small, such as a silver spoon. Sometimes silver was used for objects when it would have been more sensible to use some other metal. During the eighteenth century the dining-table glittered with innumerable devices, containers, and utensils of one kind or another, often of little in-

Mid-Victorian silver wine ewer dated 1874.

terest in themselves except that they were in silver and therefore were decorated and adorned in often excessive and counter-productive ways. Among the smaller objects are badges, bodkins, christening cups, cigar and cigarette boxes, nutmeg graters (carried around to flavour dubious meat), snuff-boxes, soap-boxes, spice boxes, tobacco boxes, vinaigrettes, buckles, buttons, card cases, whistles, corkscrews, gambling counter boxes, dog-collars, etuis, miniature furniture, hour-glasses, inkstands or standishes, dolls' house pieces, napkin-rings, pens and pencils, pipes (not satisfactory), posy holders, purses, rattles, seals and seal boxes, shoehorns, candle snuffers, sovereign cases, photograph frames, and thimbles, most of them engraved, embossed, or otherwise decorated in the manner of the time. During the nineteenth century, silver was used in immense quantities, and even ordinary middle-class households had huge and impressive pieces, for by the end of the century silver had ceased to be a really valuable metal (the price in 1850 was 5 shillings [25p] an ounce, and the price in 1896 was 2 shillings and 3 pence [12p] an ounce). The proportion of silver to alloy varies thoughout the world. The Sterling standard in English silver has been used since the Anglo-Saxon period, and the standard for coinage was established by law in 1300. The Sterling standard is 925 parts pure per 1,000; the Britannia standard, used 1697–1720, was 928 parts per 1,000. Foreign silver merely marked 925 indicates the same degree of purity as Sterling silver. The Sterling mark since 1544 is a lion passant, and in Scotland since 1759 a thistle.

SILVER DRINKING VESSELS

Until the end of the seventeenth century, covered tankards are probably the most common pieces of silver. These had flat covers, but between about 1710 and 1790 the domed top was preferred, and from about 1735 curved baluster shapes were preferred. Some of the handles were very elaborate with ornate top pieces. A tankard without a cover is technically not a tankard but a mug. Beakers, popular from Elizabethan times, were fashioned in one piece, sometimes gilded inside. They changed little except for superficial decoration from 1600 to 1800. Stirrup-cups were made from silver from about 1760 until well into the nineteenth cen-

tury in the shape of an animal's head, usually a dog's, with a circular band around the neck. They could not stand upright and were drunk from in the saddle, then handed to a servant when empty. Before the introduction of porcelain, silver teacups were used. Although not strictly a drinking vessel, beer jugs were made of silver from the seventeenth century, and are rare and valuable.

SILVERING

A form of glass decoration sometimes combined with gilding, which was unsatisfactory as it tarnished. High-priced Victorian glass vases and goblets were sometimes double-walled, the gap filled with silver. The most common application was to make mirrors, but silver is not used, only mercury and tin. Silver was occasionally applied to furniture, not very suitable because of tarnishing, and if it was done the surface needed varnishing or lacquering.

SKILLET

A pottery or metal cooking-vessel with a rounded bowl, three or four legs, and a long handle. The term was also applied in the sixteenth and seventeenth centuries to the straight-sided saucepan without legs that had come into use.

SLAG GLASS

Coloured glass, mixed in a random fashion with slag from iron foundries, was widely used in the manufacture of novelties in the nineteenth century especially in America. It is also known as 'end of day' glass as it was thought that the makers used the odds and ends left over from making more select glass articles.

SLIP-WARE

Name given to lead-glazed earthenware decorated with slip, fine clay and water mixed to the consistency of cream. Slip could be trailed on, painted on, combed on, or used as an all-over coating, and be as carefully or casually applied as the potter wanted. It was one of the earliest processes, used at least 3000BC in Japan, 2000BC in Crete. The earliest known English examples made at Wrotham in Kent in the early seventeenth century were somewhat crude, and the most interesting English slip-ware was perhaps made in Staffordshire. Typical of rustic slip-ware was Brede pottery, made in Sussex (some say Kent) from the late eighteenth until the early nineteenth centuries, with the slip red on white or white on red, with quaint motifs and odd inscriptions. The manufacturing process was brought up to date in the nineteenth century when slip was applied by multi-spouted funnels while the object to be decorated was turned on a lathe. As a peasant craft the making of slip-ware was unequalled, being cheap and easy, and is still a method employed by small potters. This should be borne in mind when looking at 'rustic' ware. It may be brand new.

SNUFF BOTTLE

Made in China of porcelain, opaque glass, and other suitable materials in a variety of ingenious naturalistic forms, and carved, gilded, modelled, or painted.

SNUFF-BOX

Tobacco inhaling (snuff taking) began in France in the seventeenth century and by the eighteenth was a consuming passion with its own rituals, one being the need to keep snuff in an expensive, decorative, little box which could be made in gold, silver, ivory, tortoiseshell, horn, lacquered tin, or enamel – in fact almost anything which could take adornment, often of the finest quality. A characteristic of the snuff-box which differentiates it from other tiny boxes is the presence of a hinge. Until about 1730 the hinge stuck out; after then it was integrated. Smoking vied with snuff taking in the nineteenth century.

SNUFFER

Implement for trimming candle wicks, usually consisting of a pair of scissors and usually with two open-sided boxes on the end of the blades which would take burnt-off wick. Often of silver, with brass, steel, iron and pewter increasingly used from the mid-eighteenth century. Snuffers were often kept in a socket on the candlestick.

SNUFF RASP

Snuff takers often preferred to grind their own snuff, and there were two kinds of rasp, large and small, some of them with a compartment for ground snuff. Early types from the seventeenth century were graters in plain wooden frames, but more decorative frames were later made from ivory or silver as well. Small snuff rasps had leather or cloth covers.

SOAPSTONE

Used to make a type of porcelain and, in its natural form, carved into intricate shapes especially in China for the tourist trade. As it is very soft, a skilled operator can turn out dozens of impressive pieces in a short time. As the name implies, the stone has a greasy texture. Soapstone is also carved by Eskimos.

SOFA

Often used as a synonym for the settee, the name originated in Turkey where it was a raised section of floor or a long bench. Often used in England for a long, informal, well-upholstered settee.

SOFT PASTE

A step towards making hard-paste porcelain, mainly using white clay and ground glass. A type of soft-paste porcelain was made in Persia in the eleventh or twelfth century; experiments were made by Venetian glass manufacturers in the fifteenth century, but the first recorded European successes were in Florence 1575-87, Rouen 1673, and Saint Cloud 1675. In England the first known examples are the 'goat and bee' Chelsea jugs of 1745. Losses in the kiln were considerable, as certain soft-paste items had to be fired several times, so soft-paste is rarer than hard-paste porcelain, particularly as little was made after the end of the eighteenth century.

SPANISH FURNITURE

Furniture reflects the prosperity of a country and in the sixteenth century Spain was incredibly rich, partly due the conquests of Mexico and Peru and vast acquisitions of gold and silver.

A carved walnut wall mirror with gilded gesso details, probably around 1750, possibly Spanish in origin.

Gothic and Renaissance influences were fully assimilated in the furniture of the fifteenth and sixteenth centuries. The most popular wood was native-grown walnut, but chestnut, poplar, oak and pine were also frequently used, plus imported ebony and mahogany. Until 1593 when it was banned for this purpose, silver was used to enrich furniture. As in England, the most valued object in the Spanish home was the chest, and trunks with velvet and leather covering with elaborate locks and much ornamental bossing were very popular. Chairs were lavish, especially for men; women sat on a dais strewn with cushions in the Moorish style. A peculiar characteristic of Spanish chairs was that they were often hinged at the stretcher to make them portable. Leather was much used in Spanish seventeenth-century chairs, as it was in England. Tables were basic but covered with rich table-cloths, and the supreme Spanish achievement in furniture was the cabinet, derived from church models, and immensely elaborate and intricate, especially the *papeleira*. Spanish eighteenth-century furniture was much influenced by French, English and Italian models. The cabinet disappeared, replaced by the commode as a prestige piece. A characteristic of eighteenth-century Spanish furniture is the spectacular use of marquetry, as well as a fondness for painted white or cream chairs with gilding, and japanned red furniture. As in all civilised countries, war or no war (and Spain fared worse than most), the nineteenth century brought in massive and ponderous furniture, called in Spain the Fernandino period, followed by a version of Gothic and a sequence of revivals, many based on early French styles. Spanish art nouveau is little known outside the country of origin, and it is not often realised that the great architect Gaudi (of Barcelona Cathedral fame) made marvellous if sinister furniture in this style.

SPECULUM

Alloy of tin and copper used for making mirror surfaces before silvered glass was introduced.

SPELTER

Zinc, sometimes alloyed with lead, was generally used for cheap cast decorative objects, furniture mounts, candlesticks, clock cases, and especially the flanking figures of nineteenth-century clock sets, the spelter often bronzed to make them appear acceptable.

SPILL VASE

A vessel for holding thin slips of wood or spills of paper with which to light fires, made in a variety of materials including ceramics, and free standing or provided with a hole for hanging up. It was a favourite subject for hobbyists of the nineteenth century, especially those keen on fretwork. A spill vase can easily be confused with a hanging flower vase.

Sometimes called sportiana, attention is focussed mainly on two sports, golf and cricket. So far as collectable items are concerned, cricket is dominated by W. G. Grace, and there is perhaps more memorabilia associated with him than with all other cricketers put together. These include Coalport plates to commemorate his hundredth century in first-class cricket, handkerchiefs bearing his portrait, a three-handled Doulton jug of 1882 portraying him in action, cast-iron book-ends, ashtrays, inkstands, iron pub tables bearing his portrait bust on the legs, doorstops, as well as Grace jewellery such as brooches and tie-pins.

Cricket memorabilia fall into five sections; early cricket up to 1865 (when Grace entered the game); 1866–95, when the county championship became organised; the golden age 1895–1914; 1919–39; and the post-war years. The earliest bat in existence dates from 1750, and throughout the years it has become the custom of teams to sign the bats. Such bats should not be confused with the commercial bats printed with players' names. Many manufacturers used cricket and cricketers to promote their products, including the firm of Fry which associated cricket with the drinking of cocoa. Engraved silver mugs and tankards are sought after, as are the novelties, including pier-end cricketing games, miniature bats in all materials, cricketing table-cloths and other household linen, board games, ashtrays, wine- and liqueur glasses with enamelled or painted cricketing subjects, ashtrays, shaped sweet containers, condiment sets, snuff-boxes with cricket motifs, belt buckles and buttons, and even pipes shaped into the head of Grace. Amongst the paper memorabilia are score-cards (sometimes made into silk replicas), autograph albums, posters and advertisements, menus, programmes, brochures, and cigarette-cards and picture postcards.

Golf memorabilia are more highly priced than those of cricket because there is an international market, with the Japanese being particularly strong. Club golf, leading to the establishment of rules and golf-course layout, began in 1744, St Andrews was founded in 1754, and the first club outside Scotland, Blackheath, came into being in 1766. Golf-clubs have been found that date back to at least 1714; nineteenth-century makers signed their names to their clubs and a club by master club-makers such as John Jackson (1805–78) of Perth can command in excess of £2,000. Anything, either clubs or balls, by Tom Morris is of great value. Early golf balls were of leather sewn round compressed feathers; gutta-percha balls (Indiarubber balls known as gutties) were

Staffordshire figure representing a cricketer.

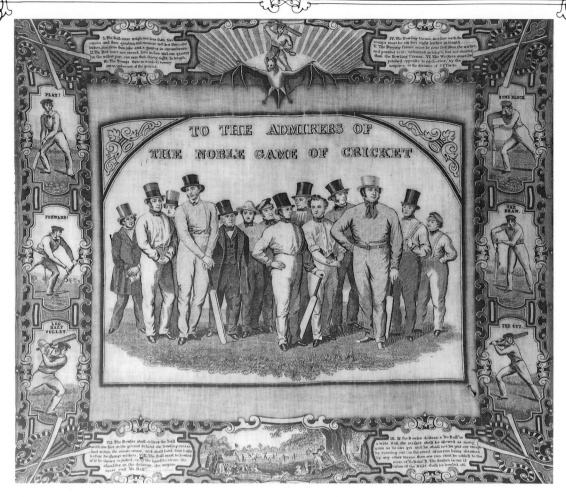

The rules of cricket presented on an early Victorian handkerchief.

introduced in 1850, first of all smooth, later dimpled, resulting in a new kind of club with leather facings and softer wood for the heads. The modern rubber-cored ball was introduced in 1902. Steel shafts replaced hickory about 1929. Amongst the novelties are lighters in the form of golf balls, biscuit tins shaped like golf-bags, biscuit barrels with appropriate finials, clocks with golfing motifs on the dial or as case ornaments, watches engraved with golf motifs, cigarette-cases, ashtrays, stands of all kinds supported by three or four golf-clubs as legs, desk sets, jewellery (the most common being the tie-pin in the shape of a golf-club), and many ceramics, Doulton being one of the main producers.

Angling antiques are amazingly diverse. Reels are much collected, especially the Hardy 'Perfect' fly reels, first patented in 1888. A complete set of all sizes and ages numbers about 160 reels. Stuffed fish in glass cases, particularly monster pike, were once commonplace pub ornaments but are now valuable collectors' pieces. There are carved wooden models of fish, especially salmon, celebrating spectacular angling coups, and numerous accessories, such as fly boxes and cabinets, fly wallets or books, tackle and bait boxes, floats, tackle winders, and a variety of fold-up line driers. Individual flies are also eagerly sought for, though their rusted hooks pose a threat to the casual browser. As with many categories of sporting memorabilia, catalogues are quite valuable. One of the most interesting angling pieces is the walking-stick that has concealed in it as many as nine rod sections. Bamboo was often used

A charming Art Deco clock of 1930. Decorations were often tailored to customer requirements, and sporting motifs were common.

for these walking-sticks, both for the ease with which the core was extracted and for lightness.

Indoor sports and pastimes have their collectables, such as dominoes in ebony and ivory; while cribbage boards come in a variety of shapes such as oblong, triangular, or strip, and were often made of rosewood with mother-of-pearl or ivory inlay. Cribbage boards can date back to the eighteenth century when boxwood was often used, inlaid with brass, ebony and ivory. Playing-cards have been fashionable from the fourteenth century, the earliest being Tarot cards in packs of seventy-eight. Single cards up to the sixteenth century can be worth well over £1,000. From about 1600 cards were printed from copperplates, some were inlaid with silk. Cards were first taxed in 1710, with a stamp on the ace of spades, and many social, satirical, political, comic and novelty packs were produced. Letterpress and lithography were employed from 1832, with the predominant maker Thomas de la Rue, and two-headed face cards appeared about 1850. Card corners began to be rounded. Card faces became standardised, but the backs gave opportunities to advertisers and illustrators of all kinds. Pin-ups and erotic subjects, which can date from the nineteenth century, are among those most collected.

Marble figure of a Victorian croquet player.

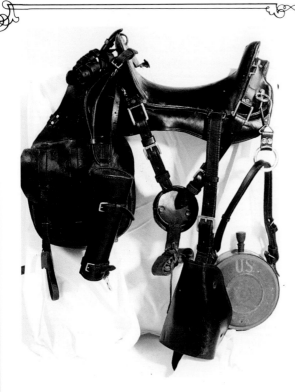

The type of antique which can achieve any price, because of its American connections and the romance of the Wild West.

Horse-racing memorabilia are exceptionally rich in artwork, extravagant silver, and models of horses and jockeys in all metals, especially bronze. Boxing and pugilism was celebrated by the Staffordshire potters in the early nineteenth century, and boxing belts and shields were often of silver and lavishly decorated; all paper memorabilia related to boxing, especially bare-knuckle fighting, are very desirable. The appeal of pugilism, or bare-knuckle boxing, was to all classes. The poet Lord Byron took lessons from a well-known pugilist called Mendoza who opened the Lyceum in the Strand, London, in 1791 to teach boxing. Being illegal the sport had even more popularity, especially amongst the aristocracy. So amongst pugilistic antiques are picture handkerchiefs and similar luxury objects. Penny farthing bicycles (known as Ordinaries) have long been collected, though the earlier velocipedes are now mainly museum pieces. The velocipede, sometimes called a dandy-horse, was introduced in the eighteenth century and propelled by the feet. In 1874 a Mr Stanton rode from London to Bath, 106 miles, in eight-and-a-half hours. At a meeting at Hampton Court three years later there were 1,500 cyclists, but cycling, along with other sports such as swimming and rowing, has not had the universal appeal of golf and cricket; nor is the equipment associated with these sports altogether suitable for novelties and mass marketing, although naturally they have their badges, emblems, and paper ephemera such as programmes and promotion material in abundance. Still undervalued are rowing oars, especially those associated with the Boat Race.

Football, despite its immense popularity, has never had the same attention as its summer counterpart, cricket, and, although collectors of football memorabilia are no less ardent, there is not the wealth of novelties and peripheral collectables. However, with many famous personages proclaiming their dedication to this or that football club, football memorabilia is being re-evaluated. Most interest is focussed on programmes (especially Cup Final programmes) and club badges. A large number of games have been based on football, and boxed and complete these are collected. The best known is blow football. Tennis and croquet memorabilia include Parian statuettes, glass vases with enamel designs depicting tennis players, jewellery, and silver cutlery with the handles in the form of rackets. There is considerable interest in the earlier sports of real tennis, brought from France in the Middle Ages, and fives, though much of the material consists of books, designs for five courts, etc. Squash is too recent a sport to have acquired collectables and there is only a muted interest in badminton. Lawn tennis was not invented until 1873, though there is a modest interest in early rackets. The Scottish sport of curling was often supported by novelties made by whisky manufacturers, and although ice skating has its devotees and its peripherals, it has been mainly celebrated in paintings, speed skating in East Anglia being especially appealing to artists. But all sports have collectables of some kind, obscure and incomprehensible as many may be.

SPIT

Rod of metal penetrating meat over an open fire, rotated by boys known as turnspits, dogs, or mechanical devices, clockwork being the most suitable driving force.

SPITTOON

Also known as a cuspidor, this was a pottery or metal receptacle. Gaily patterned ironstone was often used.

SPODE POTTERY AND PORCELAIN

A factory was established in 1776 producing cream-coloured earthenware. Bone china was made from 1800, and in 1805 stone china, with added feldspar, was introduced. Spode was especially distinguished for its fine range of blue-and-white transfer ware; some of the patterns such as 'Asiatic Pheasant' and 'Italian' are still being produced today. Spode also made Imari-style, *famille rose*, and armorial ware.

SPONGED WARE

Nineteenth-century ceramics, with colours thickly applied with a sponge through a stencil, often resulting in blotchiness and uncertain edges to the design. Sponging was sometimes combined with other techniques.

SPOON

Spoons of the Middle Ages were probably of horn or wood, silver or gold, with pewter used from the fourteenth century. They were usually made in one piece, with the only decoration a finial on the end of the stem in various shapes including the acorn. In the seventeenth century the ends of stems were hammered flat and became square-ended before being rounded off; the end and the stem, also flattened, were decorated in diverse ways with a multitude of patterns that were eventually to stabilise and are still used today. The main technical advance was the strengthening of the stem by using a reinforcement such as the 'rat tail'. Silver was increasingly used, but handles could be of other materials. Porcelain handles were sometimes used in the eighteenth century.

Mid-18th-century Staffordshire salt-glazed bear jug.

STAFFORDSHIRE POTTERIES

A concentration of large and small factories and workshops, sometimes employing one or two, sometimes massive industries, producing vast quantities of ceramics from the seventeenth century to the present day. Most of the practitioners are unknown, but some such as Toft, who introduced quality slip-ware, and John Astbury (1688–1743) who combined red and white clay under a thick glaze, sometimes splashed with metallic oxides, are almost mythical figures. Wares varied from the rustic and naive such as Toby jugs, flat-backed and summarily decorated figure pieces and groups, and innumerable spaniels to the sophisticated products of Wedgwood.

STAINED GLASS

Figures were represented in stained glass from the eleventh century, and the craft reached an amazing peak in the twelfth and thirteenth centuries in France. The effect of these windows, at a time when glass technology was limited, is rich and jewelled, but sometimes hard to decipher. In the fourteenth century larger panels of stained glass became available, together with new colouring agents, and in the sixteenth transparent enamel pigments were discovered. Stained glass returned to favour in the early nineteenth century with the Gothic revival, and in 1827 Sèvres established a studio for making stained glass. In 1861 William Morris founded a similar studio in London. In the twentieth century stained glass has been used for door panels and similar objects. Modern 'stained glass' may come from a kit, with imitation lead; it is a popular and well-established craft.

STAMPING

Process in which small metal objects are produced by pressing between shaped dies, used for coins and medals and especially buttons, the making of which was a major industry. An improved technique was invented in 1769. Large items in sheet metal could now be made, such as basins and saucepans, and in 1779 rolling cylinders with dies attached opened up endless possibilities. Much cheaper than casting, die-stamping was ideal for Sheffield plate.

STATUARY

It was customary for the old-time aristocracy to take the Grand Tour through Europe and it was equally customary for them to collect as they moved through the various countries, served by agents who are really the first antique dealers. Their acquisitions were almost wholly classical antiquities, and included marble statues and busts, which were dutifully copied or imitated. Statuary was also widely used in public places and streets. The first equestrian statue erected in Great Britain was that of Charles I in 1678 in brass, though it was founded in 1633 and hidden during the Cromwellian years. Bronze was much used for statuary, but marble was preferred, and during the eighteenth and nineteenth centuries drawing-room sculpture proliferated, sometimes tinted. Lesser items found their way into the gardens of the great, or garden sculpture was commissioned for specific places, often in association with fountains, either in marble or in lesser substances, such as lead.

STEEL

Iron plus carbon, was known from about 3000BC and used from prehistoric times to make weapons and cutting instruments. Used occasionally, but less than one might expect, for decorative objects such as boxes and jewellery and furniture, the surfaces decorated by chiselling, engraving, and inlay such as damascening (gold or silver beaten into grooves). Steel furniture was made especially at Tula in Russia and in Birmingham. Stainless steel is a steel alloy made rust-proof and stain-proof by the addition of chromium, first produced in England and Germany in the early twentieth century and developed in the 1920s, first of all for table-knife blades and then for forks and spoons.

STEVENGRAPHS

Coventry was one of the important centres of the silk industry, but in 1860 duty-free ribbons were allowed into the country from France, causing alarm and despondency amongst the silk workers. Thomas Stevens decided that there was a future in something other than in producing long runs of ribbon, and began weaving bookmarkers, gaily decorated with motifs, mottoes, messages and pictures woven on the Jacquard loom, and marketed as New Year, Christmas or Valentine gifts. He sent a sample to all the editors of magazines and newspapers, inviting readers to buy them. The book markers were registered in 1862, and were a great success, and 468 different designs were available by 1877, leading to other items in silk such as Valentine cards, scent sachets, birthday cards, fans, sashes, neckties, mechanical cards, and views. Portraits of local celebrities, and commemorative items were made to order.

STIPPLING

Technique using various tools to produce a dotted effect, most apparent in glass engraving where a diamond point or a steel needle is used.

STONEWARE

One of the most important types of pottery, types of which sometimes pretend to be porcelain. Waterproof because it is fired at 1,200–1,400°C. First produced in China, from whence the techniques were taken up in the Middle East, and then assimilated in Europe in a slow lengthy process. There is some doubt about the date of its emergence, but it was probably Germany in the ninth century, a region that remained the main centre of stoneware throughout the Middle Ages and into the seventeenth. Wares were usually grey or off-white, sometimes coloured by the glaze, customarily brown, black, purple or blue. Glazes were usually salt-glazes (lead glazes were difficult to apply because of the high temperature of firing). Similar ware was produced in England from about 1684, predominantly in Staffordshire.

STOURBRIDGE GLASS

Very important glass-making centre in Worcestershire from the seventeenth century, certainly before 1612, with 17 glasshouses in existence by 1696, many operated by Huguenot immigrants

Stourbridge cameo glass vase.

from France. The Glass Excise Acts from 1745 encouraged many glass-makers to move to Ireland but, despite this, Stourbridge flourished, manufacturing tableware and decorative pieces. The lifting of the tax in 1845 enabled the factories to compete with the long-established glassworks of Bohemia, the products of which were shamelessly imitated, especially the more flashy pieces. The Great Exhibition of 1851 gave stimulus to the intricate and over-elaborate, and machinery was introduced to produce new types of glass, including a pressing machine for decorating glass with relief ornament and in 1857 a threading machine to make filigree glass. Products included vases, scent-bottles, candlesticks, plates, drinking vessels, and paperweights, as well as large exotic one-offs reflecting the interest in the past and prestige pieces, such as the cameo (layered) glass, some of which could take years to make.

STRAW-WORK

An ornamental process, using strips of bleached and coloured straw to make landscapes or to form geometric patterns, used from the seventeenth century on caskets, mirror frames, and pieces of furniture.

STUDIO POTTERY

Pottery made in traditional manner on a small scale, maybe a one-man, one-woman show, often adventurous, sometimes self-indulgent. The term is usually applied to nineteenth-century or twentieth-century work, and perhaps the first true exponents were the Martin Brothers. Many studio potters have achieved cult status; Bernard Leach is known throughout the world. It is perhaps the most important of the crafts, and certainly the studio potter is in the tradition of William Morris and all those eminent Victorians who turned their backs on the world of commerce, whether or not they are performing for an audience of one.

SUNDERLAND WARE

Lustre-decorated earthenware made by a number of potteries that flourished between about 1800 and 1880. Large bowls and jugs were characteristic pieces decorated with pink lustre,

Pair of 19th-century Sunderland cat figures.

often splashed with white to give a marbled effect. The designs were transfer-printed and included religious and rustic subjects, animals, topical personalities and local views especially the cast-iron bridge over the Wear at Sunderland.

SUNDIAL

These can be either fixed or portable, when they are simply called dials. These are made in many varieties, are often of ivory, and have an adjustable gnomon (straight edge), adjustable so that the dial can be used away from the place where it was made. A compass is provided for alignment. The dial could be flat, or hinged and folded out for use, or it could be in cylindrical form. The ring dial worked by allowing the sun's rays to pass through a small aperture onto a graded scale.

SURGICAL INSTRUMENTS

There are two kinds of surgical instruments, those in use before the discovery of antiseptics and those after. Early instruments were ornamented and decorative, breeding grounds for germs; when it dawned on the profession that scrupulous cleanliness was essential, basic tools were stripped of inessentials. The scalpel of the sixteenth century folded into the handle like an ordinary pocket-knife; the handle was decorated with a mythical or symbolic design such as a winged female. Surgical saws were richly decorated, with a lion's mask with a ring through it to hang it up. Forceps and retractors (for holding gently the edges of a wound while an operation is being carried out) were also decorative. Sets of surgical instrucments often had handles made of unusual materials such as bloodstone. Wood and ivory instruments were discarded because they could not be boiled and immersed in carbolic solution and were replaced by all-metal instruments. After 1846 anaesthetics revolutionised medicine, giving doctors time to operate, and many of the instruments used today were invented in the nineteenth century. The ophthalmoscope was invented in 1857, making the interior of the eye possible to study; the laryngoscope, enabling the doctor to examine the patient's larynx by a combination of mirrors, arrived in 1860; the lithotrite was invented in 1839 for crushing bladder stones so that they could be voided; the tonsillitome for removing tonsils dates from 1881, though tonsillitis had been recognised since 1801. A curious group of medical instruments relating to electrolysis, were introduced in the late nineteenth century, and were largely useless.

SURVEYING INSTRUMENTS

Surveying is concerned with finding out and recording surface features so that a map can be made. The science dates back to at least 3000BC when the civilisations of Egypt and Babylon demanded the setting down of distances, the division of land into plots, and the construction of a road system. The first requirement of a surveyor is to set out lines at right angles; the first surveying instrument was probably the groma, two small sticks lashed together to form a cross, which was used horizontally with four small pieces of limestone suspended from the ends of the sticks to act as plumb-lines. Two were used for sighting; the other two determined the direction at right angles. Later more sophisticated instruments, such as the circumferentor (a circle with uprights containing vertical slits), invented in the sixteenth century, the graphometer (with a semicircular scale) invented in 1597, the Holland circle, and the optical square (a small box containing two mirrors, one partly silvered), used the same principle.

A selection of sundials of various types.

195

Mahogany waywiser as used by surveyors.

Distances in ancient times were measured with a cord, with knots at regular intervals. During the Middle Ages navigating instruments, such as the compass and the astrolabe, a circular plate and a rotating rule with sights, were pressed into service. Surveying was rough and ready, and distances were measured with the waywiser, also called a hodometer or surveyor's wheel; this is a large wheel with a handle, which when pushed registers the distance covered on a dial in the same manner as a milometer or odometer of a car. The pedometer, measuring the number of steps taken, and attached to the belt, was also used. In the sixteenth century the science of triangulation arrived, the foundation of which is a baseline of a precise length. Lengths of chain, copper- and brass-capped rods, and, most accurate, glass rods were used for accurate measurement (the tape measure was invented in the nineteenth century). In 1791 it was proposed to make a map of Britain of one mile to the inch – the Ordnance Survey. The principal instrument of surveying is the theodolite, which measures vertical and horizontal angles. It incorporates a compass, spirit-levels, means to adjust the angle of the instrument, and, from the beginning of the eighteenth century, a telescope. For greater accuracy there is a scale within a scale (the Vernier invented in 1631). A surveyor's level is a simplified theodolite. The value of all surveying instruments depended on the compass, the principle of which, the aligning of a lodestone in a north-south axis, was known to the Chinese by AD121, and probably known to Europeans by about 1400. It consists of five parts – card, needle(s), bowl, cap (usually jewelled) and pivot. In the mariner's compass the card is above the needles, otherwise not. The liquid compass, used at sea, was suggested in 1779, used about 1830. The 'boy scout' compass with a card and a needle on a pivot, does exactly the same job, if without frills and, because of friction, less accurately.

TANKARDS

The basic drinking vessel for beer, ale, and cider, and the personal pewter tankard hanging up behind the bar is still a feature of old-fashioned public houses. Silver tankards were in use in Britain and other parts of Europe from at least the sixteenth century, pewter tankards probably from the thirteenth. The shapes vary, sometimes globular, sometimes a tapering concave, and there is sometimes a hinged lid. There is a good deal of variation in the thumbpiece that holds the lid open while the tankard is drained – wedge, ball and wedge, ball, hammerhead, bud and wedge, double volute (scroll), chair-back, ball and bar, shell, double acorn, corkscrew, and ram's horn. In the nineteenth century old silver tankards were often embossed and sometimes turned into jugs by adding a spout. Tankards sometimes had pegs inside for cummunal drinking; these marked the drinker's goal. Many of the nineteenth-century pub tankards were glass-bottomed, and there are all kinds of reasons put forward. One of them is that in the days of the press-gang a shilling was dropped in the tankard while the drinker's back was turned, and as the beer was drunk the shilling could be seen on the glass, so giving the unwilling conscript the chance to make a run for it. Another reason is that a drinker could see a possible enemy through the bottom of the glass, and give him (less often her) an opportunity to change pubs. Sometimes tankards have verification marks, and the vessel is stamped with a reigning monarch's initials. These are measures.

Arguably the most important piece of furniture of all, and made in every conceivable way. Tables with a central support (pedestal tables) were used by the ancient Egyptians, but the Greeks and Romans seem to have preferred tables with supports under the table-top edges. From the fifteenth century there were two basic types of table – the trestle-table, with planks on a portable stand, and the fixed-top table with a leg at each corner. There were often conflicts between design and function. A table could look well, but be inconvenient to sit at, as with certain gateleg tables, and there were many ingenious ways to cope with this, including telescopic table-tops and one or more pedestals so that there was knee space for all. There were innumerable fancy tables going under various names such as Pembroke table, Sutherland table, sofa table, all of which were multi-purpose, and many of which had hinged outer leaves, to give different surface areas, and there were specialist tables which sometimes were not tables at all such as the work-table. There are also wall tables without legs but with supports such as the console table. There is a thin line separating tables from desks, with writing-tables often used as dres-sing-tables and vice versa. Apart from the one-piece moulded table the twentieth century has provided little that is new.

Architect's table: type of desk from the eighteenth century incorporating drawing-board and compartments or drawers for materials associated with the profession. An artist's table is similar. These tables often have intricate working parts, and ingenious fold-away gadgetry.

Bedside table: a nineteenth-century table incorporating bookshelves, and fairly uncommon.

Bed-table: a kind of tray rather than a table and made for invalids, often with folding, screw-in- or rigid legs, while others involve a pillar support with an arrangement of rods connecting it to an adjustable tray.

Bonheur-de-jour: a lady's small writing-desk, first made in France about 1760 and soon adopted by British cabinet-makers. It has a drawer or drawers in front and tiered shelves, drawers, and cupboards at the back in all per-

The bed table is an article difficult to make interesting, but it has a modest role in the world of antiques.

Edwardian inlaid table from about 1910.

mutations, with sometimes a shelf between the legs. Made in a multitude of styles from its inception until the Edwardian period, where the reproductions and re-creations of eighteenth-century examples are masterpieces of craftsmanship. A large number have painted decoration.

Breakfast table: sometimes a small table with hinged flaps to increase the surface area, or a tip-top or tilt-top table, but a term too vague to be considered definitive, and often a catch-all title for an undistinguished table with uncertain pedigree.

Butterfly table: an American table with butterfly-shaped brackets to support the raised leaves.

Card-table: usually with a fold-over top as opposed to a hanging flap table. Card-tables are sometimes equipped with built-in dishes for chips or money and occasionally a facility for a candlestick. Mostly square, but round ones – which when closed are known as *demi-lune* – are not uncommon. Somewhat surprisingly the structure of the folding-top card-table derives from the ecclesiastical credence table. The surface is covered with a material, usually baize, though velvet and other fabrics are used as well. So-called card-tables are often multi-purpose, being used for tea as well as games. There is a three-top variation, in which the extra flap, sometimes featuring a chess-board inset, provides an alternative surface. Being prestige pieces of furniture, some card-tables are of the very highest quality, as in the Chippendale style with blind-fretting and pierced and fretted brackets. A concertina action was sometimes used, which brings the back legs forward to support the top. Collapsible card-tables of the 1920s and 1930s are very common. A popular kind of card-table of the 1930s has a circular top which slots into a fold-away set of legs; the baized top can be turned over, revealing a plain wooden surface.

Carlton House desk: one of the most elegant and desirable of all pieces of furniture, first mentioned in 1788. Carlton House was a London residence of the Prince Regent (later George IV). It is essentially a writing-table with a superstructure of tiny drawers at the back and sides, leaving a clear space in the middle for writing. The best examples have square-section tapering legs and are in mahogany and satinwood, though rosewood and other expensive woods were also used in later versions. It was one of the favourite pieces of Edwardian cabinet-makers, who often copied the originals with great skill and fidelity, occasionally betraying themselves by inlay that was slightly anachronistic.

Console table: a table fixed to the wall and supported by massive legs at the front or by ornamental brackets often featuring eagles and intertwined dolphins. It was introduced into England from France, and became fashionable in the early eighteenth century. It was one of the few pieces of English furniture to reflect the European rococo style or to incorporate huge slabs of marble in its construction.

Credence table: originally an oak table holding consecrated communion bread and wine but latterly a trade term for a small side-table, sometimes with a folding top. The fold-over card-table was based on the credence.

Cricket table: a name given to a sturdy three-legged table, much used by cottagers and those of simple means because, being a tripod, it was more stable on an uneven floor than a four-legged table. A cricket was a low stool. The etymology of both is obscure.

Deception table: a coy name for a drop-leaf table with a concealed compartment for a chamber-pot.

D-end table: an eighteenth-century semicircular four-legged table, which, pushed against an identical table, made a satisfactory round-table. If the table needed to be larger there was provision for the addition of extra leaves, the back legs of D-end tables being swung out to help support them.

Dining-table: some antiques are bought for show, some for hard usage, and typical of the latter group is the dining-table, and almost any money can be paid for larger speciments. An early large gateleg table, seating ten, can be worth £20,000 and more. Many kinds of table could be used as dining-tables. The earliest is the refectory table, though contemporary with it was the smaller frame table, with the legs set at the corners. The mahogany gateleg without stretchers and with various kinds of shaped feet was favoured as a dining-table in the eighteenth century; there could be four, six, or eight legs. However, no matter how large the gateleg there was a limit on size, and the alternatives were extending tables, either D-ends or rounded-square-ends with a centre section or sections, or multi-pedestal tables, the pedestals of which often needed to be massive to cope with the weight of the wood and the food, silver, winebottles, plates, and everything on top. Fashion outmoded the long table towards the end of the eighteenth century when gatherings tended to be more intimate; for informal meals the dining-room was often neglected in favour of a breakfast room, needing smaller tables. Round and rectangular multi-purpose pedestal and tripod tables were made in huge quantities in every conceivable style and of every conceivable quality. Sometimes they had names, such as the saloon table, and for a time from the 1870s there was a fad for a table with four slender pedestals set in a platform from which the legs led, usually socketed in (a weakness in such tables as the weight of the top tends to strain these sockets). The tops themselves often had deep friezes and the wood was often in the solid.

Draw-leaf table: a table, often of rugged construction, originating in the sixteenth century in which the top is in at least three sections, one or more of which can be removed if required. The outer leaves then slide on runners to lap together, activated in Victorian and Edwardian times by a wind-up mechanism. Made in many woods, with walnut perhaps the best.

Regency patent mahogany dining table of about 1820.

The legs can be very ornamental and bulbous or elegant. Impossible to destroy, they often end up in garages and workshops, which is a pity as they are worth several hundred pounds each.

Dressing-table: this can be a misleading term, for pieces of furniture not intended for dressing purposes are used as such, the owners believing that they are absolutely genuine. In period they may be, in terminology not. What are now used as high-quality period dressing-tables were designed as sideboards (the clue lies in the cupboards at the side). True dressing-tables were often angular, long-legged and refined, often fully enclosed. What are now reckoned to be 'knee-hole desks' were once often intended as dressing-tables. What does it matter? Not a jot. Mirrors were an eighteenth-century innovation, the triple mirror a nineteenth-century refinement. In the 1930s the dressing-table lent itself to adventurous design in all the show woods, with particular attention being focussed on mirror shapes and finishes. It was the ideal piece of feminine furniture, often elegant, sometimes outrageous, occasionally enchanting.

Drop-leaf table: also called a fall-leaf or flap table, this description can cover a variety of more specific tables such as Sutherland or sofa tables. Basically it is a table with one or two hinged outer leaves which can be raised or lowered. Some of the flaps can be large, some so small that it seems hardly worthwhile adding them. They are held flush with the table surface by a gateleg, by slides which push in and out, or by hinged brackets or rudders.

Drum table: a circular table, often with a leather top, supported on a column. The frieze contains a sequence of drawers. Sometimes known as a rent table or library table.

Envelope table: invented in the 1780s, the envelope table has a top comprised of four triangles. By rotating the top slightly a concealed peg causes one leaf to pop up slightly and sufficiently for raising it fully, followed by other leaves. The now enlarged table-top rested on the four corners of the frieze.

Framed table: in early oak furniture an alternative to the trestle-table. In the framed table the legs are set at the corners of the top, and they became popular as more intimate tables for private rooms as feudal mass-feeding became increasingly unfashionable. It remains the standard table, made in all kinds of woods. The top is usually plain, though there can be a good deal of adornment on the frieze, and there is a lot of variation in the legs, which can be turned, square, baluster shape, tapered, or bulbous. Castors can be fitted.

Games table: made from the sixteenth century, by the eighteenth century the games table could be a compendium with a folding or removable top concealing such items as dominoes, chess-boards and pieces, and dice shakers. There were also drawers. The surface often had recesses to hold money or counters.

Gateleg table: The gateleg mechanism was one of the earliest alternatives to the fixed-top or trestle table. Dating from the sixteenth century, it meant that tables could be expanded in size by added hinged leaves, supported by a swinging frame (the gate). Simple gateleg tables are known as tuck-away tables in the United States. The tables could be very large with an intricate arrangement of gates, and in the eighteenth century the mechanism was beautified as the strength of mahogany meant that stretchers were no longer necessary. In the 1750s an interesting variant was the concertina action, with the frieze itself folded at each end of the table, a way of solving the problem of knocked knees, always a nuisance in anything but framed tables with the legs at the corner.

Guardroom table: a type of Spanish table with splayed trestle supports and with a wrought-iron underbrace fixing stretchers to the underside of the top.

Hall table: the hall was the main room of sixteenth- and seventeenth-century houses, and this was a large table, usually with baluster-shaped legs. This is the real name of a refectory table.

Handkerchief table: looking like a folded handkerchief, the top consisted of two triangles which opened up to form a square. One of the legs swung out to provide support for the drop-leaf triangle, so the handkerchief table is a form of gateleg.

Harlequin table: a combined breakfast- and writing- drop-end table with a concealed nest of drawers, which could be mechanically raised.

Hutch table: Tudor serving table of a long, narrow, shape with a cupboard below the top.

Kidney table: a table with a kidney-shaped top,

Described as a George I walnut lowboy, this could also be termed a side table.

201

usually used as a dressing-table or as a form of desk, introduced from France in the eighteenth century where it was known as a haricot.

Library table: term for a large table perceived for library use, often of a huge size, or a drum table.

Loo table: an oval or round table introduced in the nineteenth century for a card-game called loo, often with a pillar support. The loo table-top was one of the favourite sites for Victorian inlayers, whose work could be breathtaking.

Lowboy: a term used for three- or four-drawer side-tables used as dressing-tables or for occasional use, of immense variety, favoured by country makers in fruitwood or yew, as well as London makers, and popular from the seventeenth century because of their versatility, compact size, and serviceability. The styles echoed furniture fashions – legs with simple turning and low-slung square stretchers, legs with inverted cup or bell-like turning and cross stretchers, cabriole legs, square untapering and tapering legs, pad feet and other stylish terminations. A term used in America for a table with a hinged top-drawer-front which when opened forms a writing surface, revealing drawers and compartments for writing equipment.

Nest of tables: one of the most desirable of all pieces of furniture, a set of interlocking tables graded in size and, because of their usefulness, even the most humdrum examples can command high prices. The nest of tables was illustrated by Sheraton in 1803. He called them quartetto tables, and saw them as useful for needlework, though they soon found their more familiar role as tables for refreshment. They were made in papier mâché and other suitable materials. Lacquered wood was very popular in the 1920s.

Night table: one of the many euphemisms for a piece of furniture housing a chamber-pot, sometimes modest, sometimes with a marble top and gallery, often with a tambour-shuttered front. It often had handles at the side so that it could be secreted away in the daytime.

Occasional table: a name given to any portable table.

Ombre table: a three-sided table for the three-handed game of ombre, introduced from Spain and popular in the seventeenth and eighteenth centuries.

Pedestal table: a general term for tables supported by a central column, though certain kinds of dining-table had several pedestals. Pedestal tables could be used for dining or for games. A popular design for the pedestal between about 1820 and 1880 was triangular with hollowed sides known as a hyperboloid base, sometimes combined with what are known as 'hairy feet' (extravagant animal paws).

Pembroke table: a small elegant table in the prestige woods, oval, or rectangular with rounded corners, with flaps on the long side, supported by hinged wooden brackets. There are one or two drawers on the short side. Named after the Countess of Pembroke, it appeared about 1750 although it became popular only after about 1780. These are the kind of small portable antiques beloved of foreign buyers, and when the craze strikes they will pay astronomical prices.

Piecrust table: the name given to a circular tripod table with the rim around the top scalloped and allegedly resembling a piecrust.

Pier table: intended not for a specific use but for a specific place – between the windows of grand houses, often surmounted by a tall mirror.

Quadripod table: a table with four small legs, often nothing more than protrusions or tiny bun feet, usually set into a low platform, and so far as usage and decoration are concerned a variation on the tripod.

Refectory table: nineteenth-century dealers' term for the oak tables of the seventeenth century and after, whether they were long and massive, with bulbous legs, or smaller with pretty vase-shaped legs – or farm kitchen tables! Of all tables the refectory table is most often faked. The tops can be made from old floor-boards, so they are already conveniently aged. The stretchers, which are often at ground level, are often chamfered to simulate wear.

Sawbuck tables: American long table with X-shaped supports, popular from the seventeenth to the eighteenth centuries.

Serving table: a small oval or round occasional

1920s lacquered table with Oriental scenes.

A 1920s country-house dining room furnished in the olden style. Notice that the chairs do not match and are probably reproduction, though the table looks original. The court cupboard to the right is carrying out its traditional function – to display the family's plate. The main anachronistic feature is the Victorian pole screen by the side of the fireplace. The plates above the fireplace and court cupboard are pewter; these would not have featured in a grand house of the 17th or 18th century, as they were used by servants or the ordinary person.

table placed beside the diner on informal occasions and meant to hold wine, plates, and other dining-room items.

Settle table: a seventeenth-century example of multi-purpose furniture, a settle with a back section that is hinged to the back of the arms. When brought forward it rests on the arms of the settle to make a table.

Side-table: a vast ambiguous area covering occasional tables, lowboys, dressing-tables, occasional tables and indeed almost any type of table with drawers. Furniture historians have tried to create order by preferring the term side-table to cover tables with one or, at the most, two drawers side by side. Made in all woods and styles, often very plain indeed, often of the utmost elegance with marquetry inlay or serpentine fronts. A true side-table has one side undecorated, as it is unseen when placed against a wall.

Social table: an eighteenth-century mahogany table, in horseshoe, kidney, or semicircular shape, sometimes with a brass rail. Decanters and bottles are held in a frame that is attached centrally and which swings from one part of the table to another.

Sofa table: derived from the Pembroke table and intended to stand against the sofa, it is therefore long and thin with flaps at the end (sometimes rectangular with rounded corners, less often semicircular). There are two main types, those with a vertical at each end supported by splayed legs, and those with a central pillar, often in the form of two or four grouped pillars connected to a four-legged base, again commonly with splayed legs. As with all such tables, it was regarded as a multi-purpose table.

Stool table: a curious short-lived hybrid of the

late seventeenth century, this was a stool with a large seat with a drawer attached to the under-side of the seat.

Sutherland table: a term for a drop-leaf gateleg table of the Victorian period, usually of mahogany or walnut. Its main asset is that the flaps are very large, often almost reaching the floor, and the non-flap section is very narrow so that when folded it can be neatly tucked away. The tables are supported by a single or double column at each end, with often elaborate turning, and because of the structure the gates that support the flaps can look ungainly or out of place. Almost always it is fitted with castors.

Swing-leg table: often confused with a gateleg table, this is an eighteenth-century table where two of the four legs swing out to support flaps.

Table bedstead: gadget furniture of the late eighteenth century, a bed that folds into the body of a table when not in use.

Table de lit: French table with short legs used to place on a bed.

Table en chiffonnière: small eighteenth-century French work table with galleries.

Tea table: all sorts of tables could be used for tea, and what are described as side-tables, pedestal tables, tripod tables, or even sofa tables also doubled as tea-tables. Tables with a raised rim, sometimes pierced, are sometimes termed tea-tables, it being thought that the rim was to stop teacups' falling off. Perhaps a contingency if the tea-drinkers have been at stronger liquid refreshment.

Trestle-table: one of the earliest types of table, still used when portability is of the essence, consisting of boards laid parallel over trestle supports, with all elements dismantled and placed against the wall when not in use. It was the only type of table to provide mass seating in feudal times.

Tripod table: one of the most important types of table, made in a variety of sizes, materials (not necessarily of wood but of iron, papier mâché and other substances) and forms for almost any usage. The three legs can be set directly into the central stem, or into a platform base. Tripod tables can be rigid, or the top can be hinged to fall vertically when not in use. Be-cause of the enormous quantity made in all periods, they remain eminently buyable by those on a small budget. Some tripod tables have a gallery. The surfaces, more often circular or oval, can be very decorative with intricate marquetry, parquetry, or set with mosaics or precious and semiprecious stones.

Work-table: the work-table fitted out with receptacles for needlework, embroidery, games and hobbies appeared at the end of the eighteenth century; it was ignored by Chippendale, and mentioned at length by Sheraton, for there is no object so amenable to pull-outs, slides, novelty mechanisms, and adjustable surfaces. The main characteristic of the work-table is that the majority had a bag, pouch, or wooden compartment, often in funnel shape, beneath the table and drawers. Sometimes the wooden compartment was lined with silk and divided into sections. It was made in all styles and woods, with bases that could be tripod, quadripod, cabriole-legged, pillared, or indeed any fashionable type for it enjoyed a long run. Some tops are fixed, some can be drop-leafed or folded-over, in which case they may feature a chess- and backgammon board. Because of its size and portability, plus its feminine appeal, the work-table has become very desirable and lady antique dealers who very rarely touch anything but pretty china and jewellery often venture into the world of the work-table. Some work-tables were made without bags, with the needlework and other items kept in drawers, and these can be distinguished from other tables by the small top area in relation to the drawer capacity. Some of the cheaper non-bag work-tables have dummy drawers.

Writing-table: an ambiguous term that can mean almost anything, and the only requirement for a writing-table is that the top should be uncluttered.

All categories of tables are provisional. Any table can be used for any purpose, and sometimes names have been fostered on them hundred of years later by collectors and auctioneers, sometimes to make them appear more interesting, sometimes to categorise them. Many non-descript tables can aquire a cachet by giving them a French name.

TANTALUS

Wooden or metal open-work case made from about 1850 for holding square (spirit) decanters, locked in by a metal bar.

TAPESTRY

A fabric, usually of silk, silk and wool, or wool, woven on a loom. The subject is usually pictorial, often mythological, often grandiose, sometimes overpowering, and the weaver works from a design or cartoon, making the picture as he weaves, watching it grow in narrow horizontal strips. Tapestries covered the bare walls of

18th-century octagonal ivory tea-caddy with tortoiseshell stringing with a silver shield-shaped panel and inlay of mother-of-pearl.

medieval castles and were draped over tables and beds, bringing rare colour into an austere world. A British manufactory was established about 1560, but most tapestries were imported from Flanders and France. The most important maker of the seventeenth and eighteenth centuries was the Gobelins tapestry factory, which worked mainly for the French king, Louis XIV. Tapestries were regarded as expensive alternatives to oil paintings. Arras was the most important fourteenth-century tapestry-producing town. Only one tapestry exists that can definitely be assigned to Arras. Beauvais was another important producer, founded in 1664, its best work done in the 1730s and 1740s though it continued into the nineteenth century, copying earlier work in dull tones, which have faded still more into a depressing brown. Tapestries were not a favourite British art form. Tapestries should not be confused with other

textiles used for wall hangings such as appliqué work, Berlin woolwork, and other types of embroidery. Tapestry-weave carpets are woven in the manner of tapestries.

TEA-CADDIES

The great age of Tea began in the 1660s. It was so expensive that it was locked in a tea box, or tea canister, cube-shaped and lined with foil. A pair of canisters in silver, pewter, wood or japanned iron would be protected in a leather-covered box called a tea-trunk. There were two canisters because there were two qualities of tea which the hostess would blend at the tea-table, for in taking tea in the seventeenth century there was something of an echo of the Japanese tea ceremony (and dishes were used instead of cups). The tea-trunk gave way to the tea-chest, and a central container for sugar was provided, as well as a 'mote skimmer', for removing tea dust from the surface of the tea. As tea became cheaper, canisters became larger, and the tea-chests became substantial pieces of furniture, but there was also a demand on informal occasions for unblended tea, needing just one container. As with many articles of small furniture, the 1770s saw the use of the rarer woods, often veneered on deal, and tea containers were made by many of the celebrated cabinet-makers of the period. Design followed fashion, with restrained decoration, and about 1810 the introduction of the Regency show-woods, amboyna and rosewood, led to a heavier appearance. Attractive tea-caddies (the name was introduced about 1770) were made in the form of a melon, for throughout its reign the tea-caddy was a select article for upper- and middle-class use and whatever form it took it was expensive; therefore liberties could be taken with its design with the sure knowledge that affluent tea-drinkers would buy it.

TEACUP

The early teacups used when tea became fashionable were silver, but they were soon replaced by porcelain cups. Until the middle of the eighteenth century teacups were without handles. Although the first teacups were no different in shape to chocolate cup or coffee-cups, it gradually became customary to make coffee-cups straight-sided and single-handled and provide chocolate cups with two handles. There is no end to the variety in teacups – large, small, with a safeguard to the wearers of moustaches (the moustache cup), plain, ornate, traditional-shaped or geometric with square sides and triangular handles. It is a very popular collecting area, only slightly less so than teapots.

TEAPOT

Coffee preceded tea as a drink in the west, and consequently the first teapots were modelled on coffee-pots with a tapering cylindrical body, a straight spout, a domed cover, and, perhaps the most unusual feature, a handle at right angle to the spout. However, the orthodox teapot shape, based on Chinese models, was soon introduced, egg-shaped, with a domed lip topped by a finial. Ceramic teapots were often based on those in silver. Early eighteenth-century silver teapots could be rounded (the bullet teapot), pear-shaped, or polygonal, often panelled for strength and quite small, reflecting the high cost of tea. Eventually fashion rather than whim moulded the accepted designs – the inverted pear in the 1730s, the drum-shape in the 1760s and 1770s, and then oval, rectangular, and other angular shapes towards the end of the century. Fluting became very popular in the early nineteenth century and, as the century proceeded, all shapes were revived, or revived and rejigged with too much ornament, too little concerned with the overall shape, and supplemented with fantasies, charming or grotesque. Typical of the former was the Wedgwood Egyptian-style teapot of about 1815 with a crocodile as the teapot-lid finial, or the Wedgwood red stoneware teapot of about 1830 with a body in the rough outline of a junk with a square-shaped cane handle suspended from rings let into the body. But from the eighteenth century the potters had regarded the teapot form as something to play with, as witness the vogue for teapots in the form of cabbages. One of the most ingenious teapots produced anonymously in red clay covered with copper lustre, about 1840–50, was an exact replica of a metal tea-kettle. Minton produced a teapot in 1874 in the form of a Chinaman with the head forming a lid. The barge teapots, sometimes called Derbyshire, with bright moulded flowers against a treacle-

Worcester porcelain teapot with Chinese motifs about 1758.

brown ground, often had a finial in the form of a tiny replica of the teapot beneath it, and some barge teapots were made with twin spouts. The humorous aspect of teapots continued well into the twentieth century, epitomised by aeroplanes and racing cars as teapots (and functioning as teapots). Collecting teapots is very popular, not surprisingly. Besides silver and ceramics, teapots were also made in pewter, Britannia metal, japanned metal, and of course Sheffield plate and silver plate.

TEAPOY

A Regency piece of furniture, *tepai* is Hindi for three-legged or three-footed, though teapoys were often on a platform base with four small feet. The teapoy consisted of a box, a column support, and legs. The column was often elaborately turned or carved, and the box could be any shape, and was really a tea-caddy. Teapoys were intended for tea, but there is a thin dividing line between teapoys and work-tables and there are designs that could be either.

TEAR

Tear-shaped air-bubble in glass, sometimes accidental, sometimes deliberate. Air trapped inside glass becomes a bubble because of the heat, and can be used as a decorative motif. The tear was particularly popular in eighteenth-century wineglass stems, in paperweights, and in novelty pieces, especially in coloured glass. Sometimes it is difficult to decide whether a tear is deliberate or an accident.

TEA-TIME SILVER

The taking of tea, coffee and chocolate was a great civilising process from the seventeenth century, establishing women in a central role and bringing decorum to an often rough-and-ready society. It enabled men and women to meet in neutral surroundings, and established codes of conduct that, perhaps, last to this day even if the cocktail party from the 1920s tended to displace it. It has its own ceremonials, and its own specific equipment, usually in silver, sometimes shared with formal dining. The most important item was naturally the teapot, dealt with elsewhere, but among the other containers are the chocolate pot, a pouring vessel popular between about 1675 and 1725, often mistaken for a coffee-pot, except that some chocolate pots have a hinged or sliding piece on top of the lid so that a rod could be pushed through a hole to stir the liquid. The earliest silver coffee-pots of the mid-seventeenth century were of a tapering cylindrical shape, with straight spout and handle on opposite sides of the body, or with a handle set at right angle to the spout. The curved spout arrived towards the end of the century. In the early eighteenth century the lower part of the body became rounded, and there was a domed lid with mouldings. About 1730 a pear-shaped body became popular, elongated from the 1740s and urn-shaped on rounded or square plinth bases from the 1770s. The coffee-pot was not amenable to radical re-shaping and although there was the provision of extra ornamentation in the nineteenth century the makers could do little except revive past shapes. As with all similar domestic silver, examples were produced in Sheffield plate and electroplate. Sometimes termed a tea fountain, the tea-urn could be very decorative. The early urns were often pear-shaped, and the neo-Classical movement was responsible for vase-shaped examples with fluting, swags, festoons, and other characteristic decoration. A tea-urn often had an interior compartment for a red-hot iron so that the water would be kept hot. Less common than the tea-urn, the coffee urn was a container with a tap instead of a spout, usually two handles, often incorporat-ing a lion mask, and on feet or a stand.

The cream jug dates from about 1715, the earliest in the shape of small pitchers, very plain, somewhat squat, resting on a rim with three-legged ones appearing in the 1720s. Later ones had a longer lip, and between 1775 and 1805 the helmet shape was popular, resting on a rim. The Regency type with a more angular handle, a sensible wide mouth, and fluting around the under-side, provided the model for the perfect cream jug, as used today. Slop-basins were for tea-leaves. Sugar-bowls sometimes had covers with an inverted rim on top instead of a finial. The reason was that the cover could serve as a receptacle for the teas-poons, saucers often not being used when tea was drunk from a dish and not a cup. Sugar baskets are miniature cake baskets. The boat shape was especially fashionable. A spoon tray was an oval or rectangular dish with plain or ornamental edges. A number of small tools were created to deal with sugar, which was purchased in a loaf and needed to be broken down. A crusher was a rod with a disc at one end and a ring at the other to break pieces from the loaf; a nipper was a wrought-iron or steel contraption usually set on a wooden base and about a foot (30cm) long with strong pinchers, also for breaking up the loaf; tongs were for handling lumps; in the seventeenth century they were in the form of miniature hinged tongs, with shell-shaped, oval, or leaf-shaped pans and a scissors mechanism. The familiar spring form was introduced in the 1760s. The sifter was a small pierced ladle and the sugar spoon was often in the form of a shovel, though the term could be used for a spoon with a pierced bowl as in the sifter. The muffineer was a caster used from the late eighteenth century to sprinkle muffins with sugar or salt. The caddy spoon, for measuring tea from a caddy, had a short handle, often in fancy shapes such as a leaf, jockey cap, and a hand.

On the tea-table would probably be extras for tea-time snacks, although some might be kept in the kitchen. The honey-pot was shaped like a beehive with a ring or a bee on top. The cucumber slicer, made from the

Victorian silver coffee-pot dated 1853.

eighteenth century, was a cylinder set horizontally on a stand, with a slicing blade activated by a handle at one end against which the cucumber is pushed. Cake was important. The cake slice, not unlike the fish-slice, had a large oval or triangular blade, which was often engraved and pierced, and was used to serve cake or pie. Cake tongs were similar to large sugar-tongs, and it is possible to confuse them with asparagus tongs. Strawberry dishes were shallow with fluted sides. Cake baskets were used from the 1740s with pierced and vertical sides, and in the 1750s they had a slope. Silver wire was used over-laid with ears of corn, vines, and similar motifs, and some baskets simulated wickerwork. A popular cake basket was in the form of a shell. About 1800 there was a fashion for unpierced cake baskets with plain handles. The tea-tray is one of the best known and most useful of silver articles, usually large, and oval or rectangular. There were four feet, and the rims could be elaborately moulded and decorated. In the late eighteenth century a gallery was provided, together with hand-holes. Because of its suitability for the material, more trays were made in Sheffield plate 1800–40 than any other article. During the nineteenth century the tray itself lent itself to extravagant ornament of every kind without affecting the function. Naturally tea-trays have been made of many materials other than silver, Sheffield plate, and electroplate, with papier mâché and lacquered wood amongst the most popular.

TELESCOPE

There are two types of telescope, the best known being the refracting telescope discovered by accident in 1608. The simplest form is a tube with a plano-concave lens (flat on one side, concave on the other) at one end and another lens (the eyepiece) at the other. Later in the century the single eyepiece was replaced by two thin convex lenses. A telescope could have as many as nineteen spaced convex lenses, and did, but such an instrument was impossibly unwieldy. The simple telescope, or 'perspective glass', was very popular. The tube could be of card, covered with leather, silk, parchment or shagreen; in early telescopes the lenses were mounted in wooden rings. In the eighteenth century brass was used, the larger instruments were telescopic, extending to more than sixteen feet (4.9m); the quality of the glass steadily improved. The hand-held telescope was a valuable aid in battle, but even the longest refracting telescope was not a suitable astronomical instrument. The reflecting telescope uses a mirror, with the image fed to the object glass, visualised by Sir Isaac Newton in 1666, but mirror glass was poor and lost more than eighty per cent of the available light. The first feasible reflecting telescope was made in 1726. It is still the basic astronomical telescope.

19th-century brass reflector telescope.

TENT-STITCH

A basic needlework stitch, a series of parallel diagonal stitches across the intersections of the threads. When applied to a canvas it is known as *petit point*.

TERRACOTTA

Lightly fired earthenware, red or reddish-brown in colour, used in ancient times. Fired at higher temperatures terracotta was used in the nineteenth century for decorative vases and similar objects, but rarely for utilitarian goods. It was much used for garden ornaments.

THERMOMETER

Instrument for measuring temperature, invented about 1640, and using mercury from about 1720, often affixed to a barometer surround.

TIGERWARE JUG

Tigerware was an early stoneware product originating in Germany in the sixteenth century and exported to Britain, and there imitated. It was salt-glazed with a mottled browny surface that resembled tiger markings. The jug itself was round bellied, often with a cylindrical top, and it was frequently mounted with silver and silver gilt. It was one of the first examples of an attractive and interesting texture being deliberately sought for, rather than just found.

TILES

Slabs for surfacing floors and roofs and for providing decoration on walls, exterior and in-

17th-century Dutch Delft tiles.

terior, around fireplaces, and sometimes inset into furniture. Medieval tiles, often for church floors, were thick, and were decorated with impressed designs filled with contrasting colours, a technique known as encaustic. Tiles of great beauty and compexity were used in Persia and neighbouring countries from the ninth century, and manufacturing techniques gradually filtered into Europe via North Africa and Spain. Tin-enamelled tiles depicting foliage, portraits, heraldic devices, and grotesque animals were made in Italy from the fifteenth century, but far more important, so far as Britain and America were concerned, were the Dutch tiles, principally in blue and white, featuring a variety of themes, some Chinese, some European, which had great impact and encouraged a home industry. The importance of the tile in the Victorian period cannot be overestimated; it was perhaps the most lasting memorial to Victorian mass-production. Many were simply patterns, but others were pictures, including sea scenes made about 1860 by Copeland. Tile design attracted some of the best graphic artists of the time including Walter Crane and J. Moyr-Smith, and the tile was an ideal medium for art nouveau designers who used the characteristic sinuous line and shapes to marvellous effect. Even the tiles adorning the splashbacks of wash-stands were minor art works. Tile-pictures were widely used in the nineteenth century in dairies, butchers' shops, hospitals, and in many public and private buildings. Mercifully some of them have been preserved. The vast majority of tiles are pottery, though some porcelain ones were made.

TIN

Used in alloys to make brass, bronze, pewter, etc, and as a coating for metals, especially the interior of copper vessels to protect them from oxidisation or corrosion, a process known as tinning.

TINDER-BOX

Box containing flint, steel, and tinder and a dry inflammable material, used from the fifteenth to the nineteenth centuries to start a fire. Some boxes were fitted with mechanical devices such as a trigger and spring mechanism to produce a spark, ignited by a minute amount of gunpow-der. A strike-a-light was a tinder-box in the form of a pistol (produced in replica as a cigarette-lighter in recent years).

TIN-GLAZED EARTHENWARE

A technique first developed in Baghdad in the ninth century, lead glaze made opaque by the addition of tin oxide sometimes coloured with metallic oxide. It reached Europe via Spain about the thirteenth century, and the consequences were maiolica or faience and delftware (Delftware in Holland, otherwise delftware).

TIN-PLATED IRON

An early method of covering iron plate with tin replaced in about 1730 by a method in which the tin is completely fused with the iron, resulting in a whitish metal with a good surface, offering possibilities for the manufacture of basic kitchen gear such as bowls, basins and pans.

TOBACCO BOX

Made from the seventeenth century in most metals and shapes, the main feature being a close-fitting lid and smooth outlines so that it did not tear the pocket. English tobacco boxes tended to be plain with perhaps a monogram or coat of arms, but Continental boxes were often elaborately adorned with masculine designs – sporting, military, rustic. Their use went into some decline when tobacco manufacturers supplied their wares in tins and many smokers have long preferred a leather tobacco-pouch.

TOBACCO JAR

Whereas the tobacco box was portable, the jar was a fixture and therefore more highly decorated, widely made in most materials, the earlier ones being lead and pewter with sometimes a weight inside to keep the tobacco compressed. Early seventeenth-century examples are cylindrical, often with a domed lid with a finial. Eighteenth-century tobacco jars were often in wood, especially lignum vitae, elegantly shaped, frequently with a liner of pottery or tin. Many of the well-known pottery factories made tobacco jars. Wedgwood made very attractive examples in black basalt and blue jasper. A large

TOYS

There are two distinct meanings. The first kind of toy is a seventeenth- and eighteenth-century trifle for adults, such as the snuff-box, rouge box (with an extra division for eye shadow), scent-bottle, etui, tiny figurine and similar luxury items made in metal or ceramics. The second kind is a children's plaything. The children of ancient Greece and Rome had a wide variety of toys, including whistling birds made from clay, rattles, dolls with jointed limbs, and even the yo-yo. What children played with in the sixteenth century is indicated in contemporary pictures, such as those by Brueghel, in which can be seen tops, hoops, hobby-horses, dolls, skittles, marbles and knuckle-bones. Making toys was a cottage industry, and most were in wood, but gradually Nüremberg became the centre of toy making except for those at the luxury end of the market

Sad-looking teddy-bear-type animal on skates which made £430 at auction.

such as dolls, which, in the sixteenth and seventeenth centuries, were almost always dressed as adults. Many traditional toys continued to be used, and additions included paper cut-out toys, flat metal toys in relief (especially soldiers from 1775), and a wide range of educational toys, such as building and alphabet blocks, and the jigsaw (invented in the 1760s). During the nineteenth century toys became more sophisticated, especially dolls. Toys were mass-produced, but folk-toys such as the monkey-up-a-stick continued to be made by hand and sold by street traders. Among the toys were board games (the Victorian game Moneta eventually became Monopoly) and scientific toys such as the gyroscope, the kaleidoscope, and the various optical toys relying for their effect on the phenomenon of persistence of vision. There were also the magnetic toys, and for the older children there were kits to demonstrate static electricity by friction. Many toys were regarded as subtle instruments of education. Others were not, such as model soldiers. In about 1870 the French began to produce three-dimensional soldiery. In 1893 William Britain of England evolved a new process, hollow casting, suitable not only for model soldiers but in the twentieth century for Mickey Mouse, Donald Duck, Snow White and the Seven Dwarfs, and even footballing teams in the correct colours. Tin-plate toys date from the 1860s, and featured acrobats, performing seals, all kinds of transport especially railway stock, most of them operated by a clockwork mechanism, simple but efficient. Many of the twentieth-century toys are based on older versions, but transformed by using electricity and electronics, with model soldiers made from plastic instead of lead. Rag dolls and soft toys were perennial favourites. The gollywog dates from about 1890, and the teddy bear, the focus of a cult, from 1902. The main name in teddy bears is Steiff, the Steiff bear being recognised by its humped back and a button fixed in the ear. Rupert Bear dates from 1920, Winnie-the-Pooh from 1924. Paddington Bear and Yogi Bear will no doubt join the pantheon in due course.

Early 20th-century toy yacht.

A selection of William Britain's toy figures and accessories, including a Shell petrol pump and the types of penny-in-the-slot machines once common on railway stations.

number of tobacco jars were made from the wood of famous ships, more than one might suppose. Associated with tobacco jars and the ceremony of smoking was the tobacco cutter, a wooden-handled steel blade, hinged to a wooden block, and used to cut tobacco from a roll; not dissimilar to a small guillotine. Nineteenth-century versions were often fitted with a mechanism to feed the roll to the blade edge.

TOBY JUGS

Earthenware jugs representing a man in a three-cornered hat holding a jug of beer and a pipe or glass first made in the 1760s and speedily imitated by Staffordshire potters and later elsewhere, including potters on the Continent and, surprisingly, in Japan. Other figures in the same style include Martha Gunn (the celebrated Brighton

A quality toilet set from 1930 using silver and enamel. Many toilet sets were made in imitation tortoiseshell and imitation ivory.

bathing woman), The Thin Man, The Drunken Parson, Prince Hal, The Night Watchman and many others. Toby was probably Toby Fillpot, nickname of Harry Elwes, a notorious tippler. An enormously popular subject, toby jugs have continued to be made, sometimes in porcelain, often in miniature form. Many of the modern versions have been deliberately crazed to appear old. Character jugs have been produced by Royal Doulton since the 1930s (Ronald Reagan appeared in 1984, Sir Winston Churchill in 1940 – but he did not like it and it was withdrawn, and John Barleycorn, idiot yokel, was produced from 1934 to 1960).

TOILET-SETS

Made from the sixteenth century for the upper classes in gold, silver and silver gilt, these could encompass more than just the common comb, brush and mirror and include bowls, boxes, salvers, scent-bottles, pincushions, candlesticks, bodkins, tongue scrapers, and toothpicks, in fact anything that could find a place on

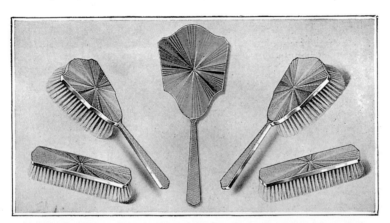

a dressing-table or its early equivalent and probably more beside. Many of the more expensive and expansive sets were made for particular customers by famous silversmiths. The silver, tortoiseshell, or imitation tortoiseshell brush, comb, and mirror set was a popular middle-class gift, and often was very elaborately packaged and presented.

TOKENS

Unofficial coins to supplement or replace official coinage, used from the Middle Ages and declared illegal in 1817. Some were for goods, some could be exchanged for official coins of a higher value, and most represented some act of duplicity. Designs could include tradesmen's names, portrait heads, and slogans. Most tokens were of bronze or copper, but some were made in porcelain by the Worcester Porcelain Company. Being collected, tokens are much faked.

TORCHÈRE

A candle stand, popular in the eighteenth century, usually a pillar support with a tripod base, sometimes plain, sometimes elaborate in carved giltwood, surmounted by a small top, which could be round, square, oval, octagonal, or rectangular, sometimes with a shaped edge. It was intended to hold a candelabrum, a branched candlestick. It was probably used from an early stage as a multi-purpose stand.

TORTOISESHELL

Hard, brittle, translucent material of mottled brown and yellow, which can be moulded under heat and retains a high polish. It is taken from the carapace of a species of turtle, and was used by the ancient Romans as furniture veneer. Usually moulded into boxes, cut into combs, or used as a veneer for caskets, mirror frames, and other objects. In association with brass it became boulle (buhl), much used especially in France as furniture facings and inlay from the seventeenth century onwards. Imitation tortoiseshell was much used in toilet services in the 1920s and 1930s, backing the mirrors and brushes and providing the material for the combs. A tortoiseshell finish was produced by Staffordshire potteries in the eighteenth century.

TOWEL- OR CLOTHES-HORSE

Wooden frame used to air clothes and dry towels, comprising horizontal bars and vertical supports at the end, simple objects which could be made fairly ornamental by lavish turning and carving and the use of attractive woods. Much reproduced in the style of the nineteenth century.

TRANSFER PRINTING

Thought first to have been practised on Battersea enamels, the techniques were taken, when Battersea closed in 1756, to the china factory at Bow and then to Worcester and Caughley. The method consists of taking a print on transfer-paper from an engraved copperplate; the image on the paper was then applied to the biscuit-fired ceramic body (underglaze transfer printing), which was fixed by heating in an oven, then glazed, sealing the picture. There were technical problems to be overcome, one of which was that cobalt was the only colour to stand firing without blurring. This means that early transfer-printed ware was blue and white. Until 1760 transfers were printed after the glazing, as the unglazed ceramic body was not hard enough to stand up to the process. Early in the nineteenth century better transfer-paper meant better definition and detail, and enabled engravers to combine line-engraving with stipple (little dots).

TREEN

A vague term but generally speaking a smallish wooden object made for a specific purpose, with a bonus for the unusual, and a nod of approval for the quaint. These include miniature wooden letter-boxes for use in country houses (with delivery and despatch times), decoy ducks, drinking vessels carved from the solid, dentists' drill-tip holders, pill silverers (to put a silver coating on pills!), body massagers, bird rattles, berry-pickers (a shovel with a comb blade), and silk winders. Often a catch-all category for items that have no natural home of their own.

TRENCHER

Originally a slice of bread, secondly a wooden double-sided plate for primitive diners, lastly a

silver, tinned copper, delftware, or pewter plate, often with a reinforced rim.

TRIVET

Three-legged stand placed in front of fire on which to put pots and utensils, made from the seventeenth century, and usually in wrought iron, but later in brass or with a brass pierced and decorated top. Some have a handle, and others have one leg and two hooks to rest on the bars of the fire.

TRUCKLE-BED

A low wooden bed designed to be pushed under one with a higher base to save space, used into the nineteenth century. These are very basic items of furniture, and easy to misinterpret as children's beds.

TRUNCHEONS

Used since the Middle Ages as emblems of authority, tipstaves or tipstaffs (staffs tipped with metal) and truncheons (a short staff) depend for their appeal on the decoration and ornamentation, and whether these are hand-painted or transfer-printed; they were increasingly used towards the end of the eighteenth century, especially with the coat of arms. Tipstaves of ebony mounted with silver or brass, with a crown at one end, are likely to be eighteenth-century. The monarch's arms will indicate the period of a tipstaff and it may be possible to identify the initials of the authority or organisation issuing the tipstaff or truncheon, which became shorter about 1830. Most truncheons are solid, but there is a variety that pivots in the centre, useful for crowd-control. About 1870 ornamentation was reduced to a minimum, with perhaps just a crown and royal monogram. Truncheons usually have a base colour of black. Sometimes a truncheon has its own leather case. Too bright an appearance may mean that a coat of arms and other interesting material have been painted on a plain truncheon, but it may merely mean that the truncheon has been well cared for, as they are usually bought for show. Scars and marks of use detract from the value of a truncheon, so truncheons should be examined for signs of filling-in or planing.

TRUNK

The difference between a trunk and a chest is that a trunk is portable; not obvious if the trunk was once a hollowed-out tree trunk, but in the Middle Ages all furniture was portable as the owners took it with them as they moved from castle to castle. The poor did not have furniture to move around. A trunk has a hinged lid, is sometimes covered with leather, and the lid is often bowed so that the rain runs off it. By about 1600 the trunk was acquiring some of the sophistication of the chest with inner compartments and drawers.

TSUBA

The tsuba is a Japanese sword-guard. Japanese hilts were made of wood with a hollow slit for the blade, which became curved about AD1000, and the tsuba is a small, flat, plate, usually circular or oval, although square, lozenge, and irregular shapes are known. The plate is pierced by an elongated slit, with sometimes a hole at each side for sword knife and sword needle. As early as the twelfth century, tsuba were artworks, with pine trees, ferns, shells, dragonflies etc, depicted in silhouette; in the fourteenth century low relief landscapes became popular, followed a century later by a fashion for heraldic subjects and flowers and plants. Early tsuba were of plain, hammered iron, but later there was inlay of bronze, silver and gold. From about 1570 tsuba became more elaborate, with silver and yellow and red copper wire used on the iron plates, and with silver or bronze studs. Enamelling came into use in the seventeenth century, and throughout the nineteenth century the piercing and the decoration became increasingly elaborate, though there was a reaction against this, as there always is in any society when craftsmanship becomes effete and overloaded. Criteria for tsuba include the quality of the forging and decoration, unusual patina, subject matter, and maker or school of manufacture. Iron is subject to rust, and corroded tsuba lose much of their value; rust removed can result in a tsuba being unnaturally bright. The patina can result not only from the effects of time, but from pickling. Tsuba are easily faked, and counterfeits were imported into Britain in bulk in the nineteenth century.

TUPPERWARE

This entry is not meant to be treated seriously, but Tupperware, sold in the recent past at highly organised parties, and a social phenomenon causing much amusement, is the kind of object that could, in twenty years time, be taken up in the same way that Bakelite has been. By its very nature Tupperware is disposable, as Bakelite was, which means that fewer examples will exist than might be expected. It could enjoy the same role in 2010 as 1950s porcelain does today, regarded as quaint and typical of its period, without any questions of individuality or beauty entering into it. An interesting comparison can be made with pewter which in earlier centuries was regarded as of no value, the mundane household articles such as dishes made from it being melted down and recycled.

TUMBLER

A drinking vessel without a handle, originally with a pointed or rounded bottom so that it could not be put down until empty. From the seventeenth century the tumbler had a heavy flat bottom. Of glass or of silver, but generally of glass. The device of making a drinking vessel which could not be placed on a table was not uncommon, perhaps best seen in a stirrup cup, the contents of which were drunk from the saddle. The word is exactly the same as that for an acrobat or a person who falls over.

TUNBRIDGE WARE

Decorative wooden pieces with a mosaic pattern formed of contrasting tiny squares, made in the Tunbridge Wells and Tonbridge areas of Kent. The early Tunbridge ware is not, in fact, mosaic, but straightforward marquetry on small boxes, followed by veneering, lacquering, and mother-of-pearl and ivory inlay. By the late eighteenth century a wide range of products was being produced such as spillholders, games boards, and napkin-rings. For a while painted designs on polished and varnished wood were popular, but in the 1820s James Burrows introduced the mosaic-type of ware, and there was no end to the variety of subjects, with small boxes the most common. Tunbridge-ware chairs and tables are museum pieces. From the 1880s to about 1910 there was less emphasis on pictorial scenes and more on geometric ornament. The more unusual objects command a premium, as do the number of mosaic squares, which on large objects could exceed 100,000. The delicacy and finish of good Tunbridge ware can be amazing, but there have been many crude attempts by amateurs to cash in on the appeal, especially by woodworkers experienced in cross-banding, where similar techniques are employed. There was a short-lived revival of good-quality Tunbridge ware in the 1930s. Sometimes marquetry pictures surrounded by a mosaic border are described as Tunbridge ware when, in fact, it is tourist work imported from the Continent, especially Italy and Spain (the marquetry subjects often give the game away). Heat and damp can play havoc with Tunbridge ware, but superficial scratching can easily be taken out; the mosaic squares are held under tension and will usually hold fast. Tunbridge ware with missing squares should be regarded with suspicion, as the odd square is difficult to replace satisfactorily. Beware of coloured wax masquerading as a mosaic.

TURKISH CARPETS

A description covering different types of carpet made in Anatolia (Asia Minor), differing from Persian carpets in that a certain knot, known as the Ghiordes knot, is employed. This is a knot tied in a symmetrical fashion on two adjacent warp threads. Until recent times, animals and figures were not used, and the natural forms such as flowers were presented in a severely abstract form. It is impossible to determine when carpets were first made in Turkey, but fragments of carpet from about the thirteenth century survive. One type of carpet is Ushak, made in two main patterns, one with a central medallion and the other featuring an eight-point star with diamond motifs and stylised plants. An interesting Turkish carpet is the 'bird' carpet, in which the main motif is similar to a bird shape, though the exact significance is unknown. Some carpets are named Holbeins and Lottos, simply because the paintings of these sixteenth-century painters include certain types of carpet. Transylvanian carpets were not made in Transylvania (Romania) at all but were simply discovered there and were actually made in Anatolia. They have quieter colours than the Ushak carpets, and often have a 'double niche' motif (prayer rugs have a niche or arch as the main design) as well as the Ushak-style medallion. Smyrna carpets are thick and heavy, with floral motifs arranged systematically, and were made in the eighteenth century. The place of origin of Turkish carpets can be doubtful, for there are many minor centres. Yuruk is not the name of a place but a word meaning 'mountaineer'; Yuruk carpets are made from a mixture of wool and goat hair. Although traditional designs were made well into the nineteenth century, using modern aniline dyes, the Turks also made imitations of French carpets.

TURKOMAN CARPETS

Woven by nomadic tribes in the area east of the Caspian Sea, these are classified by the tribes who made them, but overall colours are sombre, with reds and blacks dominating, and the carpets are often decorated with octagon shapes in rows, sometimes with stylised animal figures and with the octagons filled with sub-motifs, such as stars and flower heads. Nothing earlier than about 1850 is known to exist. Certain carpets woven near Samarkand and the east of the region show Chinese influences. Turkoman carpets have been sold since the late nineteenth century at Bokhara, and this name is often used to describe them.

TWIG HANDLES

Often used on cups, jugs and teapots from the eighteenth century, with Meissen examples recorded in the 1720s, and Chelsea pieces in the 1740s. It was one of several methods of making handles interesting without affecting their utility. A variation on the twig theme is a branch, often with the marks of cut-off sub-branches, sometimes curved as in the shape of an orthodox handle, sometimes more angular. Twig handles are customarily coloured green or brown.

Barlock typewriter of 1889, with 'down-striking' mechanism, a method soon discarded as gravity could not bring the keys back.

TYPEWRITERS

A patent for a writing machine was taken out as early as 1714, but the first typewriter-like object was not produced until 1829, the 'typographer', a lettering device with the letters on the rim of a wheel. The first typewriter that really looked like one was produced in 1872, and there were only two main improvements to make – a shift key to provide capital and lower case letters, and a front-striking movement so that the operator could see what was being typed. This was the first Remington typewriter, and was in competition with others, the Yost with a keyboard of seventy-two characters, and the Crandall, which had a type head and anticipated the IBM 'golfball' machine. The first successful front-striking typewriter was the Underwood of 1893; differential spacing was invented in 1889; tabulator keys appeared in 1898; the first noiseless machine dates from 1910. Some makers used an ink-pad, but it was clear that the ribbon method was the better. Most typewriters can be dated by a small plate or inscription, usually at the back of the machine. Because of the quantity produced, standard office typewriters of the Remington kind are of little value, but there is a demand for the oddities, if in good rust-free condition.

UMBRELLAS

Umbrellas and parasols did not acquire distinct identities until about 1800, but the use of a waterproof umbrella as protection against rain dates back to at least the end of the seventeenth century though only women used them, and the first man to risk scorn was Jonas Hanway who died in 1786. Towards the end of the eighteenth century the French made them less cumbersome and introduced refinements, such as the system of folding hinged ribs and the telescopic handle. As with many fashionable innovations, the revamped umbrella was introduced to English women via the fashion plate. The paper parasol was mentioned as being used in China in 1644, though unquestionably it had a longer ancestry there, and it enjoyed a vogue in the 1870s and 1880s with the interest in all things Oriental, and again in the 1920s and 1930s where it went with houseboats, the Black Bottom, and the Flapper.

Victorian umbrella stand of 1862.

UMBRELLA-STAND

Hall furniture in many forms, sometimes dull and straightforward such as an upright segmented frame with a drip tray, often whimsical, such as a hollowed-out elephant's foot. Although the umbrella dates from the eighteenth century, most umbrella-stands are nineteenth-century when men carried umbrellas as a badge of middle-classdom rather than because of imminent rain.

VALENTINES

Although exchanging amatory tokens dates from the Middle Ages, commercial Valentines were not produced until the early nineteenth century. These were engraved with hand-colouring and were of limited appeal, and it was not until the arrival of the penny post in 1840 that the manufacturers realised that February 14th could be a profitable date in the year. Until about 1870 Valentines became increasingly ornate, with a profusion of paper lace, heavy embossing, rich colours, and added extras, such as pressed flowers, ferns, feathers, costume jewellery, and indeed almost anything that could be stuck on a flat surface. Novelty Valentines appeared about 1870 with pop-up, trick folding, and animated cards, some of them decidedly saucy. A curious type of Valentine was the thoroughly unpleasant kind often directed at spinsters and the less fortunate in the way of looks with malicious, even sick, messages and caricature illustrations. Throughout the nineteenth century many lovesick young people made their own Valentines, often of a very high standard. Many Valentines were fragile, and broken parts may have been doctored recently, replacing damaged pieces with something similar, especially 'scraps' as used in scrap-albums. Except during World War I, Valentines have suffered a decline in the twentieth century, though there were amusing comic-postcard types issued in the 1920s and 1930s.

VEILLEUSE

An eighteenth-century pottery or porcelain food-and-drink warmer, with a covered bowl on a short drum-shaped stand holding a lamp. In the nineteenth century the bowl was often replaced by a teapot. It was made in English delftware in the 1750s, and many of the eminent eighteenth-century European factories, such as Sèvres and Nymphenburg, were involved in its manufacture. Somewhat confusingly the veilleuse is also a French sofa, often made in pairs to flank the fireplace.

VELVET

A silk textile produced by a weaving process that involves raised loops. If the loops are cut it is called cut velvet. Velvet was introduced to Europe from Persia, and plain velvets were made in Italy from the early fourteenth century and figured velvets appeared a few years later. As the most luxurious of textiles, it was much used on drawing-room furniture, especially sofas and easy chairs.

VENETIAN GLASS

Glass-making in Venice was recorded in the eleventh century, mainly associated with beads and mosaics. Fifteenth-century glass is in existence, coloured, enamelled, and gilded; and clear glass, *cristallo*, was perfected. Early Venetian glass was utilitarian but, influenced by silver forms, it became increasingly sophisticated and ornate, with jugs in the shape of ships and elaborate drinking vessels. Opaque white glass was very fashionable in the sixteenth and seventeenth centuries, as well as lace-like glass. Venetian glass could be so fragile that it could not be engraved by anything except a diamond point. With the development of lead-glass, the Venetian glass industry lost its supremacy, though there was a revival in the nineteenth century when intricacy and cleverness were valued above most other qualities.

VERNIS MARTIN

A type of lacquer invented in France in the eighteenth century, which is almost indistinguishable from English lacquer.

VESTA BOXES

Made for containing vestas or flammable matches, vesta boxes were used from the 1830s, usually converted from silver vinaigrettes or snuff-boxes, but from 1854 vesta boxes were made for this one specific purpose, following the shape of snuff-boxes. Until 1868 the lid was on the top of the box, from then on it was on the end or side and, to avoid wear and tear on clothing, the corners were often rounded. Although silver vesta boxes were made until as late as 1923 (from 1890 mostly bearing Birmingham hallmarks), other materials were used including silver plate, base metals of every kind, wood, ivory, brass, mother-of-pearl, vulcanite, and pottery and porcelain. The boxes could come in a multitude of shapes, such as violins, bottles, flasks, animals, clowns, corks, ladies' legs, miniature horseshoes, with perhaps the book-shape the most common. Vesta boxes often had compartments for coins and stamps, and could also incorporate a whistle, a tiny compass, a buttonhook, a penknife or a pencil, all virtually useless and all catering for the delight in gadgets. Until recently small silver boxes were still being converted to vesta boxes because of an insatiable demand. Vesta boxes usually had a striking surface for the matches.

Originally this was a deprecating term for odds and ends collected by effete Bohemians and intellectuals who should have known better. Even now it has a kind of giggle about it. Of course, there were oddities produced in the Victorian period, and never since, often by a bored middle class who had little to do and who expended their energies on producing curious out-of-the-way work. But being Victorians the men and women, but mostly women, did the best they could, studied the subject, and diligently worked away until it ceased to be amateur work at all. As a good deal of professional work was carried out in an amateurish way, there is a very thin line separating the products of the hobbyists and the paid hands. Amongst the activities that must come under the heading of Victoriana was the making of artificial flowers, popular between about 1840 and 1865. Flowers were shaped from waxed paper, feathers and gauze stiffened with wax, with dried leaves and ferns used as foliage. They were often set under glass domes. Bead-loom work was making wristbands; these were flat panels sewn with rows of tiny beads, without any kind of back-

An American advertisement for a do-it-yourself page flower outfit in the 1880s.

ing. Beads were used for decorating clothing, covers, antimacassars, and for making bags and 'miser' purses. After 1860 beads became larger and were used to adorn footstools, tea-cosies, book covers, screens, cushions, and almost anything that stood still long enough. China mosaic was the gluing of bits of broken coloured china onto dishes or plates to form a pattern. Cork pictures were made, often incorporating foliage, and framed against black or crimson velvet. Cut-paper work involved cutting and pasting pieces of coloured paper onto a board to create pictures, landscapes for the learners, portraits for the experts. Sequins, paste, semiprecious stones, gold and silver thread, tinsel and coloured silks were used for jewelled embroidery on clothes, evening bags, hats, and other suitable objects. Feathers were often used by hobbyists, curled with tongs and glued to coloured paper, setting them in hot wax, or stuck onto painted ivory figures as clothing (the so-called butterfly-wing work). Hairwork used human hair (blonde, dark, but never red) to make pictures; the individual hairs served as pencil lines, and the surface was usually white satin. It became unpopular about the 1850s, when hair became associated with mourning jewellery. There was a craze from 1851 for hand-painted glass. Pinpricked pictures had their enthusiasts; a wide border was

◆ J. C. VICKERY ◆

Buhl smoker's tray of 1902.

left round a water-colour painting, and it was pricked out in designs of shells, foliage and flowers. Potichomanie was the decoration of vases in plain glass from the inside, gluing coloured bits of paper onto the glass and varnishing over them. Pressing flowers was not a particularly Victorian hobby, but it was treated as a serious art form, and pressed flowers, as well as skeletonised leaves and seed pods, were mounted on black velvet and framed. Scrapbooks were popular amongst adults as well as children; scrap-work was covering screens with scraps, either with pictures sold for this very purpose or with coloured pieces of paper to create a pattern. Seaweed pictures were popular, but the pictures were not made from seaweed (mercifully) but surrounded by it in a wreath. The seaweed album was started by Queen Victoria; two fan-shaped shells were tied together with ribbon, and inside the shells were sheets of thin paper to which various kinds of pressed seaweed had been glued. Sand pictures were made from coloured sand obtained from Alum Bay on the Isle of Wight, and the seaside also provided the raw material for shell-work, shells painted to look like fruit and flowers, shells stuck to boxes and vases, and shells grouped together to form grottoes. Tinsel work was embellishing prints of famous people with tinsel and colourful material. It was a hectic life for the well-to-do.

VINAIGRETTES

Tiny silver boxes made to hold a sponge soaked in something sweet smelling, usually aromatic vinegar, to counter offensive smells, popular from 1780 to about 1860. The characteristics of a vinaigrette are a gilded interior to stop corrosion and a perforated inner lid, usually elaborately pierced, to hold down the sponge. Lack of a hallmark on a silver vinaigrette of the early years is not suspicious; it may have been exempt on account of its size. Vinaigrettes were made in numerous shapes, and although silver, usually engraved or embossed, sometimes with china, tortoiseshell, or mother-of-pearl panels, was the favourite material, silver-mounted glass and ivory were later used. Vinaigrettes in enamel and porcelain, as well as silver, were produced on the Continent.

VITRINE

Glass or glass-fronted display cabinet introduced in a modest way in the eighteenth century in France but a major piece of furniture in the late nineteenth and early twentieth centuries in mahogany, or other woods, with ebonised finishes very popular. Some vitrines could be very elaborate, with mirrors and subsidiary glass units.

WALKING-STICKS

Every man in the nineteenth century had his collection of walking-sticks probably kept just inside the hall in a stand, sharing space with umbrellas. Walking-sticks and canes derive from the cudgels and staves carried for defence, evolving into dress accessories topped with silver or ivory, with a ferrule to cut down wear. Many had elaborate carved heads that sometimes unscrewed to reveal space for a snuff-box or other article. During the eighteenth century 'dandy' sticks became popular, sometimes six feet (1.8m) in length, often with a spiral twist. About two hundred articles are known to have been put into sticks, the best known being the sword or other defensive weapon. Sword-sticks date back to the sixteenth century, and often just slide out, the stick itself acting as a sheath. Other weapons were on a spring mechanism and dart out on the principle of a flick-knife. Other sticks pull apart, revealing a dagger with a handle for the left hand, and a stick with a blade for the right hand. Two steel blades sliding into the shaft from each end probably represent duelling weapons. The poacher's gun was a simple weapon in the shape of a walking-stick; more sophisticated was a six-barrelled revolver, exposed by pressure on a trigger-spring that expelled part of the cane, and which had a dagger in the centre of the barrels. Most extravagant was the Browning machine-gun in a rectangular cane. The kit, as it was known, was a pocket violin; this was developed into a violin fitted into a cane with a two-inch (5cm) diameter. Other canes contained music-boxes, harmonicas, flutes, piccolos, pipes (including opium pipes), vesta boxes, cigarette-holders, candles, battery torches (dating from as early as 1882), contraceptives, poison, and a whole tribe of canes known as working companions (scalpels for doctors, small spades for botanists, safety lamps for miners). Among the most curious is the voyeur's cane with a mirror above the ferrule (to look up women's skirts).

WALL CLOCKS

Wall clocks carried on an independent existence, and many are public clocks for public places, so have a large easily-read dial. In 1791 an annual tax of between 2s 6d (12½p) and 10s (50p) was levied on all clocks and watches and, to help their more impecunious drinkers, innkeepers put up large circular clocks. These were known as Act of Parliament clocks, and the name stuck though the tax was repealed within a year. Typical of the standard-dial wall clocks were those in railway stations. Smaller, more elegant, clocks were made for domestic use, in all woods. Typical of the ornate hanging clocks was the Girandole, an American banjo-shaped clock with a plain dial at the top, a circular base often painted with scenes, and with a mercury barometer often set in the neck. Octagonal dial clocks were popular, often inlaid with brass and mother-of-pearl, and some were made from papier mâché. The better clocks are called cartel clocks, many of the more spectacular ones being made in France. The wall clock with a sunburst surround, made in quantity in the 1930s, was perhaps the last individualistic wall clock.

WALLPAPER

The earliest surviving patterned European wallpaper dates from about 1510. Wallpaper designs echoed those of textiles, and the wallpaper and lining paper used in Elizabethan times was similar to the black-work embroideries. The flock wallpaper of the seventeenth century derived from brocades and velvets; the flock was sheared cloth scattered onto a design previously prepared with glue. Hand-painted Chinese paper-hangings were imported by the East India Company, painted in water-colours, often depicting birds, butterflies and foliage in perspective, and of a non-repeating design. These were in large panels, sometimes twelve feet (3.65m) high. These, as with all imports from China, were imitated. There was a tax on wallpaper, resulting in printers producing simple patterned papers, which was rescinded in 1836. About 1840 the first successful wallpaper printing machine (adapted from a machine that printed calico) was introduced. Generally speaking, nineteenth-century wallpaper avoided the excesses of many three-dimensional objects. Flowers were a popular subject, as were variations on the Regency stripe, which was still a favourite. In the 1860s William Morris produced hand-printed wallpaper, using carved pearwood blocks, depicting 'misbegotten sunflowers and poppies, inane sham-medieval dicky-birds intermixed with geometrical patternings'. At the same time wallpaper designers were producing wallpaper imitating old tapestries. Art nouveau introduced more refined and elegant flowers, especially irises and tulips, and promoted plain-coloured papers topped with a scenic frieze. Wallpaper suffered a modest decline in the 1920s and 1930s with modern-thinking people preferring plain wall surfaces. Twenty years ago Chinese wallpaper panels were fetching more than £40,000, and wallpaper collecting has long been fashionable in America. Wallpapers have a personal appeal; or the reverse. Oscar Wilde's last words as he lay dying in a Paris hotel were, allegedly, 'My wallpaper is killing me, one of us must go.'

WALL POCKET

Ceramic vase flattened and pierced on one side, often made in quaint shapes such as a fish, a mask, or a cornucopia, popular from the eighteenth century in delft and other pottery. Porcelain examples were made by Worcester in a very elaborate form. Wall pockets have continued to be made; those of the 1930s were streamlined and often in pleasant pastel colours.

WARDROBE

The later name given to the clothes press, with the shelves replaced by hooks and rails to hang clothes. Eighteenth-century examples in mahogany are now highly regarded. During the nineteenth century wardrobes could become of monstrous size, often measuring upwards of ten feet (3m) across, with drawers and compartments for everything, but the Edwardian examples based on eighteenth-century models, in oak and walnut as well as mahogany, can be admirable, both useful and good-looking, though the chain-store suite with wash-stand and dressing-table lent itself to debasement with the use of tired art nouveau motifs and mean inlay. One of the characteristics of the twentieth-century wardrobe is the use of a full-length mirror, sometimes on the front, preferably inside the door. Black-staining and aimless beading typified the cheap 1920s wardrobe, but the better quality were rich, often too much so, in exotic veneers, hand-painted plaques, and good lacquer work.

WASH-STAND

A pedestal, tripod or cabinet two- or three-tiered stand designed to hold a wash-basin, usually with the accompanying jug as well, mostly from the eighteenth century when they were elegant affairs mostly made for the corner with a wooden splashback to prevent water getting on the walls. There were often drawers in the bottom tier (if two-staged) or the middle tier (if three-staged). The later wash-stand was a plain table with a splashback and usually three drawers, but the Victorians refined this model, providing a marble top and decorative tiles as the splashback in place of wood, and also taking off the sides and putting in towel-rails. Although there were some fancy types in the art nouveau style it was usually a no-frills piece, quintessential boarding-house furniture before the coming of running hot water.

WEDGWOOD

The most important English pottery as distinct from a porcelain factory, founded in 1759, and making an immediate impact with its cream-coloured earthenware with simple elegant patterns, transfer-printed or painted in enamel colours. Red stoneware (before 1763), black basalt (from about 1769) and blue jasper ware (from 1774) followed. The range of products was immense and adventurous, including not only the standard vases and table-wares but large busts, incense burners, furniture plaques, show-buckles, chessmen, opera-glasses, tiny cameos for jewellery, and snuff-boxes, imitated at home and abroad (Wedgewood & Co, operating 1796–1800, with an extra 'e' in Wedgwood, was one of the more brazen imitators). During the nineteenth century Wedgwood extended its range, producing maiolica, the so-called Moonlight pink lustre, orthodox transfer-printed blue-and-white household pottery, and Parian statuary. From 1878 porcelain was made as well as pottery, and throughout the century eighteenth-century models were repeated, especially the blue jasper ware. Notable designers such as Walter Crane and C. F. A. Voysey were used. One feature of Wedgwood's nineteenth-century ware was that however startling the product there was rarely a lapse in taste, even

Pair of Wedgwood Fairyland lustre vases.

227

Wedgwood tile, one of a set c1860 illustrating the seasons.

when dealing with potential disasters such as Egyptian burial urns. And this is true of the twentieth-century products, including humorous pieces such as a jug and beakers set produced in 1927 and printed with *Punch* subjects.

Wedgwood made its own version of Parian ware. The veiled lady was a popular subject not only in Parian but in other materials as well.

WATCHES

The first watch appeared in the early sixteenth century in Nüremberg, which was the centre of the industry in the formative years. The first watches were spherical, then they became oval, and then they became shaped into stars, skulls, crucifixes, and sea shells. These are known as form watches. Conventionally shaped watches often had multiple cases, one within the other. In succeeding years, cases were engraved, enamelled, decorated with gold filigree, and set with diamonds, but the most important development was not in looks but in the application of the hairspring (more correctly the balance-spring) in 1675, which made it worthwhile putting on a minute hand. In about 1725 the cylinder escapement was invented, enabling

Two high-class French watches made by Breguet (1747–1823), simple and classical in design.

the watch to become less bulky; self-winding watches had been introduced in the eighteenth century but were not adopted. There was constant improvement in escapements, and there was technological progress. Many Swiss watchmakers emigrated to England and France in the eighteenth century, and the Swiss were in the vanguard of innovation, producing complicated work and automata. The main contribution of the nineteenth century was the widespread use of the lever escapement and mass production, in Switzerland from 1865 and, more significantly, in America by the Waterbury Company from 1880. Britain lost ground in the nineteenth century because of the reluctance to mass produce. The characteristic British watch of the period is the silver hunter, with the lid entirely covering the glass and dial. The half-hunter has an aperture cut in the lid to show the position of the hands when the lid is closed, and is sometimes known as a Napoleon, who is supposed, for some reason or other, to have cut a hole in the cover of his watch for convenience. The term is sometimes applied to a plain silver watch without a lid or cover.

WATCH STANDS

The watch stand converts a watch into a clock by simply putting it on a convenient stand. Dating from the seventeenth century, it has been made in wood, porcelain, pottery, glass, silver and brass, but fell into disuse in the 1920s with the widespread use of the wrist-watch. The simplest is a wooden pillar topped by a recessed circular disc. The 'Well-head' type consists of two pillars surmounted by an arch from which the watch is suspended. Novelty watch stands were made, imitating gongs, chairs, and other unlikely subjects. The box holder concealed a watch stand which, when the box was opened, popped up on a spring.

WAX FLOWERS

Incredibly popular in the Victorian period, often moulded with great skill, and invariably kept under a glass dome so that they did not deteriorate. Home wax-flower making was given a fillip in 1851 with *The Royal Guide to Wax Flower Modelling* by Mrs Peachey (Artist to Her Majesty). Even more popular were wax fruit, and animals and human figures were also modelled.

WAX JACK

Open-frame stand for coil of sealing-wax taper, threaded on a central pin and led through a nozzle. Used from the eighteenth century, there were several variations. It must be remembered that before the penny post of 1840 almost all correspondence was sealed with wax, and the wax jack was not merely a piece of desk equipment for occasional use.

WELLINGTON CHEST

A vertical nineteenth-century specimen cabinet, plain or fancy, with a multitude of drawers, with a hinged flap at the side that folds back over the drawers, is locked, and prevents access. Its connection with the Duke of Wellington is vague.

WHATNOT

Stand with several open tiers, sometimes with shallow drawers, made from the eighteenth century but flowering during the Victorian period.

The best examples were in walnut, inlaid with marquetry, and with elaborate uprights.

WIG STAND

Wooden stand for holding wigs when not in use, made for a single wig or several, consisting of a turned pedestal with a sturdy base and a knob on top to hold a wig, or projecting arms to take several wigs. Some were made in delft. Used from the mid-seventeenth century; probably wig stands still are used by barristers and judges as they do the job perfectly well.

WILLOW PATTERN

Not a Chinese design, but thought to epitomise the romantic East. The components are a willow

(Opposite) An unusual Victorian rosewood piece, perhaps best described as a whatnot, characterised by marvellous fretwork.

(Below) The Willow Pattern design is perhaps the best-known English pottery decoration, and this cartoon by George Cruikshank (1792–1878) shows that there was a demand for some variation in the stereotyped motifs.

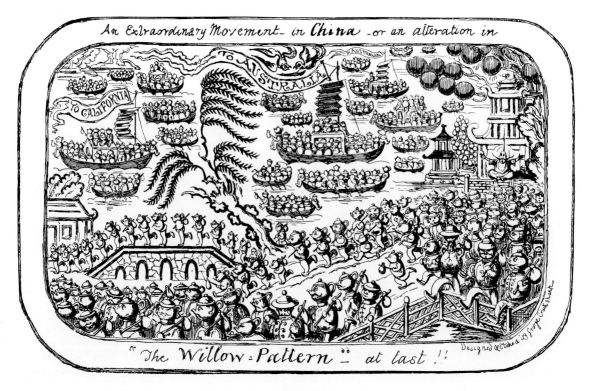

tree, a temple, a bridge with figures on it, a boat and a distant island, which can be shuffled around. It probably originated about 1780 at the Caughley pottery, but all the potteries used it and it is still made. It was so universally popular that the Chinese took it up themselves.

WILTON CARPET

The Wilton Carpet Factory was founded about 1740 in Wiltshire, making simple tapestry-weave carpets but soon developed the Wilton carpet, similar to a Brussels carpet but with more rows of pile to the inch and a richer, more sumptuous, velvet-like surface.

WINE-COOLER

A piece of furniture dating from the eighteenth century in which wine was cooled. It was made in various shapes, usually mahogany, sometimes brass-bound and invariably standing on four short legs. Castors were often fixed to allow easy movement of the wine-cooler. It went out of fashion with the widespread acceptance of the sideboard with its integrated wine-cooler. Amongst the most handsome are those, largely Regency, in the form of a sarcophagus. Rendered obsolete by the refrigerator.

WINE LABELS

A steady collecting area for use and display, the wine ticket, a silver name-plate, came into use in the 1730s after the change in shape of decanters meant that they could no longer be engraved with the contents. Early silver wine labels or tickets may not be hallmarked, and are likely to be escutcheon or shield shaped. Later labels were also rectangular, eye-shaped, or crescent. Enamel labels were also made from the 1750s, and these sometimes bear images as well as the name of the wine, anticipating the free style of silver labels of the 1820s onwards featuring vine leaves and tendrils. Sheffield plate and electroplate were also used as these came into fashion and, less frequently, porcelain, ivory, tortoiseshell, mother-of-pearl, and bone. Labels bearing the names of unusual or unlikely wines are especially sought after, so commonplace wines such as Madeira are sometimes replaced by the more exotic.

WITCH BALL

Hollow spheres of coloured glass made in England from the eighteenth century and alleged to ward off evil spirits, though they were more likely to be fishing-net floats especially if in green, the most common colour.

WORCESTER PORCELAIN

The longest-lived of the British porcelain factories, founded in 1751. In 1752 it acquired the stock and trade secrets of the Bristol Porcelain Factory. Worcester had the largest output of any of the eighteenth-century porcelain factories, and there is almost as much Worcester blue-and-white china in existence as that from all the other factories put together. The first era until 1783 is known as the 'Dr Wall Period' after the name of one of the founders, and the factory specialised in useful wares, particularly for the tea-table, and vases, with only a few figures. From 1757 Worcester pioneered transfer printing, at first overglaze in black, but from 1760 underglaze in blue. Products were fairly simple, except for dishes moulded like leaves, cauliflower-shaped tureens, and leafy jugs. In the 1760s there was a pronounced Sèvres influence, more certain after 1768 when artists employed at Chelsea joined the company. Finer products were decorated with gilding. There were also a large number of pieces produced in the Japanese style known as the 'Worcester Japans' as well as accurate copies of Chinese *famille verte* and *famille rose*. In 1783 the factory changed hands, and the period 1783–1792 is known as the 'Flight period'. A severer style, more in tune with the neo-Classicism sweeping through the decorative arts, appeared; 1793–1807 is known as the 'Flight and Barr' period when new co-owners appeared, 1807–13 is 'Barr, Flight and Barr' and 1813–40 is 'Flight, Barr and Barr.' This may seem odd, if not incomprehensible, but the products of Worcester are often discussed in such terms. In 1840 it amalgamated with a factory founded in 1783 by R. Chamberlain, and left its workshops in favour of Chamberlain's. In the 1840s Worcester went resolutely downmarket, but new blood appeared in 1850 and until 1862 the Worcester factory was Kerr and Binns, whereupon the Royal Worcester Porcelain Company emerged.

*Worcester tea set in the Imari style known as
'Worcester Japans'.*

From then on the products were elaborate, rich, jewelled, and decidedly for the luxury market, with 'Limoges ware' porcelain (painted white enamel on dark blue), ivory-tinged Parian statuary. child groups in the manner of Kate Greenaway, and when the Aesthetic movement arrived in the 1870s Worcester contributed its share. Splendidly painted 'cattle-in-a-misty-landscape'-type vases with plenty of pieces to break off were made well into the 1920s, and, indeed, many of the twentieth-century products could well be taken for Victorian decorative pieces. Amongst the most amazing products were the pierced wares of George Owen, seeming to emulate the finest ivory carving. Since the mid-nineteenth century Worcester has made a niche for itself in the manufacture of fine-quality figures and figure groups.

A Royal Worcester ewer of the mid-nineteenth century.

Late-Victorian Royal Worcester porcelain vase depicting swans in flight, dated 1900.

WRIST-WATCHES

Wristlets, or wrist-watches, were introduced in 1880 and were derided, as it was thought that dust, humidity, and rapid arm movements would damage the movement. Rolex under the name of Wilsdorf & Davies began production in Britain in 1905, moved to Geneva and invented the Rolex 'Oyster' dust-proof and weatherproof watch in 1926. Ingersoll began business in England in 1905 with their Midget ladies' watch, converted into a wrist-watch by fixing it in a leather strap with a cup to hold the watch. Soldering hoops for a strap was attributed to a London leatherworker in 1906. Until World War I men did not wear wrist-watches as they were regarded as effeminate, but wearing them in the trenches was mandatory for officers. Wrist-watches became jewellery in the 1920s when no expense was spared in the use of platinum, gold, and gemstones.

*The great range of Rolex wrist watches of 1930
including the long-established Oyster model.*

WROUGHT IRON

The manipulation of iron has continued from the Iron Age and still flourishes for both functional and decorative purposes. It was employed for strengthening doors, the doors themselves, and gates, screens, and grilles in churches, becoming increasingly decorative with the spaces between the strip filled with scrolls, rosettes, arabesques, and repeated patterns. Smaller articles were made in great quantities, such as brackets, candlesticks, locks, as well as much kitchen and household equipment such as pothooks and other fireplace accessories. In the seventeenth and early eighteenth centuries, wrought iron was a valued art form, with marvellous staircases and gates, but with the widespread use of cast iron, which was much cheaper, wrought iron tended to languish and to be regarded as a luxury.

YARD OF ALE

Monstrous drinking glass, three feet (.91m) long, with a trumpet mouth, made from the seventeenth century, but known mainly by nineteenth-century replicas and made in order to make an ambitious drinker look foolish (unless drunk slowly the liquid splashes on the victim's face). Half a yard of ale, also made, was perhaps easier to manage.

ZINC

A hard brittle bluish-white metal alloyed with copper to make brass; pure zinc first used in brass in 1780. Named spelter, zinc was a popular material for cheap statuettes and the like. When suitably treated, spelter can easily be mistaken for bronze. Discreetly scratching the base will show up a counterfeit.

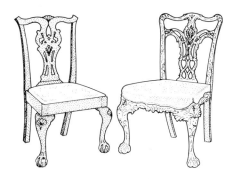

Famous Personalities

To select twelve people from the thousands of craftsmen, even geniuses, who have contributed to the history of antiques is no easy task. Any person who has had anything to do with antiques would make his or her own individual selection, though Thomas Chippendale would surely be in everyone's list. Some of those below are important not for what they made but for their influence on others, both their contemporaries and those who came later – sometimes a hundred years later.

BREGUET, ABRAHAM LOUIS (1747–1823) Breguet was a watch- and clock-maker who brought new techniques, such as newly invented escapements, to a peak of perfection and was credited with the invention of the self-winding watch. He was famous throughout Europe, even providing watches to Turkey in the Eastern style, and even throughout the Napoleonic Wars continued to supply the English market. His English agents tried in vain to persuade him to settle in England, though Breguet made several visits. In 1802 Breguet received a gold medal at an exhibition of French industrial products for a 'new, constant-force, free escapement'. Breguet also made fine and complicated carriage clocks. He eschewed mass production methods and numbered his creations.

CHIPPENDALE, THOMAS (1718–79) Best-known English furniture-maker and author of the first fully comprehensive book of furniture designs, *The Gentleman & Cabinet Maker's Director* (1754), which included rococo, Gothic, and Chinese-type styles, some of them too fantastic to be viable. Chippendale's life is scantily documented. He was born in Yorkshire, son of a carpenter, and some authorities say that Chippendale and his father moved to London in 1727. Certainly he was in London in 1748, when he married, having a shop, timberyard and workshops in St Martin's Lane from 1754. He was a designer rather than a maker and stamped none of his work, and he had two partners, one of whom survived him and carried on business with Chippendale's son, also Thomas (1749-1822). Chippendale's later work was inspired by the neo-Classicism of Robert Adam, and it has been suggested that some of this furniture was made by the younger Chippendale.

CLIFF, CLARICE (1900–72) Born in Tunstall, Staffordshire, the pottery of Clarice Cliff is regarded by many as the greatest manifestation of the art deco style in the United Kingdom. She trained at the Burslem School of Art, served an apprenticeship with A.J. Wilkinson, who appointed her director of Royal Staffordshire Pottery and its Newport Pottery subsidiary in 1939. Her brightly coloured geometric and boldly patterned pieces often show the influence of the various crazes such as the Diaghilev ballet, and she was responsible for enlisting the services of famous artists of the day such as Dame Laura Knight, Duncan Grant, Graham Sutherland, and Ben Nicholson to design pottery.

GALLÉ, ÉMILE (1846–1904) Educated at Nancy and

Weimar, where he studied mineralogy, he was apprenticed to a glasshouse in 1866, and later worked for his father who decorated pottery and glass. He travelled widely, finding inspiration in the Oriental glass at what is now the Victoria and Albert Museum in London, and after a visit to Italy in 1877 began exhibiting under his own name Italian- and Islamic-style enamelled glass. In 1884 he began to develop his own style, emphasising the ductility and versatility of glass, and by 1890 was internationally known with a large factory producing marvellous innovative glassware, no two pieces of which were the same. From the 1880s he also designed elegant fantasy furniture, amongst the best in art nouveau. Although he died in 1904 the factory existed until 1914.

GRAHAM, GEORGE (1674–1751) George Graham is by far the earliest of this group, and in his own way is perhaps the most important, for he was an inventor and it was through the pioneering work of such as Graham that Britain became such a dominant force when the Industrial Revolution arrived. Graham went to London in 1688, where he was apprenticed to the clock-maker Henry Aske for seven years. In 1695 he entered the service of the great clock-maker Thomas Tompion, and a year later married his niece. After Tompion's death in 1713 Graham invented the dead-beat escapement in 1715 and the mercury pendulum in 1726, making for increased accuracy in long-case clocks. Graham made about 3,000 watches and 174 clocks. He was elected to the Royal Society in 1721, became a member of the council the following year and published twenty-one scientific papers. He was greatly interested in instrument making and astronomy, and about 1709 made the first orrery, a clockwork-driven scientific instrument illustrating the movement of the planets, and demonstrating how intricate gearing could be used other than in clocks and watches. This orrery was copied in 1712 by John Rowley for the fourth Earl of Orrery – thus the name. Graham was buried in Westminster Abbey.

MORRIS, WILLIAM (1834–96) The most important figure in Victorian decorative arts, educated at Marlborough and Oxford, beginning as an architect in the office of G. E. Street, taking up painting without success, but finding a career in the reforming craze of the time, believing that 'all the minor arts were in a state of complete degradation'. In 1861 he started a firm, Morris, Marshall, Faulkner & Co, to remedy this, renamed Morris & Co in 1875, and moving from London to Merton Abbey in 1881. The firm made many objects – embroideries, wallpapers, stained glass, textiles, tapestries, carpets, and furniture. 'Have nothing in your house that you do not know to be useful or believe to be beautiful', he stated in 1880. He was an inspiration to what became known as the Arts and Crafts Movement, and anticipated Ambrose Heal's simple no-nonsense furniture designs of 1898 as well as, distantly, Utility furniture of World War II and G-plan. One of his most important ventures was the Kelmscott Press, founded in 1890 for the production of fine books, often written by Morris himself. Best known today for reproductions of his furnishing fabrics, but his importance in English and European taste cannot be overestimated.

PHYFE, DUNCAN (1768–1854) Said to be the greatest of all American cabinet-makers and certainly the best known, eventually employing several hundred men in his New York workshop and leaving what was then a vast fortune of half a million dollars. He emigrated with his parents from Scotland in 1783 or 1784, settling in Albany. By 1795 he was a well-established cabinet-maker in New York, and at first made first-rate copies of English Sheraton and French furniture but from 1830 his work takes on an opulent massive air in tune with American adventure. He anticipated later US developments in that he was one of the leaders in transforming the workshop into the factory.

PUGIN, AUGUSTUS WELBY NORTHMORE (1812–52) Pugin was an architect and designer and more than anyone created the Gothic Revival which was so important an influence on Victorian taste right up to the end of the century, culminating in Tower Bridge. When he was fifteen Pugin designed a set of chairs for Windsor Castle which are still there, and he also designed silver for the royal goldsmiths. By the 1830s he was insisting on historical accuracy, and published a number of influential books including *Gothic Furniture in the style of the 15th century* and *Designs for Iron and Brass Work*. He was responsible for furniture in the Houses of Parliament (1836-7), designed wallpaper and also ceramics for Minton. He became a Catholic in 1833, and he and his son Edward Welby Pugin (1834–75) designed and built several churches. He married three times, and died mad in Ramsgate.

SHERATON, THOMAS (1751–1806) Born in Stockton-on-Tees, Sheraton settled in London about 1790, and although he described himself as a cabinet-maker no definite piece of furniture can be assigned to him. Nevertheless he was immensely influential and his *The Cabinet-Maker and Upholsterer's Drawing-Book* (1791–4), in which he dismisses Chippendale as 'wholly antiquated', was addressed to the furniture-making trade, who often used the designs simplified or modified to suit their own preferences. Sheraton furniture is marked by restraint and sophistication, elegance and discretion, though he also found time to invent fanciful combination furniture. He published religious tracts as well as furniture designs and in 1800 left London to become a Baptist minister in the town of his birth, but seems to have returned to London two years later. In 1804 he went mad and died in poverty – as he had lived. His income was mostly derived from teaching drawing.

STORR, PAUL (1771–1844) Perhaps the leading silversmith of his time, apprenticed to Andrew Fogelberg, a Swede who had established himself in London in the 1770s. After his apprenticeship Storr engaged in a partnership with William Frisbee from 1792 to 1796, whereupon he set up on his own. He then worked for Philip Rundell and John Bridge, major silversmiths, from 1811 to 1819 being a partner. Storr's earlier work is in the fashionable neo-Classical style with an abundance of Greek motifs, but he seems to have later reacted against it, introducing a rococo note to his work as well as being engaged in large show pieces very popular during the Regency period. In 1819 he started up again, but in 1822 took another partner, John Mortimer. This business was soon facing bankruptcy, but was rescued by a nephew of Storr. Storr retired in 1839, though the firm continued under the name of Mortimer and Hunt, later Hunt and Roskell.

THONET, MICHAEL (1796–1871) Decidedly not a household name, Thonet is immensely important in that he perfected the bentwood process for chair-making and pioneered the mass production of furniture of a simple practical nature, certain items still being made without change. He is one of the pioneers of the fitness-for-function movement, and of furniture suitable for informal occasions, gardens and hotel verandahs. He was born at Boppard in Prussia, started a cabinet-making business in 1819, specialising in parquetry (patterned veneer) and experimenting with bending beechwood under heat from 1830. The advantages of bentwood were low production costs, lightness, and strength, without the need for hand-made joints. A typical Thonet chair had six parts and ten screws, and could be assembled in a matter of minutes. He moved to Vienna in 1842, but was unable to open his first factory until 1849 because of lack of money. He immediately prospered and salerooms were opened throughout Europe. By the end of the century the Thonet factories were employing 6,000 workers, making 4,000 pieces of furniture a day.

WEDGWOOD, JOSIAH (1730–95) Born into a family of potters of Burslem, Staffordshire, he was working by the age of ten, apprenticed to his brother 1744–9 and in 1754 entered into partnership with T. Whieldon, but they soon parted and in 1759 he founded Wedgwood Pottery, an immediate success and enlarged greatly in 1764. In 1769 he opened a new factory called Etruria with a Liverpool merchant, Thomas Bentley. Wedgwood was a man of many parts, involved in the improvement of turnpike roads, the construction of the Trent and Mersey canal, and the founding of schools and chapels. He was a member of the intellectual Birmingham Lunar Society (which included Boulton, Watt, the printer Baskerville and the scientist Joseph Priestley), a supporter of the American Revolution, and advocated the abolition of slavery. He gave pottery which was regarded as a very poor relation of porcelain a prestige which it never had before. His creamware, a service of which he gave to Queen Charlotte, was immensely popular, as was his blue jasper and black basalt ware, and many of the original designs are made today. Wedgwood married in 1764 and he had a large family, one of his daughters becoming the mother of Charles Darwin.

Potteries and Porcelain Factories

A complete list of potteries and porcelain factories would be unimaginable. The criteria for inclusion here are importance and the possible availability of the pottery or china at a reasonable cost, especially with regard to European producers. So small Italian potteries of the seventeenth century, no known pieces of which survive, are not mentioned. European makers of the middle rank, especially of porcelain, who survived into the nineteenth century are included; those who failed in the later years of the eighteenth century, as many did, unable to compete with an improved range of pottery, are not. The makers of porcelain are usually referred to as porcelain factories, and this convention has been respected. So potteries on this list do not make porcelain. Many of the famous potters of the present century, such as Clarice Cliff, worked for large firms such as Royal Staffordshire, though Susie Cooper did have a small pottery called Susie Cooper Pottery (established 1929). Some of the dates vary from one source to another, but the most reliable authorities have been taken. It must be remembered that many potteries worked in almost total anonymity; without the overbearing presence of the Commissioners of Inland Revenue there was no need for them to keep records. They also show a propensity to change their names without apparent reason.

Abtsbessingen Factory founded in Thuringia in 1739.

Adams A pottery dynasty from John Adams (1624–87) to William Adams (1798–1865), all more or less related, whose work ranged from crude slipware to Wedgwood-type ware and massive quantities of blue-and-white.

Alcock, Samuel & Co Staffordshire pottery c1828–53.

Aller Vale Devon pottery 1865–1901, when plant and goodwill acquired by Watcombe Pottery Co.

Amberg Bavarian factory 1759–1910.

Ansbach German factory 1708–1860.

Aprey French pottery 1744–1885.

Ashworth, G. L. & Brothers Staffordshire pottery founded 1862, still in existence.

Ault Burton-on-Trent art pottery founded 1887, merged with Ashby Potters' Guild 1923 to form Ault & Tunnicliffe, renamed Ault Potteries in 1937.

Baden-Baden German pottery and porcelain factory founded 1770.

Belleek Irish factory founded 1857, famous for its translucent white porcelain.

Belper Derbyshire pottery producing light brown stoneware 1750–1834.

Bennett Baltimore USA porcelain factory founded 1846.

Bennington Vermont USA porcelain factory 1793–1894.

Berlin The first porcelain factory 1752–7, second founded 1761, acquired by Frederick the Great in 1763 and state-run ever since.

Bing & Grondahl Founded in Copenhagen 1853. Products akin to those of Royal Danish Factory at Copenhagen.

Boote, T. and R. Pottery founded 1842 at Burslem, Staffordshire.

Booths Staffordshire pottery 1891–1948.

Bourne & Son Pottery at Belper and Denby from 1812.

Bovey Tracey South Devon pottery 1841–1956.

Bow With Chelsea, first porcelain factory in England 1744–75.

Brampton Group of Derby potteries from early 18th century to early 20th century.

Brannam, Charles Art pottery in Barnstaple, trade name Barum, established in 19th century, surviving today and formerly an 18th-century pottery owned variously by Lovering and later Rendell.

Bretby Art pottery established 1883.

Bristol Porcelain factories 1749–82. Potteries from late 17th century until late 19th century.

Brownfield, William Staffordshire pottery 1850–91.

Burmantoft Leeds pottery founded 1858, art pottery 1882–1904.

Cadinen Factory established in Germany by Kaiser Wilhelm II, active until 1945.

Capodimonte Italian porcelain factory founded 1743.

Carlton Staffordshire pottery founded 1890, still in existence.

Castle Hedingham Pottery founded for production of imitation 16th and 17th century ware in 1837, sold in 1901 to Essex Art Pottery Company. Closed 1905.

Castleford Yorkshire pottery under name of David Dunderdale & Co c1790–1821.

Caughley Pottery established 1755, porcelain produced from 1772, amalgamated with Coalport Porcelain Factory c1799, plant transferred to Coalport 1814.

Chamberlain Worcester pottery founded 1783, porcelain from 1792, amalgamated with other Worcester factory 1840, trading as Kerr & Binns 1852, the Royal Worcester Porcelain Co from 1862.

Chantilly French porcelain factory c1725–1800.

Chelsea Keramic Art Works US pottery 1866, renamed Dedham Pottery 1896, closed 1943.

Chelsea Porcelain factory c1745–84.

Choisy-le-Roi French pottery 1804–1934.

Clews, James and Ralph Staffordshire blue-and-white pottery 1817–35.

Clyde Scottish pottery 1815–1903.

Coalport & Coalbrookdale Shropshire porcelain factory founded c1796, moved to Staffordshire 1926, still exists.

Cocker, George Porcelain factory at Derby 1826–40.

Cockhill Pit Derby pottery 1751–9.

Codnor Park Derbyshire pottery 1821–61.

Commondale Yorkshire art pottery 1872–84.

Copeland Proprietor of Spode from 1833, Copeland & Garrett 1833–47, Copeland 1847 onwards.

Copenhagen Danish porcelain factory founded 1774, styled Royal Danish Porcelain Factory 1779. Several potteries in the city from 1722.

Creil French pottery initially imitating English ware 1795–1895.

Crown Staffordshire Porcelain factory founded by H. Green in 1830, known 1859–c1890 as M. Green & Co, and present name from that date.

Dartmouth South Devon art pottery founded in 1947.

Davenport Pottery founded at Longton, Staffordshire, in c1793, porcelain made from c1820, closed 1887.

Deakin & Son Staffordshire pottery 1833–41.

De Morgan Art pottery 1869–1905.

Delft At least twenty-three major Dutch potteries from early 17th century.

Della Robbia Art pottery in Cheshire 1894–c1906. Denholme Yorkshire pottery.

Denaby Yorkshire pottery trading 1864–6 as Wilkinson and Wardle. Closed 1870.

Denholme Yorkshire pottery c1790–1893.

Deptford Pottery Sunderland pottery founded 1857, noted for lustre ware.

Derby Porcelain factory founded c1745, Crown Derby from 1877, Royal Crown Derby from 1890.

Devonmoor Devon art pottery 1913–14, re-opened 1922.

Devonshire Small factories in North Devonshire making slipware from 17th century.

Dixon Austen & Co Sunderland pottery c1820–65 noted for lustre ware, from 1840 Dixon, Phillips & Co. Also known as Garrison Pottery.

Doccia Italian porcelain factory founded 1735, still in existence.

A group of South Devon art pottery pieces.

Don Yorkshire pottery c1790–1893.

Doulton London pottery from 1815, Doulton & Watts 1815–58, Doulton & Co from 1858, porcelain factory in Burslem added in 1884. The name Royal Doulton dates from 1902.

Dresden Dresden is the same as Meissen, but 'Dresden' can mean porcelain in the Meissen style, or straightforward fakes of Meissen. Or Dresden can be used to refer to later Meissen work. Pottery was made at Dresden 1708–84.

Dudson, James Staffordshire pottery. Dudson lived 1838–88.

Duke, Sir James & Nephews Staffordshire pottery 1859–63.

Eagle Glasgow pottery established by Frederick Grosvenor, founded 1869, continued into 20th century.

Eccleshill Yorkshire pottery 1835–67.

Elkin, Knight & Bridgewood Staffordshire pottery 1827–40.

Faubourg Saint-Denis French porcelain factory 1771–1810.

Fell & Co Tyneside pottery 1817–90.

Fenton, A. & Sons Staffordshire pottery 1887–1901.

Fielding, S. & Co Staffordshire pottery founded 1879, still extant.

Frankenthal German porcelain factory 1755–99.

Fremington Devon pottery late 18th century–c1906 later specialising in 'olde worlde' ware.

Fulham Established by John Dwight c1671 producing stoneware. Dwight died 1703.

Fulper US pottery founded 1805, known for later art pottery.

Fürstenberg German porcelain factory in Brunswick, founded 1747, best period c1769–90.

Gera German pottery 1752–80, and porcelain factory from 1779.

Giustiniani Italian pottery at Naples founded c1760, porcelain made from 1829. Closed 1885.

Glasgow Pottery 1748–1810. Another pottery in Glasgow existed 1842–1940.

Gmunden Austrian pottery near Salzburg founded 1863, art pottery made 1908–10.

Goodwin, J. & R. Staffordshire pottery 1829–31.

Gorbunovo Russian porcelain factory c1800–1872.

Goss Porcelain factory near Hanley 1858–1940.

Gotha German porcelain factory founded 1757, existing into 19th century.

Grainger Worcester porcelain and pottery

founded 1801, acquired by Worcester Porcelain Co 1889, but operated independently until 1902.

Gray, A. E. & Co Art pottery 1907–62, when absorbed into Portmeirion Pottery.

Greatbach, William Staffordshire pottery 1759–87.

Green, Stephen Lambeth pottery c1828–58.

Griffen, Smith & Hill US art pottery 1879–90.

Grueby US art pottery 1894–1919.

Gutavsberg Swedish pottery founded 1827, making bone china from 1860s, and copies of Wedgwood from c1897.

Hackwood, William Staffordshire pottery 1827–43.

Hall, John Staffordshire pottery 1814–32.

Haviland Franco-American porcelain factory founded in 1839, concentrating on exporting French porcelain to the US.

Heath, Joshua Staffordshire pottery 1770–c1810.

Heider German art pottery established late 19th century under name of Max von Heider & Söhne.

Herculaneum Liverpool pottery founded 1793, porcelain from 1801.

Herend Hungarian pottery and porcelain factory founded 1838.

Heubach German porcelain factory founded 1822, with little of interest until early 20th century.

Hicks & Meigh Staffordshire pottery 1806–22.

Höchst German pottery and porcelain factory 1746–96.

Holitsch Hungarian pottery 1743–1827.

Hull Pottery 1802–25 when taken over by Belle Vue Pottery.

Ilmenau German porcelain factory 1771–1871. From 1808 to 1871 named Nonne & Roesch, the new owners. Other factories in area were founded later.

Isleworth Pottery 1760–1820.

Jackfield Shropshire pottery c1750–c75.

Johnson Brothers Staffordshire pottery founded 1883, still in existence.

Jones, George Staffordshire pottery (Trent Pottery) 1864–1907.

Lakin & Poole Staffordshire pottery 1770–97.

Lambeth Potteries founded c1665 producing delft, and later blue-and-white ware.

Langenthal Swiss porcelain factory established 1904.

Leeds Several potteries c1760–1878.

Lennox US porcelain factory founded 1889.

Lille French potteries and porcelain factories 1696–c1817.

Limoges French pottery, founded 1736, large

An interesting engraving of the 1860s of one of the Liverpool potteries.

PART OF PENNINGTON'S WORKS.

number of porcelain factories from 1784.

Linthorpe Art pottery near Middlesbrough 1879–89.

Liverpool Potteries and porcelain factories founded c1716, porcelain by Richard Chaffers from 1756, bone china from c1800.

Lloyd, John Staffordshire pottery c1834–52.

Longton Hall Porcelain factory in Staffordshire c1750–c60.

Longpark South Devon art pottery 1905–40.

Lonhuda US art pottery founded 1892.

Lovatt & Lovatt Nottinghamshire pottery founded 1895, still in existence.

Lowestoft Porcelain factory 1757–1802.

Ludwigsburg German pottery and porcelain factory 1756–1824.

Lunéville French pottery founded 1731.

Madeley Shropshire pottery 1825–40.

Magdeburg German potteries, one 1754–1839, one 1799–1865.

Malling, C. T. Tyneside pottery 1850s–1963.

Marblehead US art pottery founded 1905.

Marieberg Swedish pottery and porcelain factory 1758–88.

Martin Brothers Studio pottery 1873–1914.

Mason Pottery 1813–48, famous for ironstone china.

Meigh Pottery c1780–1861 when it was renamed Old Hall Earthenware Co. Old Hall Porcelain Co from 1886.

Meissen German porcelain factory founded 1710 (some say 1713), but not systematically marked until 1724 with the famous crossed swords.

Mennency French porcelain factory 1734–1806.

Methven, David & Sons Scottish pottery founded first half 19th century, closed c1930.

Mexborough Yorkshire pottery c1795–1844.

Middlesborough Pottery c1831–87.

Minton Pottery and porcelain factory founded 1796.

Moore, S. & Co Sunderland pottery 1803–74.

Moorcroft Staffordshire art pottery founded in 1913. Founder died 1946.

Morley, Francis Staffordshire pottery 1848–58.

Mortlock, John London manufacturer and retailer of pottery and porcelain.

Moustiers Group of French potteries founded in the 17th century.

Münden German pottery c1737–1854.

Nafferton Yorkshire pottery 1848–99.

Nantgarw Welsh porcelain factory 1813–14 when the founders moved to Swansea, and 1817–22 when they briefly returned, probably as decorators.

Naples Italian porcelain factory 1771–1821.

Nevers Group of French potteries founded 1588. Pottery still made in the town.

New Chelsea Staffordshire pottery c1912–51 specialising in reproductions.

New Hall Staffordshire porcelain factory founded 1781, bone china from 1810, closed 1835.

Newcomb College US art pottery 1895–1930.

Newport Staffordshire pottery founded 1920, still in existence.

Niderviller French pottery founded 1754, porcelain made from 1765, factory still active.

Nove Italian potteries and porcelain factories founded 1728 and still active.

Nüremberg German potteries c1530–c1840.

Nymphenburg Porcelain factory founded 1747 (some say 1755), still active.

Nyon Swiss porcelain factory c1780–1860.

Oettingen Schrattenhofen German pottery in Bavaria founded 1735. From late 18th century into 19th century noted for cream-coloured earthenware.

Ott & Brewer US porcelain factory founded 1863 under name of Bloor, Ott & Booth.

Ottweiler German pottery and porcelain factory 1763–94.

Paris French potteries founded in 17th century, porcelain from late 18th imitating Sèvres.

Pecs Hungarian pottery founded 1855, still active.

Pewabic US art pottery founded 1903 by Mary Chase Perry.

Phillips, Edward & George Staffordshire pottery 1822–34.

Phillips, John Sunderland potter 1815–64.

Pinder, Bourne & Co Staffordshire pottery 1860–82.

Pilkington Royal Lancastrian pottery 1892–1938.

Pinxton Derbyshire porcelain factory 1796–1813.

Plymouth First hard-paste porcelain factory in England founded 1768, factory moved to Bristol in 1770.

Poole Carter, Stapler & Adams of Poole, Dorset, founded 1921.

Poppelsdorf German pottery founded in 1755, still active.

There is one Wedding Present that will be welcomed and prized for many a year. It is a Shelley Tea-Set—made by master craftsmen who have worked with their brains as well as their hands to produce this, the finest and most exquisite of all Shelley Fine China.

The pattern illustrated is one of many : most Pottery and Glass Stores will be glad to show you this fine china. In the meantime, may we post you a folder which shows a selection of these Shelley Tea-Sets in their true colours ?

Write for coloured illustrations of Shelley Tea-Sets, Shelley Children's Ware by Mabel Lucie Attwell and Hilda Cowham. Shelley Dainty White China, Shelley Jelly Moulds and name of nearest supplier. To Dept. I.

CHINA

SHELLEYS *Potters (Advert Dept.)* LONGTON

Portobello Scottish potteries established on Firth of Forth in 1786 producing household wares.

Potsdam German pottery founded c1739, continuing into the 19th century.

Pratt Staffordshire pottery 1812–1920, best known for pot-lids and decorated terra-cotta ware.

Proskau German pottery 1763–1850.

Quimper French pottery founded c1690 in Brittany, in the ownership of same family well into the 19th century.

Rennes French Breton potteries existing from the 17th century.

Many potteries who worked in a progressive Art Deco style in the 1920s and 1930s also continued to make traditional ware, as revealed in this 1927 advertisement.

Ridgway, J. & W. Staffordshire pottery active from early 19th century until 1830.

Ridgway, W. Son & Co Staffordshire pottery 1838–48. The Ridgways a very confusing lot.

Riessner & Kessel Bohemian art nouveau porcelain factory founded in 1892.

Roanne French potteries operating from 16th century until c1866.

245

Robinson & Leadbeater Staffordshire pottery 1864–1924.

Rockingham Yorkshire pottery and porcelain factory 1745–1842.

Rogers Pottery in Longport, Staffordshire, 1780–1836.

Rookwood US art pottery founded 1880, still active.

Rörstrand Swedish pottery and porcelain factory founded 1725 and still in production.

Rosenthal German porcelain factory founded in 1879, famous for its Art Deco figures, still active.

Rozenburg Dutch pottery and porcelain factory founded in 1883 to make delft, known for its art nouveau and Art Deco wares.

Ruskin Art pottery 1898–1935.

Sadler, James & Sons Staffordshire pottery founded 1899, still active.

Saint Amand les Eaux French pottery and porcelain factory 1718–1882.

St Anthony's Pottery Newcastle-on-Tyne pottery 1780–1820.

Saint Clément French pottery founded 1758, surviving into the latter part of the 19th century.

St Cloud French pottery and porcelain factory c1667–1766.

St Petersburg Imperial Porcelain factory founded 1744, surviving Russian Revolution to become state factory.

Samadet French pottery 1732–1836.

Sarreguemines French pottery founded c1770 and in the 19th century one of the largest with 2,000 workers.

Schleswig German pottery 1755–1814.

Schrezheim German pottery 1752–1872.

Sèvres French porcelain factory founded 1738.

Shelley Pottery founded c1913.

Sherwin & Cotton Staffordshire pottery 1877–1930.

Shorthouse & Co Staffordshire pottery c1817–22.

Sinceny French pottery 1733–1864.

Smith, William & Co Durham pottery c1845–84.

Southwark Potteries founded 1618 for making delft.

Southwick Sunderland pottery 1788–1897.

Spode, Joseph Pottery and porcelain factory founded 1776, Spode & Copeland 1797–1816.

Staffordshire potteries The largest group of English potteries, centred in the Five Towns (Burslem, Stoke, Hanley, Tunstall and Longton), producing vast quantities of ware from the 17th century to the present day. Besides the potteries there were individuals such as Thomas Toft (d 1689), John Walton (fl c1805–50) Ralph Wood, renowned for his Toby Jugs (1715–72), and Obadiah Sherratt (1755–1845) who transcended their medium (usually figures and figure groups), and whose products are often unmarked.

Steele, Edward Potter mid-1870s–89.

Stevenson, Andrew Staffordshire blue-and-white potter 1816–30.

Stevenson & Williams Staffordshire pottery fl c1825.

Stockelsdorf German pottery 1771–1811.

Strasbourg German pottery and porcelain factory 1720–81, in its day of immense importance and widely copied.

Sussex Group of 18th and 19th-century potteries at Chailey, Brede, Rye, Cadborough, Wiston, Dicker, Burgess Hill etc., making crude slipware.

Sutherland & Sons Staffordshire pottery 1865–75.

Swansea Potteries and porcelain factory, pottery at Cambrian Pottery from 1765, porcelain 1814–22, pottery only 1822–70 when it closed.

The Hague Dutch porcelain factory 1776–90.

Tournai Group of potteries and porcelain factory founded 1751 and most important in the Low Countries, active until 19th century.

Tucker First US porcelain factory of note 1825–38.

Union Major porcelain factory in US 1848–c1910.

Vienna Austrian porcelain factory 1719–1864. After Meissen the first European factory to make hard-paste porcelain.

Vincennes French porcelain factory 1730s–88, factory moving to Sèvres 1756.

Vinovo Italian porcelain factory 1776–1825.

Volkstedt Porcelain factory founded c1760, still in existence.

Wallendorf Porcelain factory founded 1764, still in existence.

Walley, Edward Pottery 1841–56.

Walton Burslem pottery late 18th century to 1835.

Watcombe South Devon art pottery 1867–1962.

Wedgwood Pottery founded 1759, still thriving.

Weesp Dutch porcelain factory 1757–c1820.

Weller US art pottery founded late 19th century.

Wemyss Pottery in Scotland c1883–1930 when rights and moulds bought by Bovey Tracey Pottery.

Westerwald German potteries founded in 16th century and still in existence.

Wiltshaw & Robinson Staffordshire pottery founded 1890, still in existence.

Wincanton Somerset pottery 1737–48.

Wood, Enoch Staffordshire pottery 1790–1818 as Wood & Caldwell, continued until 1846 as Enoch Wood and Sons.

Worcester Porcelain factory founded in 1751 and still in existence. Royal Worcester founded 1862.

Wrisbergholzen German pottery 1735–1834.

Wrotham Group of Kent potteries with dated pieces 1612–1739.

Zerbst German pottery 1720–1861.

Zurich Swiss pottery and porcelain factory 1763–1897.

Bibliography

Aaronson, J. *Encyclopaedia of Furniture* (1966)

Andere, M. *Old Needlework Boxes and Tools* (Newton Abbot,1971)

Andrews, J. *Price Guide to Antique Furniture* (Woodbridge,1969)

Andrews, J. *Price Guide to Victorian Furniture* (Woodbridge,1972)

Angus, I. *Medals and Decorations* (1973)

Armstrong, N. *A Collector's History of Fans* (1974)

Ash, D. *Dictionary of British Antique Silver* (1972)

Aslin, E. *Nineteenth Century English Furniture* (1962)

Baines, A. *Musical Instruments Through the Ages* (1961)

Banister, Judith *English Silver* (1985)

Barilli, R. *Art Nouveau* (1969)

Barnes, R. M. *History of Regiments and Uniforms of the British Army* (1950)

Battersby, M. *The World of Art Nouveau* (1968)

Battersby, M. *The Decorative Twenties* (1970)

Battersby, M. *The Decorative Thirties* (1972)

Battie, D. and Turner, M. *Price Guide to 19th and 20th Century British Pottery* (Woodbridge, 1979)

Beard, G. W. *Modern Glass* (1968)

Bedford, J. *All Kinds of Small Boxes* (1964)

Bedford, J. *Paperweights* (1968)

Bemrose, G. *Nineteenth Century English Pottery and Porcelain* (1952)

Bennett, M. *Refinishing Antique Furniture* (1980)

Bernal, J. D. *Science and Industry in the Nineteenth Century* (1953)

Bickerton, L. M. *Eighteenth Century English Drinking Glasses* (1971)

Boger, L. A. *The Complete Guide to Furniture Styles* (1961)

Boger, L. A. *A Dictionary of World Pottery and Porcelain* (1972)

Boothroyd, A. E. *Fascinating Walking Sticks* (1973)

Bradbury, S. *Evolution of the Microscope* (1967)

Bradshaw, P. *18th Century English Porcelain Figures* (Woodbridge,1981)

Bristowe, W. S. *Victorian China Fairings* (1971)

British Optical Institute *Dictionary of British Scientific Instruments* (1921)

Britten, F. J. *Old Clocks and Watches and their Makers* (1973)

Bruton, E. *Clocks and Watches* (1968)

Buchner, A. *Mechanical Musical Instruments* (1921)

Butler, R. *Arthur Negus Guide to Antique Furniture* (1978)

Calvert, H. R. *Globes, Orreries and Other Models* (1967)

Chapuis, A. and Droz, E. *Automata* (1958)

Chinnery, Victor *Oak Furniture; The British Tradition* (Woodbridge,1979)

Claxton Stevens, C. and Whittington, S. *18th Century English Furniture* (Woodbridge, 1985)

Clifford, A. *Cut-Steel and Berlin Iron Jewellery* (1971)

Clutton, C. and Daniels, G. *Watches* (1965)

Colby, A. *Samplers* (1964)

Coleridge, Anthony *Chippendale Furniture* (1968)

Collard, Frances *Regency Furniture* (Woodbridge, 1985)

Cooper, D. and Battershill, N. *Victorian Sentimental Jewellery* (1972)

Cooper, G. R. *The Invention of the Sewing Machine* (1968)

Cousins, F. W. *Sundials* (1969)

Cowie, D. and Henshaw, K. *Antique Collectors' Dictionary* (1962)

Coysh, A. W. *Blue and White Transfer Ware* (Newton Abbot, 1970)

Coysh, A. W. *British Art Pottery* (Newton Abbot, 1976)

Cross, R. *China Repairs and Restoration* (1972)

Culff, R. *The World of Toys* (1969)

Cunnington, C. W. and P. *Handbook of English Costume in the Nineteenth Century* (1966)

Current, R. N. *The Typewriter* (1954)

Cushion, J. P. *Pottery and Porcelain* (1972)

Daumas, M. *Scientific Instruments of the Seventeenth and Eighteenth Centuries and their Makers* (1972)

David, D. C. *English Bottles and Decanters 1650–1900* (1972)

Delieb, E. *Silver Boxes* (1968)

Dilby, A. U. *Oriental Rugs and Carpets* (1960)

Distin, W. H. and Bishop, R. *The American Clock* (New York, 1976)

Dunhill, A. *The Pipe Book*

Elville, E. M. *English Table Glass* (1951)

Elville, E. M. *Paperweights* (1954)

Evans, J. *A History of Jewellery 1100–1870* (1970)

Fastnedge, R. *English Furniture Styles* (1969)

Fleming, J. and Honour, H. *Penguin Dictionary of Decorative Arts* (1977)

Flower, M. *Victorian Jewellery* (1967)

Folson, R. S. *Handbook of Greek Pottery* (1967)

Foster, K. *Scent Bottles* (1966)

Fraser, Lady A. *A History of Toys* (1966)

Gardner, P. *American Glass* (Washington, 1977)

Garner, F. H. *English Delftware* (1972)

Garner, P. *The World of Edwardiana* (1974)

Garratt, J. G. *Model Soldiers* (1961)

Gelatt, R. *The Fabulous Phonograph* (1956)

Gernsheim, H. and A. *History of Photography* (1969)

Gloag, J. E. *Short History of Furniture* (1954)

Goaman, H. *English Clocks* (1967)

Godden, G. A. *British Pottery and Porcelain 1780–1850* (1963)

Godden, G. A. *Encyclopaedia of British Pottery and Porcelain Marks* (1964)

Gorden, H. *Antiques – the Amateur's Questions* (1951)

Haggar, R. G. *English Country Pottery* (1950)

Haslam, M. *English Art Pottery 1865–1915* (Woodbridge, 1975)

Hayward, H. (ed) *Handbook of Antiques Collecting* (1960)

Hayward, J. F. *English Cutlery* (1956)

Hill, H. and Paget-Tomlinson, E. *Instruments of Navigation* (1958)

Hillier, B. *Art Deco* (1968)

Hillier, B. *The World of Art Deco* (1971)

Hillier, M. *Dolls and Dollmakers* (1968)

Holmes, E. *An Age of Cameras* (1974)

Honey, W. B. *Glass* (1946)

Honey, W. B. *English Pottery and Porcelain* (1962)

Howarth-Loomes, B. E. C. *Victorian Photography* (1975)

Heutson, T. L. *Lace and Bobbins* (Newton Abbot, 1973)

Hughes, G. B. and T. *Small Antique Furniture* (1958)

Hughes, G. B. and T. *English Painted Enamels* (1951)

Hughes, G. B. *English Snuff Boxes* (1971)

Hughes, T. *Small Decorative Antiques* (1959)

Hughes, T. *English Domestic Needlework 1680–1860* (1961)

Hughes, T. *Cottage Antiques* (1967)

Hughes, T. *Old English Furniture* (1963)

Jervis, S. *Victorian Furniture* (1968)

Jones, M. E. *A History of Western Embroidery* (1969)

Joy, E. T. *Country Life Book of English Furniture* (1968)

Joy, E. T. *Country Life Book of Clocks* (1967)

Kiely, E. R. *Surveying Instruments* (New York, 1974)

Klamkin, M. *The Picture Postcard* (Newton Abbot, 1974)

Klein, D. and Ward, L. (eds) *History of Glass* (1984)

Lang, D. M. *The Georgians* (1966)

Larson, K. *Rugs and Carpets of the Orient* (1966)

Laver, J. *Victoriana* (1966)

Lewis, M. D. S. *Antique Paste Jewellery* (1970)

Lloyd, H. A. *The Collectors' Dictionary of Clocks* (1964)

Luddington, J. *Antique Silver* (1971)

McCausland, H. *Snuff and Snuff Boxes* (1951)

Mackay, J. *An Introduction to Small Antiques* (1970)

Mackay, J. *Price Guide to Collectable Antiques* (Woodbridge, 1975)

Mackay, J. *Nursery Antiques* (1976)

Marquoid, P. and Edwards, R. *Dictionary of English Furniture* (1954)

Masden, S. T. *Art Nouveau* (1967)

Michaelis, R. *British Pewter* (1969)

Moody, E. *Modern Furniture* (1966)

Mount, S. *Price Guide to Eighteenth Century Pottery* (Woodbridge, 1972)

Murray, P. *Toys* (1968)

Musgrave, C. *Regency Furniture* (1971)

Naylor, G. *The Arts and Crafts Movement* (1971)

Newman, H. *Illustrated Dictionary of Glass* (1977)

Norman, A. V. B. *Arms and Armour* (1964)

Oman, C. C. *English Domestic Silver* (1959)

Ormsby, Thomas *The Windsor Chair* (1962)

Osborne, H. (ed) *Oxford Companion to the Decorative Arts* (1976)

Owen, M. *Antique Cast Iron* (Poole, 1977)

Pearsall, R. *Collecting Mechanical Antiques* (Newton Abbot, 1973)

Pearsall, R. *Collecting Scientific Instruments* (Newton Abbot, 1974)

Pearsall, R. *Making and Managing an Antique Shop* (Newton Abbot, 1979)

Pearsall, R. *Joy of Antiques* (Newton Abbot, 1988)

Pearsall, R. *Antique Furniture for Pleasure and Profit* (Newton Abbot, 1990)

Peterson, H. L. (ed) *Encyclopaedia of Firearms* (1964)

Pevsner, N. *Pioneers of Modern Design* (1960)

Pinto, E. *Treen and other Wooden Bygones* (1969)

Polak, A. *Modern Glass* (1962)

Quennell, M. and C. H. B. *History of Everyday Things in England* (1938)

Ramsay, L. G. C. (ed) *Concise Encyclopaedia of Antiques* 5 vols (1955–60)

Ridley, M. *Oriental Antiques* (1977)

Roche, S. *Mirrors* (1957)

Savage, G. *Glass* (1965)

Savage, G. *Dictionary of Antiques* (1970)

Sevensma, W. S. *Tapestries* (1965)

Singer, C. Holmyard, E. J. Hall, A. R.

Williams, T. I. (eds) *A History of Technology* 5 vols (1954–8)

Smith, A. *Illustrated Guide to Clocks and Watches* (1975)

Smith, D. J. *Discovering Railwayana* (Tring, 1971)

Spero, S. *Price Guide to Eighteenth Century English Porcelain* (Woodbridge, 1970)

Staff, F. *The Picture Postcard and its Origins* (1966)

Symonds, R. W. *History of English Clocks* (1947)

Thoday, A. G. *Astronomical Telescopes* (1971)

Toller, J. *Discovering Antiques* (Newton Abbot, 1975)

Toller, J. *Treen* (Newton Abbot, 1975)

Turner, H. A. B. *Collectors' Guide to Staffordshire Pottery Figures* (1971)

Wakefield, H. *Nineteenth Century English Glass* (1961)

Wardle, P. *Victorian Lace* (1968)

Webb, G. *Cylinder Musical Box Handbook* (1968)

Webb, G. *Disc Musical Box Handbook* (1971)

White, G. *European and American Dolls* (1966)

Whittington, P. *Militaria* (1969)

Whittington, P. *Undiscovered Antiques* (1972)

Wilkinson, P. *Swords and Daggers* (1968)

Wills, G. *Victorian Glass* (1976)

Wills, G. *Collecting Copper and Brass* (1962)

Wills, G. *Candlesticks* (Newton Abbot, 1974)

Wood, V. *Victoriana* (1960)

Woodhouse, C. B. *Victoriana Collectors' Handbook* (1970)

ACKNOWLEDGEMENTS

Henry Spencer & Sons, Sheffield: 6, 15, 18, 38, 39, 43, 50, 51, 91, 95, 99, 118, 142, 158, 163, 170, 171, 182, 191, 206, 227, 230, 234

Sean Hickey: 203

Dee & Atkinson, Driffield, Yorkshire: 62

Robin Fenner, Tavistock: 55, 86, 139, 146, 166, 190, 194, 210, 215

Hetheringtons, Amersham, Buckinghamshire: 23, 26, 29, 66, 148

Sotheby's, Billingshurst: 111, 186

Christopher Wray, London SW6: 34

Index

The alphabetical arrangement of this encyclopedia is, of course, an index in itself, but sometimes the categories need to be split down into their components, and entries will naturally include items which have their own heading. So this index is a guide to cross-referencing. To prevent the index being long and laborious, the actual objects are the main entries rather than the processes, the materials, and the technical details contained in the main body of the book. Naturally the individual entries in the book are not duplicated.